TWELVE GRAND

Jonathan Rendall was born in 1964. He was educated at Campion School, Athens, and Magdalen College, Oxford. His first book, *This Bloody Mary Is The Last Thing I Own*, won the Somerset Maugham Award. He lives and writes in Suffolk.

T0316149

For Susie

Twelve Grand

The Gambler as Hero

JONATHAN RENDALL

YELLOW JERSEY PRESS

Published by Yellow Jersey Press 1999

2 4 6 8 10 9 7 5 3 1

Copyright © Jonathan Rendall 1999

Jonathan Rendall has asserted his right under the Copyright, Designs
and Patents Act 1988 to be identified as the author of this work

First published in Great Britain in 1999 by
Yellow Jersey Press
Random House, 20 Vauxhall Bridge Road,
London SW1V 2SA

Random House Australia (Pty) Limited
20 Alfred Street, Milsons Point, Sydney,
New South Wales 2061, Australia

Random House New Zealand Limited
18 Poland Road, Glenfield,
Auckland 10, New Zealand

Random House South Africa (Pty) Limited
Endulini, 5A Jubilee Road, Parktown 2193, South Africa

Random House UK Limited Reg. No. 954009

A CIP catalogue record for this book
is available from the British Library

ISBN 0 224 05149 0

Typeset in Bembo by MATS, Southend-on-Sea, Essex
The Random House Group Limited supports The Forest Stewardship
Council® (FSC®), the leading international forest-certification organisation.
Our books carrying the FSC label are printed on FSC®-certified paper.
FSC is the only forest-certification scheme supported by the leading
environmental organisations, including Greenpeace. Our
paper procurement policy can be found at
www.randomhouse.co.uk/environment

Printed and bound in Great Britain by Clays Ltd, St Ives PLC

Contents

'He said: I believe in poetry, love, death –
that's precisely why I believe in immortality. I write
    a line of verse,
I write the world. I exist, the world exists.
A river flows from the tip of my little finger.
The sky is seven times blue. This clarity
is the primordial truth, my last will.'

Yannis Ritsos, *Mortgage*

'That is a complete liberty. That is rubbish. I never
done 30 grand at cards in my life. My downfall was
horses.'

Jimmy White, snooker player

Pig City

I had never liked Dr Marlsford. All right, I had never actually met him before. But I had seen him about, ambling down Market Street with his brown bag, and driving a little too fast along the country roads in his rather flashy saloon, always with the same look on his face: mildly bored, but also immensely self-satisfied, as if to say, yes, well, all in all, Dr Marlsford has everything nicely under control. He was probably only a few years older than me. 36? 37? 40? I bet he was 40 when he was 17.

And every time I'd passed him I'd thought, now there goes an opposite: put us in a room together, it would be two magnets repelling. Maybe I envied him, his obvious stability. Mind you, these had only been idle, fleeting thoughts; nothing significant. After all, I had the constitution of an ox. I'd never have to go and see Marlsford anyway.

But now I did. The receptionist called my name. I put down my copy of *Hello!* and stood up. I walked through the waiting room, past the benched old folk snuffling into their Reader's Digests, then out into the brightly lit corridor and through Marlsford's surgery door. Airily he gestured at me to sit down. I started to tell him about the seize-up, but quickly realised he wasn't listening. He was looking out of the window at the car park, an expression of mock-horror fixed ostentatiously on his face. No doubt it was something trivial. He'd be used to the regulars in here paying rapt attention to his every facial tic. Dr Marlsford, what a character.

'Incredible, I've never seen that before,' he said, employing the classic diversionary gambit of the arrogant fucker. 'Seven parking spaces, seven red cars. I wonder what the odds are about that!'

Jesus. I stood up and peered out of the window, feigning interest. Better to stay on-side. His type could be malicious. He had the power. He could book you into hospital for enemas when there was no need.

I looked out at the red cars. Granted, their simultaneous presence was an unusual coincidence. And what he hadn't noticed was that they were all hatchbacks. The odds against that were, let's see . . . I was never any good at odds.

'The bookies would probably only give you a hundred to one,' I said, in a friendly voice. 'But it's worth more than that. And if you included the hatchback factor, you could add a nought . . .'

Marlsford raised an eyebrow and went back to his notes. He hadn't expected a reply. It was all rhetorical, of course. He wasn't interested. Dr Marlsford a betting man? I don't think so. Then again, neither was I. It was all bravado, and ancient history at that, of diminished interest even to myself. A real betting man would skin me alive.

I started again on the seize-up. How I always kept a balance. Well, I knew it wasn't really a balance, but maybe it could delay things. I'd be 45, probably 50 before it caught up with me. So every morning I used to run: five, six miles; on Saturday mornings I did a nine-miler through the empty woods and bridle paths, pheasants and hares scattering ahead.

Then I could drink. I'd sweated it out, you see, in the mornings. Look at my face: no blemish. God, I love drinking, doctor. But only if you keep the balance. As a writer, you have to use it as a tool. Go slowly; only pick up the right tool, only when necessary. The afternoons are best. Mid-afternoon, when the sun comes to the study window across the unkempt lawn, and your mind just . . . *reaches*. Except, I know, I know, it's not really reaching. I'm quite aware. It's not expansion, it's contraction, depression, the shutting down of parts of the brain. But the thing is, doctor, it helps you find words – isolates them, eliminates alternatives, leads you to them with mystical certainty. In the right hands, it can be quite a beautiful process. A gamble, really: to get your best words down, before the drink catches up. It's either that, or decades of sunless attrition. I know which I'd choose. Sorry, have chosen.

'And when did these, er, symptoms begin?' Marlsford said.

'Begin? Well, I suppose when I was 26. That's when I started in earnest.'

'And you are now?'

'33. 33 and a half.'

'Yes. Mmm.' Marlsford drummed his fingers, adopting his mildly bored look. He looked at his watch.

OK. OK. Symptoms. Well, it happened about three weeks ago. A Saturday morning: I was setting off on my run and . . . nothing. I stumbled and stopped. Started again, stumbled, found myself sitting down among the nettles and spiders. Normally, you see, you can tell the exact state of your health when you're running. If you've a cold coming, or a virus, your legs will tell you: almost the exact proximity and strength of it, like an advance-warning system. Any runner will tell you that. But this time there'd been nothing. Just a few steps and – total shut-down, a seizing-up.

So, I'd panicked. I mean you had to keep the balance, sweat it out. I hauled myself back to the cottage – at Red House Farm, doctor, do you know it? I've seen you drive past – and got this bike I've been borrowing out of the stable. Cycled out towards town; four miles downhill, usually it's a breeze. And it took me an hour. Don't know how I made it; I just kept on, like in a dream. I was in the

Gents at the station for ages, stuff coming out of every orifice. Tried to get back on the bike; couldn't. Got a taxi back instead. The bike's still there, incidentally, chained to that old British Rail sign.

'Oh, that's yours, is it?' the doctor said, in his previously unpublicised capacity as chairman of Stray Bike Watch. 'And, um, had you done anything different that might have precipitated all this?'

Well, yes, actually, I told Marlsford: Bacardi. Normally it was beer, wine, a few gins – I saved the gins till the evening, but not too many, three trebles, because you can taste the strength in gins, to remind you; that's why I avoid vodka. I was behind, you see, doctor? I needed to write another book. *Needed*. But I couldn't think what . . . I did one before, *Road Star*, but it's two years ago now. It was one of those books that got good reviews and crap sales (56 hardback, 812 paperback). But this new book I was supposed to be writing – I couldn't, sort of, get on to it.

So to pay the rent I started doing these celebrity interviews, for a Sunday paper. I've done Gary Glitter, Max Bygraves, Jimmy White the snooker player. The old ones or the ones in decline, because they were easier and you might get something from them. Having said that, next I'm supposed to be doing Noel Edmonds – Christ – and he's not yet in decline, unfortunately. Ah, Jimmy White. What was it someone said? 'If you ever need some quick money, ask Jimmy for a game of cards.' Poor, sweet Jimmy. I still had his phone number. 147147. Maximum break. 'They can't take that away, can they?' Jimmy said. When Jimmy loses, a part of me bleeds. Just to think of Jimmy makes me smile. Are you a White fan, herr doctor?

'Jimmy, er? I'm not sure I know . . .' he bumbles. No, of course you don't.

So anyway, what with all these celebrity articles, I was getting distracted. Time was running out. And I was drinking hard all the time – didn't hold back when I was doing the articles, just to get through them. The drink was catching up with the words. But I still hadn't crossed the line.

Then I had this idea, a sudden angle, for the book. I had to pursue it. You see, many years ago, doctor – well, several – I was in New Orleans. I was in pursuit of something else, a person. In reality I think I was probably in pursuit of an idea, a lost, impractical idea at that, but the idea manifested itself in this person. And while I was there I drank these Bacardis, Cuba Libres, rum-and-Cokes. I didn't think anything of it at the time. What I drank was an irrelevancy. I was involved in the central business.

Now, melancholy is an important and difficult tone in writing, doctor, and this would be a melancholic story. It had to be delicately wrought. You couldn't let it tip over. But at the same time, you had to re-experience it, at least a *frisson*, to know how you were going to infuse it. So I started drinking the Cuba Libres again, to try and get the picture back. I think that's when I crossed the line, what caused the seize-up, all these other things that have been going on since. Because I drank them like beers, day and night for a month, getting the words down in my head. Not your pub rum-and-Cokes, mind you. Proper Cuba Libres. A jigger each of lime and lemon juice to cut it. Plenty of crushed ice. Some of the Cubans put mint leaves in, like *mojitos*, but I prefer not to. Beautiful. You could drink it for breakfast, easy, which in fact I did . . .

'Yes, yes,' Marlsford said impatiently. 'And these "other things", how exactly have they *manifested* themselves?'

'The vomiting and diarrhoea,' I said. 'Pretty constant. And when not, this feeling of nausea. Chronic fatigue. Can't eat. Just thinking of food makes me feel sick. Sometimes I even find it hard to drink, which is a new one. So then I drink cider. Only thing I can keep down. The sweetness and additives – fools the liver, thinks it's apple juice, lets you take it. That's why it's wino-fodder. Cheap gut-rot. A nasty mean thing to get drunk on. Emergencies only. Women and their half-a-dry-ciders – I've never understood it. On Sundays at the pub before lunch: 'Mmm, half a dry cider please. Lovely.' Mad.

And weight loss. My trousers fall down. I'll be a welter-weight soon. I used to be a light-heavy. Looking on the bright side, I'll have a reach advantage. Ha bloody ha.

Not the flicker of a fake smile from Marlsford. But I could tell he was interested.

'Stomach?' he almost barked.

'Eels.'

'What?'

'Eels,' I repeated. 'Like a load of eels swimming around in there. Sometimes when they're sleeping, I can crawl to the desk.'

'I see.'

'Basically I don't know what the fuck's going on, doctor. Oh, sorry.'

Marlsford brushed it aside. He was now on operational footing, starting with reconnaissance. With a few quick gestures and mutters he ordered me to strip and get on the trolley. His fingers were soon at work – away at my stomach disturbing the eels, delving around the liver, kidneys, liver again (found something?), briefly up my arse (serves him right). A nurse came in to take some blood. The syringe lay dangling on my arm, filling up, thick red against the green plastic trolley. I was sick into a grey cardboard bowl, proffered by the nurse with excellent timing. There must be a reading crisis in the waiting room by now.

From my elevated position I could see beyond Marlsford's whippet-like brow, beyond the line of red cars, out into the flat Suffolk countryside, with its thin trees. I thought, what the hell am I doing on this edge of England, where I know no one, have nothing? Well, I knew why. But maybe I had lost the gamble.

At least there were no flies in here. How was I to know Red House was a pig farm when I rented the cottage? You can't see over the hedgerows at ground level. The house-flies I can deal with. I must average 30–40 kills a day, three fly-swats in the study alone, strategically placed. No, it's the bluebottles. Horrible bastards. And so fast. You end up hypnotised. You can spend an hour chasing one bluebottle around.

I found myself dressed and back sitting opposite the doc. He was scribbling away on his prescription pad. He had a computer screen there as well. Outside, darkness had fallen. The screen glowed light blue, with my name at the top. No escape now.

'If you could just get me running again,' I heard myself saying. 'To restore the balance. Obviously I've cut out the Bacardis . . .'

'Look,' he said firmly, angrily even. 'You can forget about *running*. I'm sorry, but you're . . . fucked.'

'Eh?'

Fucked. This was a bit of a liberty. I mean, if I was my mother in there (God rest her soul), would he have said, 'I'm sorry, Mrs ——, but you're fucked'? I bet he wouldn't speak to his wife like that. Obviously, it was the only language he thought I'd understand. All right, I'd started it, but it was still a hellish liberty.

'How badly fucked, doctor?' I said anyway.

'Mmm, I'm not sure,' Marlsford said, with an air of ascetic reflection. 'The blood tests will show conclusively. And we'll have to book you in. Hospital. But pretty badly, I'm afraid, yes.'

'Right.'

'Your liver's very swollen. I'd be surprised if you don't have cirrhosis. And chronic pancreatitis, too. Certainly the

7

beginnings of it seem evident.' Marlsford paused, shooting me an eagle-like glance. 'Oh, and I'm fairly sure there's some hepatitis in there as well.'

'Right.'

'Plus a stomach ulcer. But we can sort that out.'

'OK.'

'You'll get a letter. About the hospital. You should get it tomorrow. I'd like to book you in immediately but . . .' But alcos come low on the list. It's all right, doctor. *Capito*, man.

'And I don't want to take you off booze entirely,' Marlsford went on. 'Because you won't sleep. You need sleep. Just stay off spirits. *And three meals a day.*'

I felt anger coming on. Jesus: as if I couldn't stay off the bottle for a few days. Fags, now there's a different matter. I wanted to tell him: if it's an operation I need, I can raise the dough. Don't you realise? Drink is endemic to what writers do. If not drink, something. It's like a plane to a carpenter. But you wouldn't condescend to a chippie like you do to me. So I am not 'fucked', as long as I am unfuckedable. Ask the 812 (868 including hardback) who read *Road Star*. It may not sound a lot, but it is. 868! They'd give a fiver each, no problem, to save me for another book. I bet you. That's over four grand. That should pay for putting me under the knife, push me 'up the list'. Because they write to me, these people. I've had two dozen letters. I've re-read them lovingly, carried them around (and yet I've never replied, the shame, can't face it: but I will, I will). And there was one from this man in Stoke, fourteen pages long, about this Cuban dancer called Johnny Tango. Amazing. It must have taken him a week to write that.

So you see, doctor, ours is a PUBLIC SERVICE, with unfortunate but unavoidable occupational side-effects – indeed debilitating ones, as you have seen – which MUST, where possible, BE CURED. And the most I ask is that, after appropriate adjustments on the occupational scale, I

receive EQUAL CURING RIGHTS TO ANYONE
ELSE.

But I didn't tell Dr Marlsford any of this. Instead, I stood
up, putting my hand out to receive the clump of
prescriptions he was peeling off his pad. Standing there, I
felt dizzy.

'Pancreatitis, cirrhosis. That's pretty serious,' I said.

'Yes.'

'Irreversible?'

'Well, yes.'

'But you're not sure.'

'No. As I say, the blood tests will be conclusive . . .'

'Terminal?'

'Look, you're an intelligent man . . .'

'Put it this way. If I went back on spirits, how long would
I last?'

Dr Marlsford paused, pursing his lips. This calculation
was of some interest.

'You mean, *heavily* on spirits?' he enquired.

'Heavily. Cuba Libres all over the place.'

'Well, if you did that, you could be a goner in, say, three
months. But I'm sure you're too sensible for that.'

I must have wavered, swayed a bit, because suddenly
Marlsford was doing his uncle routine, stretching out his
hand towards my shoulder, to steady me, if somewhat
distastefully.

'Now listen, erm, there are things we can do, so don't go
and do anything silly, old son,' Marlsford soothed. 'Top
yourself or anything like that.' As if. Stupid idiot.

I drove back up the slope of Market Street into the empty
town. Well, they call it a town round here. Population:
1,200. A chemist, a newsagent, Co-op, hole-in-the-wall
bookie's (no TV or free pens), another food shop, un-
frequented estate agent, much-frequented off-licence, impres-
sive church, Chinese take-away, megalomaniac butcher.

The bakery has just closed down. Along Market Street they lie grouped, across a cobbled road. It is picture-postcard, but it is deceptive. It is poor; not by international standards, but British poor, just out of range of weekenders. You could buy a broken-down mansion for a quarter of a mill. The farmers are doing all right, whatever they say. But in the town and in the villages they are generally ageing or skint or both, like me.

I loaded up at the chemist; then into the food shop opposite; stood gazing at the cans of food for ages. The barren wire basket swung in my hand. Is this 'shock'? I would give myself a treat. I deserved it. I would go for *haute cuisine* as a gesture to Mr Jimmy Gruber. The problem is, the shop does not cater much in this line. Just cans, mainly. I put a can of lobster bisque in, and a can of asparagus tips. No booze. I would show Marlsford. Fancy juices instead. They're extortionate, but who cares. Elderflower *pressé*, V8, ginger cordial with ginseng, Clammato: in they go. I'll drink them out of champagne flutes. Paid by cheque – goes through slower (if, indeed, it goes through). Almost forgot. Back across to the chemist for a packet of Nytols, to knock me out before the jitters set in.

The snakes came at around 3 a.m. Two or three dozen, all over the bed, plus a few eels too. What the hell were the eels doing there? I let them writhe over me for a while. But then five snakes got hold of a foot, one on each toe. I hopped downstairs, opened a window, pulled the snakes off my toes, flung them out. It wasn't difficult. They were only baby ones.

Back in the bedroom I put a heavy blanket over the snakes, tucked the blanket into the mattress, quickly and tight. Fastened the edges with books. Lay across two chairs, waiting for the crying dawn – crying with happiness when it came. Nytols. Got a couple of hours' light sleep. Woke up. Peeked under the blanket and the snakes had gone.

After a couple of fags I felt restored. I walked over to the window to view the legions of my immediate neighbours, snouts foraging, huge peach and apricot bellies swinging. Steam rose from the roofs of their little corrugated-iron houses, up into the bracing morning air. Another day in Pig City.

Downstairs I drank a Coke and surveyed the confusion of the kitchen – champagne flutes half full of murky liquids, the green and pink contents of the cans untouched in bowl and on plate. I headed for the study, pausing at the mirror in the hall. It was not somewhere I had lately dwelt. But something about my skin made me look closer, the texture . . . curiously fine-grained, with a sort of illuminated glow, sepia almost. It must be a paradox of ill health, I reflected, that in my current disgusting condition I had attained an unprecedented handsomeness.

In my absence, the flies had multiplied in the study. No bluebottles, though. I annihilated seven or eight of the slow house-flies and sat down at the desk, opening a notebook I used for lists, and placing the bloodied swat within reach.

Lists had comprised my whole output for the last month, instead of Noel Edmonds. They had started out, a few years before, as sincerely drawn plans, setting out the future conquering of my objectives. But they were ludicrously optimistic, and very quickly out of date. Once I overcame this realisation, I still did them. They no longer took the form of plans. They could be called, I suppose, post-modern lists. Or, just lists. They were aimless and therapeutic, yet raised the amusing illusion of order. At least now I had a real reason for a list, like a reckoning. Yes, this would be a proper list, with no silly names this time, like Jimmy White (sorry, noble Jimmy), or ancient boxers, or the names of favoured horses or cocktails.

I wrote:

BAD PEOPLE: Uncle Paul (?); Jimmy Gruber (very); Walter.

And then, underneath:

GOOD PEOPLE: Carol; Walter (despite himself); Johnny; Tony Bamber (?), Stanley.

I sat looking at the list, and then out of the window, at the tangled summer green. An hour must have passed. It was afternoon. The sunlight crept to the study window. But it wasn't the same without booze. It seemed raw and unfiltered; a metallic glare.

I wanted a drink. A large gin in a tumbler, lots of ice, a splash of tonic from a new bottle (nice and fizzy), with a chunk of unwaxed Greek lemon plucked straight from the tree, two leaves still attached. Run the rest of the cut lemon round the rim of the glass just to freshen it up. No. Can't.

I started rifling through the desk drawers instead. There was some dope in there that someone had left. It must be a year ago now. My last agent. She only brought it because she thought I was a dope-fiend. But I'm not. Can't write on dope. There'd be no writing today: start tomorrow. Nice of her, though.

I fished out the silvery packet, rolled an amateurish joint with the ancient dope. Drug people have always rather intimidated me with their dextrous cool. Now drink, though . . .

Lit up, inhaled. Disgusting. Stubbed it out and poured myself a small gin. Not the deluxe model but it was a runner nonetheless. I could feel the eels massing at the mere sight of it.

I anaesthetised them by putting down the whole lot; three greedy gulps. Felt better immediately. Poured another. Ah, the soft deadening, the introspective calm.

The light got better as well; its warmth on my face. So, three months, eh? I looked at Uncle Paul's name on the pad. What if he was misunderstood? Could be. I was only a kid after all.

For a moment I imagined I was back there, ten years old, in the house in the dip, by the conker trees, the Downs stretching out, with the only thing to look forward to a pure, long and blameless life. Then again, if I was back there, I suppose Stuart and Julian would have to be there too. Hmm. My God, that was a weird time, looking back. I picked up the pen, crossed Uncle Paul's name off the BAD PERSONS list, and wrote in those of Stuart and Julian.

The phone rang. Must be the paper. Christ. About Noel . . .

I picked the phone up – a woman's voice, quite posh. That new one on the features desk? Whatsername. Caroline?

'Sorry I haven't been in touch,' I said. 'But I've been . . .' No, don't tell them. Never admit frailty. You'll be out. And you need the rent. Act insouciant, in-demand. 'Yeah, sorry, I've been away on assignment for this magazine. Anyway I've been on to Noel Edmonds' people, and frankly they're not keen. I suppose we could do it without Noel. I could go down to that theme park of his. Y'know, Mr Blobby? Have a snoop around, go on the rides. Mind you, I'll be a bit conspicuous, the only one over twelve. But don't worry, I can work it out.'

'Really?'

'Yeah. I mean, if security collars me, I can always say I'm a teacher, checking things out for the kiddies in advance.' I attempted an insouciant chuckle. Caroline did not respond. 'But to be honest, Caroline, what I am thinking is: Noel Edmonds, is he worth it without access?'

'I'm not calling about Noel Edmonds.'

'Oh.'

13

'And my name's not Caroline.'

'I see. Sorry . . . Who are you then?'

'My name is Rachel. I'm calling from a publisher's called Yellow Jersey Press.'

'Yes . . .?'

'I'm thinking of giving you £12,000.'

'Are you?'

'Yes, I am.'

'Great,' I said.

'But the catch is, you have to spend it on gambling – horses, the dogs, casinos, boxing, footie, that sort of thing – and then write a book about it.'

Didn't sound like a catch to me. Always unfortunate when m-class use the term 'footie' but let it pass, of course, in the circumstances. Twelve grand eh. So there is a God after all.

Perhaps prompted by spiritual reference, found myself drifting off a bit. Holding the phone receiver, I looked out at my view. That funny stray dog had got into the garden again. I've got two doves that live on the chimney, with occasional flights down to the lawn. Always after the doves, this dog. Sort of creeps up on them pawing at the air. But they're always long gone. He's got no chance at all. There'd be more chance of 14 red hatchbacks in Marlsford's car park.

Doves flew off and the dog slunk away. I lit another fag and listened to this Rachel going on about the 12-G idea. Sounded quite bossy. Not complaining, naturally, . . . not in my state. Jesus Christ! One dove's come back, and that dog's still lolling quite near. Stupid dove hasn't seen it. Bloody risky and . . . oh yes it has. Just a bit of dog-baiting. Clever dove. Sorry kid. Sorry?

'. . . I said of course any profits made are entirely yours. But if you lose it all, I still want my book . . .'

2

The Pond in the Fields

When I was ten years old I was living with a family called the Pratts. They were thinking of changing their name from Pratt to something else, because of the things people sometimes said. Prattley, Prattham and Partt were being considered. But in the end they decided to stick with Pratt.

Auntie Jean (Pratt) was my godmother and my mother's best friend. My mother died trying to give birth to my younger brother, Ben, who was stillborn. Afterwards, Auntie Jean became my guardian. She had a son called Stuart who was 18 months older than me and together we lived in a tiny cottage near Epsom Downs. There was another son called Julian who was two years older than Stuart, but he wasn't there most of the time, because he was away at boarding school, and only came home on exeats.

All around us during the day racehorses were being exercised. The cottage was a lodge at the foot of a drive that led to a mansion owned by an elderly couple called the Greaveses. They owned all the racehorses. The cottage was in a dip, so you couldn't see the mansion, only the tall conker trees that stood on either side of the drive like sentries.

The Greaveses had no children, but Auntie Jean said they didn't need to, because to them each racehorse was a special child. Auntie Jean was very fond of horses herself. She wore jodhpurs all the time, even when she wasn't riding. She didn't eat much, and so was very thin, with black hair that she said had a mind of its own, because it stood up in the mornings. Auntie Jean had two horses, but they weren't like the Greaveses'. They were two mares called Nobbin and Noggin, who were very old and very fat.

In the mornings Auntie Jean rode out the Greaveses' horses and, in the afternoons, after school, she tried to teach me and Stuart how to ride like jockeys. When she was younger Auntie Jean was a stable lass at a yard in Newmarket and her ambition was to be a jockey, but they didn't allow lady jockeys then.

The only horses we rode were Nobbin and Noggin. Auntie Jean groomed them before breakfast. Then she came in and combed her hair in the mirror in the hall. She pulled the comb through her hair the same way she pulled it through Nobbin and Noggin's manes. When she'd finished she always looked at us and said, 'Not bad for a 21-year-old, eh?' Stuart said it was true that Auntie Jean was 21 years old, but I wasn't sure, because I knew that she and Mum were at the same class at school when they met, and Mum was 29 years old when she died.

Nobbin and Noggin were kept in the garden of the cottage in a stable built by Auntie Jean's husband, Uncle Paul. The stable was higgledy-piggledy because Uncle Paul got fed up half-way through and built the second half in a rage.

Stuart told me that in court, when they decided whether Auntie Jean should have me or I should be put up for adoption, Auntie Jean had said she and Uncle Paul were still happily married, but that this had been a lie.

Uncle Paul wasn't even living at the cottage by the time I moved in, but I remembered him from before. He'd been a very good cricketer. He was a fast bowler and played two county cricket matches for Surrey. There used to be a photograph on top of the television in the cottage, of Uncle Paul appealing for a catch. But then he'd got injured and he couldn't play any more.

He wasn't like other boys' dads. He was taller and younger and more handsome, and he didn't seem to like boys. The only boy he liked was Julian. He especially didn't like Stuart. He was always teasing him and cuffing him and making him cry. Then when Stuart cried Uncle Paul got really angry and hit him. I saw him kick Stuart once when he was down. But mainly Uncle Paul just ignored us. He was either watching football or horse-racing on television or going off to the pub in his little white Mini with stripes down the side which he drove very fast.

My mother, when she was alive, didn't like Uncle Paul at all. She used to talk about him with Auntie Jean on the phone. 'He's a bad man, Jean,' I heard her say. All the Pratts except Uncle Paul once turned up at our house in the middle of the night, because of something Uncle Paul had done, and we all shared two beds.

After I went to live at the cottage, I only saw Uncle Paul twice. Once was when the police came to arrest him. Stuart and me had just gone to bed. Then the whole cottage was engulfed by dazzling light and noise. Outside was Uncle Paul's Mini. He was still in it, revving the engine as hard as he could, and shining the headlamps on full beam at Auntie Jean's room. He stayed there for ages. Then the police car arrived, and Uncle Paul drove off. As he went whizzing past our bedroom window his face was lit up by the police car's headlamps. He had a grin on his face, but he also looked sad. I don't know if they caught him or not.

Every summer we took the day off school for the Epsom Derby. We always watched from the same place on the Downs, up by the start, looking down on Tattenham Corner to the right and the grandstand to the left. We used to go there when Mum was alive, and have a picnic with the Pratts on the grass. From our position, we could see hundreds of thousands of people swarming over the Downs like ants. Normally, when I played on the Downs, there were only a few people walking dogs, and, on Saturday mornings, a group of men I used to watch flying model aeroplanes, using the racetrack as a runway. You could walk right across the empty concrete steps of the grandstand and no one would stop you.

I preferred the Downs on Derby Day. It was always sunny – at least in my mind, it was. There was a funfair across the main road from the racecourse. The caravans of the gypsies who ran the fair began arriving a week before the race. Soon dozens of other caravans arrived, because the Derby was a gypsy celebration, and they came from all over the country. By the time we had our picnic, the air was full of the delicious smell of frying food, and the sound of galloping hooves and the distant tunes of the funfair rides. For a day it seemed as though the Downs was the centre of the world.

But on my first Derby alone with the Pratts, when I looked down at all the people, it was different. It seemed unfair that they could all be there and Mum couldn't. Mum loved Derby Day. It was the only time she ever put a bet on racehorses. She always used to bet on the horse ridden by a jockey called Geoff Lewis. This was because once, when I was a toddler, I got away from Mum and ran out under the rails in front of the stalls at the start. Geoff Lewis was about to get on his horse, but instead he rushed over and picked me up and handed me back to Mum over the rails. She said Geoff Lewis might have saved my life.

I didn't remember that, but I did remember Mum saying 'Good luck!' once to Geoff Lewis as he walked to the start, and him patting me on the head and saying something nice to Mum.

Mum also used to take me to look at the funfair after the Derby was over. But Auntie Jean said me and Stuart couldn't go because it was too dangerous. The gypsies were all pickpockets and they carried knives. Stuart and I pretended to be disappointed but we weren't too much. For the last two evenings we'd sneaked off to the funfair on our bikes while Auntie Jean was over at the Greaveses' stables looking after their Derby horses.

Stuart hadn't wanted to stay long at the funfair. He said that if we did, the gypsies would steal our bikes. Because Stuart was 18 months older and bigger than me, we always had to do what he said.

Before the Derby started, Auntie Jean went off to put our bets on. She was going to bet £1 on the Greaveses' horse, and 50p each for me and Stuart on the Queen's horse. Normally I never answered back to Auntie Jean, even when she made me eat the whites in boiled eggs, which Mum never made me do. But this time I said, 'Auntie Jean, I don't want to bet on the Queen's horse. Please may I bet on Geoff Lewis's horse?'

Auntie Jean opened her mouth wide and looked at me sternly. Sometimes she did this look jokingly, so I examined her to see if it was fake or true. When I realised it was true, I looked down at the picnic things.

Auntie Jean said, 'You *can* be an ungrateful boy, can't you, John?'

'It's only, Mum always bet on Geoff Lewis's horse,' I said.

After that Auntie Jean didn't say anything except to tell me and Stuart to clear up the picnic things while she went to put on our bets. Then she came back and handed me a yellow ticket and told me that Geoff Lewis's horse was called Mill Reef.

A few minutes later we saw the jockeys ride past on their way to the stalls. As usual they were chatting and joking to each other, but in a way that was different from the earlier races. As Geoff Lewis rode Mill Reef into the stalls his face was deadly serious.

After the race started we could keep track of the leaders until Tattenham Corner, but after that the horses and jockeys zoomed down a slope, and we had to rely on the tannoy. Then in the finishing straight they reappeared as coloured specks between gaps in the crowd. The cries of the crowd were so loud that they drowned out the announcer's voice, so we went right up beneath the tower that held the dark green cones of the tannoy. I heard the announcer shouting, 'It's Mill Reef! It's Mill Reef!'

Once Stuart saw Mill Reef had won, he kicked me in the shins. But I didn't care. In the distance I saw Geoff Lewis trotting back to the winner's enclosure. Mill Reef was rolling his head as though he was laughing. Then Geoff Lewis looked up and gave a wave. The crowd opposite the grandstand roared and clapped, thinking he was waving at them, but I was sure he was looking over their heads, to where I stood on the hill, and waving at me and Mum. I waved back. It was our secret victory. No one else could break the secret happiness that only Mum, me, Geoff Lewis and Mill Reef knew about.

Auntie Jean gave me my winnings. I put the money in my pocket and she said, 'Well, aren't you going to count it, John?' I didn't want to make her cross again, so I took it out and counted it on the grass. There was £2 and 10 pence. I made sure to say thank you. Then when we got home I thanked her again and she smiled. I could tell Auntie Jean thought the reason I was so happy was because of the winnings, but I didn't tell her it was because of something else.

That evening she and Stuart walked up to the Greaveses for a Derby dinner. Mrs Greaves was Stuart's godmother so he had to go. As soon as they were gone I got on my bike and rode back to the funfair. It was a windy evening and as I cycled over the Downs millions of little balls of litter rolled around the empty racecourse as if they were having their own races.

It was eight o'clock when I padlocked my bike beneath

the clock on the grandstand. The lights from the funfair lit up my combination lock in strange colours when I moved the numbers. The funfair was packed. By then there were hardly any boys my age around, apart from the gypsy boys who were working on the rides. Gangs of teenage boys in bell-bottoms and leather jackets were crashing into each other in the bumper cars. Their girlfriends sat beside them smoking cigarettes and laughing and screaming. A beer tent had been set up, and a strip-tease tent which was dark. The beer tent was full of men. The sun was setting, and the wind made whipping noises across the top of the tents. The wind mixed the smells of beer, smoke and horses together, and the sound of bumper cars and music, the voices of the men and the screams of the teenage girls.

I spent about half my winnings. I bought a fizzy drink and a hamburger (delicious) and for a while I played the game in the arcade where you push coins off a shelf. Some of them dropped but not as many as I put in. Mainly I walked round and round the grass alleyways between the tents. Lots of things were piled up in the grass: candyfloss sticks and cigarette packets, and half-eaten toffee-apples with lipstick on them that crunched under my feet.

It started to rain, and then suddenly the strip-tease tent lit up. Almost all the men came out of the beer tent and crowded round. A gypsy man stood in front of them calling out, 'See your money to see the girls.' Some of the men fumbled in their pockets, clenching their cigarettes between their teeth, and then held up pound notes above their heads. Two gypsy ladies stood on platforms made of beer crates, one each side of the gypsy man. They were wearing raincoats with the buttons undone. All they had on under the raincoats were bikinis. They were swaying and staring at the men. Every time they swayed, the men cheered and laughed and whistled. But in between laughs they took quick puffs on their cigarettes and their faces looked serious, like the faces of the jockeys just before they went into the Derby stalls.

More and more men put up pound notes. Then the gypsy ladies went inside, and gypsy boys got up on the crates, taking the notes from the men's hands as they followed the gypsy ladies into the tent.

I rode back over the Downs. I'd forgotten what the time was so I rode very fast, even though I didn't have any lights. I got into bed just before Auntie Jean and Stuart came back. When Stuart went to bed, I pretended to be fast asleep. Then when I heard him sleeping, I opened my eyes again and lay for a long time in the dark. I looked through the bedroom window at the conker trees swaying in the wind, thinking of the gypsy ladies, and wondering if when I grew up I'd be a good man like Mum would have wanted, or a bad man like Uncle Paul.

That was the other time I saw Uncle Paul. He'd been standing holding his pound up in the air, as if he was appealing for a catch again. For a while I was worried that he'd seen me, but I was pretty sure he hadn't. And, anyway, I never saw or heard of Uncle Paul again after that.

The next year my horse won again at the Derby. This time I didn't bet on Geoff Lewis's horse, but on a horse named after a ballet dancer called Nijinsky. Mum used to do ballet when she was a girl. Sometimes she read things out about ballet from the newspaper at breakfast. Her favourite dancer was Margot Fonteyn, but I knew she liked Nijinsky too. Once she put up a picture of him dancing with Fonteyn half-way up the stairs, but it fell down and broke when I was six and trying to beat my world record at stair-jumping.

When Nijinsky won the Derby Auntie Jean said I must be psychic, or something like that. She gave me my winnings (£1.90, because Nijinsky was the favourite), and said, 'You could at least look happy, John.' I was looking unhappy because Julian had just kicked me. His bet was on the Queen's horse, and Julian kicked a lot harder than Stuart. But I didn't tell.

Since Christmas Julian had been living with us at the cottage all the time. Stuart told me it was because Auntie Jean couldn't afford the fees for boarding-school any more. Julian's fourteenth birthday was two days before Derby Day, and Auntie Jean said that was why he was a little full of himself. Julian being there meant that since Christmas he had Stuart's bed, Stuart had mine and I had the camp-bed.

Julian thought about his willy all the time. His willy was like a man's willy with pubic hair. Stuart had a few pubic hairs but I didn't have any yet. Julian was always taking his willy out and making it go hard like a stalk, then waving it around and sticking it into things.

Auntie Jean didn't know about Julian's willy things, but she was always getting cross about other things we did, like firing conkers with our catapults at the Greaveses' car from the tree-house we'd built, and sawing down one of the Greaveses' conifers to make a Christmas tree.

But then Auntie Jean got ill. She was always tired and stopped bothering to be cross. She stopped combing her hair, so it stood up on end all the time, and she didn't say 'not bad for a 21-year-old' any more. Auntie Jean didn't seem to eat anything, and for our tea on most days we had leftover fish-fingers that we chucked in the fireplace when Auntie Jean wasn't looking and covered with ashes.

We started not going home for tea at all. We stayed out on the Downs or up the tree-house, and went on expeditions through the woods with our catapults and strangling ropes in case we met enemies. If you went far enough through the woods you came out on to a grass bank overlooking the dual carriageway to London. Usually we started off by sitting on the bank and firing conkers and stones at all the cars. But then Julian got bored and took out his willy and waved it at them instead.

Sometimes Julian stuck his willy in Stuart and me. Once, in the tree-house, Julian told Stuart to stick his willy in my mouth and I was sick. Another time, we went down to the stable at night and Julian tried to stick it in Nobbin. But Nobbin started kicking so Julian made a hole in a hay bale instead and stuck it in there until white stuff came out.

As Stuart got more and more pubic hairs, he got much stronger and more like Julian. I could feel his new strength in our fights. Before, I was almost equal to Stuart, and sometimes when I hit him I could make him cry. Now, Stuart could ambush me more easily, and hit me much more than I could hit him when he pinned me down. I knew I would catch up once I got more pubic hairs, but I decided that I should try and avoid fights with Stuart until I did.

But Stuart wanted to do everything Julian could do. He started getting his willy out when we were on our own, without Julian asking him to. I never let Stuart stick it in me. I had to fight him then. It was difficult but I found that if I kept getting in a few hits in between all his hits, Stuart would still cry in the end, and his willy would go soft.

I never cried, not even when Stuart used his strangling rope, because if I had ever cried, Stuart would have won.

The summer after we sawed down the Greaveses' conifer, Auntie Jean felt better and we went on a working holiday to a village near Newmarket. Just Auntie Jean, Stuart and me went. Julian stayed behind to look after Noggin and Nobbin. It was there I went to the pond in the fields.

Stuart had told me about this pond before. The pond, Stuart said, was deep in a wood surrounded by miles and miles of countryside, and contained the biggest fish you could ever catch in a pond in England. Stuart recounted all the huge fish he had caught when he'd been there before – carp, tench and pike, but mainly carp – and all the monster fishes that had got away. All the time he had been catching these fish, Stuart said, he had never seen another soul at the pond.

This was because the pond lay in the middle of a great estate owned by an American lady called Mrs Abercrombie, a spinster millionairess who owned Derby horses. But she was never there. She lived in America. When Auntie Jean had been a stable lass in Newmarket, she'd exercised Mrs Abercrombie's horses. Mrs Abercrombie had always remembered her, and that's why she still asked Auntie Jean to go on working holidays from time to time. Stuart said the pond was a secret place that only Auntie Jean, Stuart and a few others who exercised Mrs Abercrombie's horses knew about, but I didn't really believe him.

The pond was up a steep hill about twenty minutes' walk from the village. Me and Stuart walked carrying our rods up a narrow road to the top of the hill. Then we walked across a field to another road which was even narrower, with green hedgerows so high that they folded over the road like a magical tunnel.

The way to the pond was after a sign saying 'by-road'. Stuart was very proud of knowing the way. After a couple of fields we could see the wood ahead. Stuart waved at it wildly. And it was just like he'd said. You'd never think there was a pond in there.

But there was. The water was deep green and still. Its mirrored surface made a green picture of the summer sky. The lily pads went across the pond like flat green stones being skimmed. Sometimes the mirror was broken by fish coming up and rolling over.

We put the bread on the hooks. First cast, my float went under, right down to the deeps. I struck with the rod, but the line broke. I'd fished before, at the reservoir, but I'd never felt a fish like that. My hands were shaking with excitement when I slid another float on.

I didn't get another bite, but it didn't matter. The pond was the most beautiful place I'd ever seen. I cast the float out again and watched the sky come back together from the ripples. I could have watched the float for ever.

But I could tell Stuart was getting bored. That was when I knew that although what Stuart had said about the fish was true, it wasn't true that he'd caught any of them. After a few minutes Stuart threw down his rod, and walked jauntily to the other side of the pond. First he tried to build a dam with stones from the path, but the river was too deep. Then he began picking up the stones and lobbing them at my float. Finally he walked back round to me.

'I'm going to live here when I grow up,' Stuart said.

'Are you?' I said. 'Are you really going to?' I didn't think Stuart really wanted to live at the pond. But when he was bored he was most likely to start fights, so I tried to be as eager as I could.

'Yeah, I am,' Stuart went on. 'I'm going to be the owner. Because I found it.'

I agreed with Stuart, and then asked him if I might be able to come and live at the pond sometimes too, even though he would be the owner. Stuart liked that question, and said he'd think about it. Soon we were discussing excitedly what we would do when we lived at the pond.

We got up before dawn every day to go down to the Newmarket gallops with Auntie Jean. It was dark when we left the holiday cottage. When the sun came up it was as though we had arrived in a city of horses. There were far more than in Epsom. All the top horses in the world lived in Newmarket. Every dawn was golden, and steam came off all the horses like gold mist.

Because Auntie Jean was busy, for lunch she gave us some

money and we walked into Newmarket town, to the Wimpy or the fish-and-chip shop. When we had fish and chips we went across the road and ate them on the steps by the statue of Hyperion. Auntie Jean said Hyperion was the most famous Derby horse ever. He won the Derby in 1933, and lived to be 30, which was very old for a horse.

Once a jockey came up to us while we were eating our chips and said the statue was wrong. Hyperion's face was looking down, when it should be looking up. Everyone knew that Hyperion was always looking up at the sky, the jockey said, because during his life had come the dawn of air travel, and it was trying to find out the secret of flying that kept Hyperion going so long. 'A pilot is what the old fella really wanted to be,' the jockey added.

Every evening, after tea, we went to the pond in the fields. We never saw anyone else there. We built a camp overlooking the pond, and a proper dam in front of it with logs from the wood, like a harbour.

Sometimes we took cigars we'd found in a box at the holiday cottage. We didn't like the taste, but the cigar smoke kept the midges off. There were loads of midges swarming round in the evening. They made the wood like the jungle. Holding the cigars made us feel grown up, as though we were living at the pond already.

Then the two weeks ended. It was the best time I'd had since moving in with the Pratts. Thanks to the pond, and being more expert at camps, damming and fish, I'd managed to get equal with Stuart again. As we drove back, I thought how Mum would have liked the pond, and Newmarket, especially the gallops. I imagined us having a picnic breakfast in the middle of the gallops, watching all the horses go round.

The Epsom Downs came into view, and I realised it was time I stopped thinking what Mum would have thought all the time and started thinking for myself. The pond had also made me realise that one day I would leave the Pratts, and I imagined a world beyond Stuart, Julian and Auntie Jean.

Auntie Jean parked the car in her spot under the first conker tree. I saw Julian dropping down from the tree-house with his catapult in his hand. As we unpacked the things from the car I decided I would still remember the pond after everyone else had forgotten about it. And probably I really would live there.

3

Dead Meat

The more I listened to Rachel telling me about this 12-grand book, the more I realised it was a con. From her voice, she genuinely didn't seem aware that it was. Telephone voice-imaging of Rachel: tall, theoretically beautiful with brutal dyed-black bob; yet considering herself worldly and fashionably hard-living – this despite only ten fags a day, half a bottle of dry white per night, max. Drugs? No, though dropped coke references; late twenties, ambitious and so far unstopped; knew everyone there was; jackboots? But it was. A con, I mean.

For a start, she wasn't really proposing to 'give' me the 12 grand. I would get the money all right, but it would be held against me on account, as an 'advance'. Except, a normal advance can be invested entirely at an author's discretion (in my case, booze, fags and travel costs had consumed 100 per cent of the *Road Star* advance): this money, however, *had* contractually to be invested wholly in gambling bets. Only winnings could then be dispersed in the way that a normal advance could be.

Of course, as Rachel could no doubt argue, I had the chance, thanks to my 12-grand stake, to make far more than a normal advance, far more indeed than 12 grand: one sensational winning bet, or more likely one run of winning bets with bold but judiciously adjusted stakes, could result in fantastic spoils.

But there were two fundamental impediments to this argument. The first was that Rachel, in what no doubt was a misguided attempt to guarantee material, did not intend to pay the money in one go. If she had, naturally I would have taken the whole 12 grand down to London to a casino roulette table, had a word with the manager about raising the single-bet limit (which he would have done, because roulette is the ultimate mug's game), and put the lot on Red. Twenty-four grand or nothing. Admittedly, it would have been a short book.

Instead, Rachel proposed paying it out in monthly instalments, a grand at a time. This was going much too far. You could fritter that away on pensioner bets without knowing you'd had it.

The most popular bet among pensioners in my little hell-hole bookie's in the town, U–Bet (where pensioners make up the entire clientele apart from, occasionally, me), is the 5p-win Heinz. It is so named because over six races it allows for 57 varieties of bets in singles, doubles, trebles, quadruples, quintuples and sextuples. It costs 57 × 5p: £2.35, plus optional 9 per cent tax.

If all six bets came in, you would arithmetically be at least a millionaire, even if they were all favourites, were it not for U–Bet's stingy £250,000 upper pay-out limit. Yet even this swindling quarter-mill was prospect enough to encourage a certain cavalier perspective about finance among the pensioners, to the extent that most didn't bother paying the tax in advance, figuring they would have quite enough spare to pay it later on. And if you had asked them what a grand a month meant to a betting man, they would without hesitation all have replied: peanuts.

Moreover, this slow twelve-month drip – leaving aside Marlsford's scare-mongering prediction that I would not live through a quarter of it – would mean prolonged exposure to gambling environments. Each tiny detail of these places is designed to fleece the gambler by the relentless and accumulated availability of temptation. Go into the bookie's once a year – on that one, exceptionally rare, occasion when all the conditions surrounding a particular bet, I mean *all*, appear to converge favourably – and you could win, if you're lucky. But go in every day? Then you're dead meat. No one can survive. You might as well leave the money at the door and go home.

The second impediment was that, though by most people's standards I have spent an excessive and ruinous amount of time in gambling environments, I am not by temperament or inclination a betting man. The bets themselves generally bore me. I don't care whether I win or lose. I find the sight of overt and obviously heartfelt satisfaction in an experienced gambler as he collects on a winning bet (as opposed to pretending to be pleased, which we all do) morally repugnant. In an inexperienced gambler, it is of course sweet.

The wider, recent advance of new gambling forms into the former heartlands of non-gamblers, via the Lottery, scratch-cards, 'spread'-betting (you can bet on the number of yellow cards in a football match. Thus you watch the match. Can there be anything so mundane, mind-numbingly trivialising, so anti the noble precepts of sport?), plus the novelty will-it-be-snowing-when-Elvis-returns odds which are eagerly published as fillers by naïve subalterns while the bookies look on smiling – all these I find more sinister. Though disguised as 'leisure activities', I regard them as rip-off scams borrowed from America, with worse odds. Mainly it is just naked commerce, but there are cynical proselytisers, enemy strategists in the silent war, deriving satisfaction too, at another strike. Personally I hold the quaint view that the British lottery is a tax on the poor. S'why in supermarkets the lot'tree tickets are by the fag counter, right?

And professional gamblers? I suspect Rachel wants her author to aspire to this tiny breed, mythologised by

Hollywood. To aspire, yet to fail. That would make a good book. With a certain innocence. Like Buster Keaton walking along while civilisation tumbles about his ears.

Actually, I've met a few professional gamblers. In Vegas when I have been there over the years, indulging an interest in boxing. And they're not like in films, the pro gamblers. In fact they all struck me quite forcibly, and unexpectedly, as a banal and cowardly bunch. They existed in the environment, but failed to see its necessarily tragic dimension. Their life was scoring points. Since the game was so stacked against them, it took great reserves of attritional energy to find ways of lessening their disadvantage and clawing their points.

They had developed complicated, devious systems and formulas to do this. They analysed stakes and odds to the nth degree. Their mantra was 'value': its seeking and the ways it might be denied them. Reckless frontal charges and other desperate acts of heroism were ruled out as despised anathema to the vital concentration of resources.

Theirs were small-casualty battles composed of intricate flanking movements. The longer war was all. It was a cumulative process of tiny victories. In this, they mirrored exactly the approach of their enemies, the odds-setters, who were only doing it as a job. At each tiny victory, I have never seen anyone so happy. They had extinguished the spark that makes the rest of us bet.

I prefer losers. They're more self-aware. I once interviewed this theatre director for the paper. He'd been a terrible gambler from his early twenties to his mid-thirties. Blackjack. He hated winning. The small wins were worst: 'A gambler coming out of a casino at four in the morning with £5 in his pocket feels terrible. When I came out with nothing I felt elated.' Soon he devised a sure way out. He started playing blackjack as if he was the House, taking cards up to 17 every hand. OK, some of the other punters weren't happy. But without the House's other built-in advantages, he was guaranteed the failure he craved. For twelve years he did it every night.

No, it's not the bets I like. It's the environments. Racetracks, casinos. I like the punters, the horses, the 'peripheral' people manning it all: old stewards, croupiers. They have a strange mixture of devotion and detachment. It's all cash in hand. Tomorrow, who knows? Much of it is inexplicable. The snap of the stalls opening; the flicking card-decks as they're expertly shuffled.

I knew therefore I would be doubly handicapped if I did the 12-grand book. Though I can be well-versed, I don't pay proper attention to form, odds, 'value'. Even if I do, I am liable to last-minute hunches and hasty frontal assaults. I am not a 'mug' punter. I am simply the type who should be kept away from the environment, its temptation. Yet it is only the environment that attracts me.

Let's say, optimistically, that I land one bet out of three. Casino blackjack bets – even money. That's a 4-grand advance: not enough to keep me in fags unless I dropped down to one pack. Then after the gambling was over there would be a book to write. About what? After the book was written, it would require sales of – say a pound a book as my share – approximately 11,008 more copies than *Road Star* had sold, before I'd see any royalties. And this was not compulsion, art: it was a deal proposed by someone else.

One had to be sceptical. In fact, one would be a fool to even countenance such terms. These things went through my mind.

'When do I start?' I said.

'Oh good,' Rachel said bossily. 'I'm so glad you'll do it. You're a very difficult man to find.'

'In certain circles I am known as "always available".'

Rachel ignored this.

She said, 'I've been talking to someone else but I decided he was pissing me around.'

Someone else? *Someone else?* This was not on. So I wasn't even No. 1, eh. And for someone else, read someone elses. I was probably No. 3 or 4. Or 5. How many people had turned down this book?

'Who was it you were, er, talking to then, just as a matter of interest,' I said as disinterestedly as possible.

'Oh, Tom Layburn.'

I had read Layburn. He wrote a column in the paper. It was one of the paper's few readable bits (along with my own contributions, of course – savagely mutilated by the sub-editors though they were). He had a picture byline at the top of the column: mid-thirties; a drinker's face. His columns went off at weird tangents towards the end. They were the best parts, funny. Mine used to do that, when I first started. It's always a sign. Now I can control it, keep the same sober tone right through, however raving pissed I am.

This meant either Tom Layburn had started drinking recently, or he had been drinking a long time and was now suffering tolerance fatigue: a drastic drop in tolerance to alcohol, experienced after approximately a decade of hard drinking, and generally presaging a chronic deterioration of health. Then, a few weeks ago, the paper went colour. As far as Tom Layburn's picture byline was concerned, it was illuminating, if not flattering: a red full moon stamped in the middle of his face, the gin blossoms of broken arteries spreading out from his nose into the cheeks. So, tolerance fatigue it was.

'I wanted someone dissolute and louche,' Rachel was saying.

'I'm not sure I qualify for louche,' I said. 'I live on a fly-blown pig farm.'

'Well, dissolute then.'

'Dissolute I can do.'

'Tom Layburn was *very* dissolute. I think he was too

34

dissolute even for me. He's a terrible drinker, you know.'

'I know.'

'Oh, you know him?'

'No, but you can tell, from the picture . . .'

'I took him to lunch. He smelled of meths.' Yes, darling, and he speaks highly of your *odeur* too.

'So what was his objection, to the book I mean?' I said.

'That the twelve thousand was held as an advance. He said it was unfair. Tom kept fussing about it.'

'It is unfair. But necessary, in order for the twelve grand to mean anything. For it to be the only hope the author has left. So he can really live it. For the . . . *purity* of the book.' Jesus, the things we say. 'For the same reason, it has to be three months, not twelve,' I added.

'Why?'

'Because.'

So it was settled. There was a compromise over the payments. She wouldn't do the whole 12 grand up front. It was to be 4 grand in three monthly instalments. The first 4 grand would be at a bank in Ipswich by Monday. Poor Tom. Well, lucky Tom probably.

And she asked me to lunch in London. But I said no. The dissolution and loucheness might not be up to scratch. It's best to keep your distance. And though I take pains not to smell, there was a 50-50 chance I would unintentionally vomit all over the table.

'Oh, and I've already got a title,' Rachel said.

'Have you?'

'Yes. "Twelve Grand." And a sub-title.'

'Yes?'

'"The Gambler as Hero." I hope that's OK.'

'Why "The Gambler as Hero"? I mean, do you think we really need a sub-title . . .'

'Yes, we do. And I don't really know why. I just thought it sounded nice.'

'Right.' Christ. All the years of aspiration, suffering, lists, attempted art. For this: 'It sounded nice.'

'OK, bye then,' Rachel concluded, and the line clicked dead, with what no doubt was her trademark control-freak sign-off.

I relit the crumbling joint on the desk. Get a kick out of pretending to be a druggie. OK, so dated: all the squares are on it now. Well, pills actually. Bloody jackers. Nevertheless, forced down the whole joint's antediluvian fruits. Something happening. I was giggling by the end. No more Noel Edmonds! Then I was sick. Gin-sick. Slept. Woke up breathing sick. Remembered. Things were still an improvement, then.

Went to the kitchen. Swallowed some of Marlsford's pills. Put a bottle of Cava, Spanish champagne, in the crusted freezer compartment. Order: cleaned the kitchen; hoovered the sitting-room; had a shower; swathed myself in my trusty blue towel. It was getting dark already – must have slept a long time. The Cava was now cold enough. Underestimated as well as surprisingly cheap, Cava. Got a box of it for doing a reading of *Road Star* at a festival; been buying it since. All but the tenderest stomach can take it. Bad hangovers admittedly. But a lot better than the bloody cider.

Opened the cupboard. Shot a covetous glance at the still half-full bottle of Bacardi. You've got a nerve hanging around half full in this place. Saw the bag of 'luxury crisps', seized them (forgot about those), poured some into a bowl, as a gesture to Greek civilisation. Imagined there was a Greek crone in the kitchen, setting out beautifully simple bowls of *meze*. Yes, unconsciously, habitually artful, that was the difference. Doesn't exist in England.

I took the glass of Cava and the bowl to the study, holding the towel in place with a finger. The flies were dormant. They just crouch around inertly after six o'clock.

I put down the glass and laid out the *meze*. No shakes in my hands: I still pulsed from the warmth of the shower. Nothing wrong, really: it must be all in the mind. Just a bit of 'louche' neurosis. I was Maggie Smith in *California Suite* before the Oscars, wrapped in her towels.

I began shadow-boxing round the study. Aware it was ridiculous; did it anyway; did actually have a short if unsuccessful ring career when I was 19. Jab, left hook off the jab, straight right, then down for the body, a right to the short rib, now the killer blow . . . Weave low to the left. He's expecting me to come back up with the left hook. But I don't. I stay low, swivel to the right, explode upwards with the right uppercut, everything in it. He crumples.

My towel fell off. Who cares, no one can see. I did the move again; caught sight of my reflection in the old bent window. Shit, looks all right. Haven't done this for years. I can still put them together.

Then again, I always looked good in the gym, when I boxed. I used to outclass this plodding heavyweight, admittedly he was useless, a great 15-stoner, bloody his lip; always said sorry, because it was sparring, but I loved it really. And yet . . . when it was for real, and the time came to climb the dim-lit ring steps . . .

So childish. Who am I kidding? I picked up the towel and wrapped it back around. Sat down at the desk. Had to address this 12-grand thing, the three months. Tipsters, allies, a lover: this is what I need. And not just any. No journalists, lit. mafia, agents. No point in cultivating them any more. Rachel? Unlikely. No, go back, back to the only ones who'll ever know you, forgive you your very self.

Yes. And to think I've been ashamed of them 'on my way up'. Down more like. Those odd people over there, they're not with you, are they? What, them? Oh no.

I dived back down into the desk drawers. Found the tattered coverless address book. The As and Bs have long flown away. I've scribbled down the ones I remember at the top of the Cs. Looked for O'Neill. Nothing. Must be under Handsome. How long has it been?

Johnny O'Neill, Walter Bentley, Carol Duplessis, that's who I need. Johnny my ally, Walter for tips, Carol, Carol, my girl; if I could find her. New Orleans? No, left years ago.

Need my past, like water bottle being handed up from ring steps to battered old fighter coming out for eleventh.

4

Pink Lips and the Old Music Room

When I was 13 I left the Pratts and went to a boarding-school near Epsom. Thanks to Mum a trust paid my school fees. The school was for boys with less than two parents and the sons of clergy. It stood behind high iron gates on the main road. The buildings were 100 years old and were all made of dirty red bricks. When I said goodbye to Auntie Jean and walked through the gates I felt excited, and it was there on my first day that I met Johnny Handsome.

He wasn't called Johnny Handsome then. He was called Johnny O'Neill. The first morning we were supposed to go to French in a room called 8-C. I linked up with Johnny in the corridor but when we got to 8-C we were the only ones there. We waited and waited but no one else arrived.

Johnny had curly blond hair and very piercing blue eyes. He was friendly and wasn't worried about anything. He wrote things on the blackboard and pretended to be the teacher, and we played football with the wooden blackboard rubber.

Johnny knew about horses, too. Mainly he knew about jump horses, because his dad bet on them. I already knew about Red Rum winning the Grand National. Johnny told me about other famous jump horses, like Arkle and Flying Bolt and Brown Lad, and I told him about Mill Reef and Nijinsky.

Johnny never stayed still. He stood up on the desks and shrugged his shoulders and shook his head. But he wasn't just silly. When you said something he listened intently, staring at you with his blue eyes. When it was his turn to speak again, everything he said seemed true.

Later we found out that the lesson was in a classroom in another block, 8-A. In the corridor afterwards Mr Heath-Page came up to us. He was the French teacher, and he also taught Art. He was young compared to the other teachers, and looked shy. He had funny wiry hair in a side parting. His hair sprang up on either side of the parting, and as he walked along the corridor he patted it down nervously with his hand.

Mr Heath-Page said we had to see him in his study later to explain our absence. I was worried we'd get lines, which I'd heard about in the morning from the older boys in the common room where we went during break. But Johnny said not to worry. He had an older brother, Rick, at the school, so he knew what to do.

'It's all right,' Johnny said. 'They won't do anything on our first day. Fuck 'em.'

Johnny was a day boy in Powell House and I was a boarder in Fairlow. That afternoon Johnny came in to the Fairlow common room and said we should go and have a smoke to talk about what we'd say to Mr Heath-Page. I still didn't like smoking but pretended I did.

We walked down to the back entrance where the old music room was. It was a disused shed with bashed-in wooden panels where the instruments used to hang. The bad boys from the year above had smashed some of them in so hard that the light and the wind came through. All across the panels they'd written the names of bands, like the Sex Pistols, X-Ray Spex, the Vibrators and Sham 69. Johnny cupped his cigarette between his thumb and finger. He held it behind his back between drags and I copied him.

Johnny was right about Mr Heath-Page. We got let off without lines. In fact Mr Heath-Page was quite friendly. He said he'd only come to the school the term before, and it was difficult finding your way round. At the end he shook our hands and said, 'Well, there's more to education than geography.' When he put his hand out he seemed more nervous than we were.

Johnny and I were best friends from that day. Soon I realised that I was lucky, because everyone liked Johnny. His brother Rick was the hero of the school. Rick was captain of the 1st XV rugby, and should have been Head Boy instead of Coulthard. Every Saturday we watched the 1st XV from the touchline. The players were allowed guests. Most of them were the players' girlfriends. We watched them more than the rugby. They wore jerseys in the school colours. Their hair fell down over the green and blue stripes, and when you went past them they smelled clean.

You had to win your House tie in inter-house games. Luckily I was quite good at games, though not as good as Johnny. Anyone without a House tie was called a Spac.

All the masters had nicknames. The headmaster was called The Cod, because when he read Revelations out in the old chapel he blew his cheeks out and looked like a fish.

The most hated master was Sperm. He was head of PE and drama. He was only as tall as us first-years, but he was always in the weights room in the evenings, and was as wide as he was tall. He was called Sperm because he was so slimy. At first he pretended to be your friend, but he was only deciding who his favourites were. Then when he'd got his favourites sorted out, he gave all the others lines and extra cross-country runs, and went round squeezing people's arms during dinner and teasing them that they were weak.

Sperm's main favourites were the 1st XV rugby pack. But no one really blamed the pack, because it wasn't their fault they were chosen. At Christmas Sperm gave the pack all the best parts in the school play as well. You could tell the pack didn't really want to be there, because they were always forgetting their lines.

41

Mr Heath-Page's nickname was Lurch. This was because of the way he walked in his DM shoes with air-wair soles. All the bad boys from the year above wore DM boots, to be cool. They put Blakeys on the soles so you could hear them coming down the corridor a mile off. But Mr Heath-Page was not cool at all. He wore his DM shoes because they were 'practical'.

When he walked, Mr Heath-Page's air-wair soles seemed to take him by surprise, bouncing him upwards in between steps, and that was why he was called Lurch.

Before his lessons we wrote things on the blackboard, like 'Lurch Is A Spac', and Mr Heath-Page would go red and rub them off without saying anything. Then he would try to make jokes and be friendly to us. Because of Sperm, we were suspicious of teachers being friendly.

It was Mr Heath-Page who first called Johnny 'Handsome'. He was deciding who should read next when he pointed at Johnny and said, 'Ah, what about Handsome over there.' Afterwards, it just stuck.

Mainly, the more Mr Heath-Page tried to be friendly, the worse it was for him. Grainger put the blackboard rubber on top of the door hinge, so that when Mr Heath-Page came in, it bounced off his head and covered his DM shoes in chalk.

Almost everything at the school was broken – the chairs in the common room, the desks in the classrooms, the equipment in the language lab. The window in our dorm had a hole in it, and the wind rushed through, but it was all right under the sheets. I thought that was what all boarding-schools were like. A bonus was that work was easier than at my last school. You could do almost nothing and still get good reports.

On days when there were no games you could get a down-town chit and go into town for an hour. Johnny and I always went together and drank teas reading the NME in a café called Harringtons. Sometimes the local skins picked on Johnny because of his curly blond hair. If there were lots of them we ran away. But if there were only one or two we gave as good as we got. At school people were always trying to start fights with Johnny, because he was Rick O'Neill's brother. He had a big fight in the corridor with Grainger which Sperm split up. Johnny was winning. I never saw him lose one fight. But he never boasted about it. Afterwards he was friends with the boys he'd fought with.

That summer came cricket. I got into the Junior Colts XI. The best players were Johnny, me and an off-spinner from my house called Pridwell. Before Pridwell started playing cricket he was known as a Spac. He was a scholar who wore glasses and his dad was a vicar. Pridwell knew every player's initials in *Wisden's Cricketers' Almanack* off by heart. On away matches I noticed that all the other schools we played seemed much bigger and less broken down, but I dismissed such thoughts.

When we could, Johnny, Pridwell and I lay on the grass and watched the school 1st XI cricket team, dreaming of being in it one day. In summer the 1st XI were allowed to take their guests on to the quad after the match for drinks. Their girlfriends wore white cricket sweaters that the 1st XI had given them and their laughter echoed off the dirty red bricks. I had my house tie by then, and proudly ran my hand through its blue and pink colours.

Two more summers went by and another winter came. Johnny and I were sitting in the old music room having a smoke. It was a cold Friday afternoon with no games and an exeat coming up. We'd smashed a few more panels in by then and written The Jam, Vapors and Echo and the Bunnymen over the old Sham 69 graffiti. We ground out the cigarettes with the Blakeys on the heels of our DM boots and then set off across the playing fields to see Lurch at his bungalow for extra Art.

It wasn't really extra Art. I think Lurch was just lonely. He hadn't made friends with any of the other masters. He said that he had been born two thousand years too late, and that he would have been more at home in Ancient Greece or Rome or, failing that, modern Greece or Rome. Lurch was always applying for teaching jobs abroad, though we had to keep that secret. 'You must travel!' he was always saying to us. 'Across the wine-dark sea!'

Every Friday we went over to Lurch's place for extra Art. Only Johnny and me went. I suppose it was like Sperm having his favourites in the 1st XV pack. Lurch had us. He said he had to civilise us. In his bungalow, books were piled up beside all the walls. He had to keep a foot gap between the books and the walls because of the damp. He was always leaping about and reading from the books and then handing them to us as gifts. He'd bring some snacks out for us, strange snacks like olives with anchovies in them that he opened from tins. As Lurch popped the olives in his mouth he would say things like 'Mmm, a taste of the ancient sun.' They were disgusting but we forced them down, because after the snacks Lurch usually opened a bottle of wine.

We had one glass each, watered down, and Lurch had the rest. While we were drinking it he lay back on his chair talking about the Parthenon or the Colosseum or Odysseus while me and Johnny nodded, letting the wine drift up into our heads.

Lurch never let on he was sad, but you could tell he was. When we were first- and second-years he took the whole French and Art classes up to London for classical concerts. Lurch was in bliss during the concerts, moving his head from side to side with his eyes closed and waggling his DM shoes. But then at one concert half the class didn't come back after the interval, thinking that Lurch wouldn't notice with his eyes closed. But he did, and when he'd finally collected everyone afterwards and was sitting in the minibus in a rage, he found out that someone (Grainger) had let the tyres down as well.

After that Lurch didn't take us to any more concerts, because he said we were such unimaginative and neanderthal boys, and we had no sense of poetry. He stopped training the 3rd XI soccer team too, and in the afternoons after lessons he stayed in his bungalow alone, except for Fridays when we went round. He even stopped calling Johnny 'Handsome'. He called him 'Loathsome' instead. At the bungalow he called Johnny 'Loathsome 1' and me 'Loathsome 2'.

But we knew we were still Lurch's favourites, even when he got angry and flustered and said we were 'taking advantage' because we 'clearly' hadn't read the books he'd given us. Well, we hadn't read the books, but we could persuade Lurch we'd tried to. It was just that we needed more civilising before we could succeed. It was easy to con Lurch.

That Friday as we trudged across the playing fields Johnny said he didn't think Ancient Greece would have suited Lurch as much as Lurch thought, because the wars were terrible and you had to be a warrior to survive. 'I mean, it's not exactly him, is it?' Johnny said, handing me a fag.

We'd just cleared the fence at the end of the playing fields, on to Lurch's road. You couldn't risk a fag before then, because Sperm was always hovering around the playing fields, putting out sprint marks on the lawn outside the old swimming pool, or tinkering with the scrummage machine to make it harder for the 1st XV.

We finished the smokes and walked up Lurch's garden path. I rang the bell and Lurch opened the door with a flourish wearing an unusually smart black suit. 'Ah, the Loathsomes,' he said, beckoning us in.

Lurch told us it was his thirtieth birthday. He could hardly conceal his excitement. He had a load of new snacks laid out, cheese straws and crisps as well as the disgusting olives, and a bottle of fizzy wine that he said was like champagne except it was Spanish.

We all sat down and Johnny said innocently, 'Happy birthday, sir. And sir, would you mind very much if we smoked?' Lurch went red and flustered for a second, but then acted as if it was the most natural question in the world and said, 'Of course not, Loathsome. Of course not. Puff away.' Then he went into the kitchen and came back with an empty olive can for us to use as an ashtray, and while he was gone Johnny winked at me and we managed to contain our giggles even though it was killing.

This time Lurch didn't water down our Spanish champagne, and my mind soon drifted off as he went on about some job he'd virtually got in the bag at this school in Athens. Lurch opened another bottle and refilled our glasses at least twice. I thought about the exeat – I hardly ever spent exeats and holidays with Auntie Jean and Julian and Stuart any more, and almost always spent them with Johnny at his dad's house – and I thought about the snogging party we'd be going to on Saturday night. Being a day boy, Johnny knew some day girls from Manor House school. When their parents went out they held the snogging parties. They turned the lights out and you French-kissed whoever you were next to until their parents came back and your lips and tongue were sore. I fell in love with everyone I snogged, but Johnny said I took snogging too seriously.

Sitting there on Lurch's sofa, I started having a strange daydream. First a pair of lips appeared and kissed mine. I could tell they weren't real lips, because through the lips I could see Johnny nodding and Lurch talking away. But they were beautiful lips, like the Manor House girls'. And with every sip I took from my glass, more lips appeared, coming towards me, whispering and then French-kissing me, until all I could see or feel were hundreds of wet pink lips and warm red tongues.

I pulled my head free and let it drop over the back of the sofa to get some air in. Then the picture changed. Summer had come. Johnny, me and Pridwell were playing cricket for the Colts XI. The warm breeze sent ripples through the umpires' white coats and the handkerchiefs we'd tied round our necks to be like Test players. I hooked the winning runs to the boundary. Even the opposition players applauded as I walked back to the pavilion. I could see Johnny coming down the pavilion steps to congratulate me, his blond curls traced with sweat from the century he'd scored, and the Manor House girls crowding round in cricket sweaters with their pink lips glistening in the sun.

I woke to see Johnny standing in front of me tapping ash into the olive can. Fag butts and oily ash spilled out of the top of the can. Johnny made a face to say Lurch was really out of it and that we'd better make a move. I looked over at Lurch. He was stretched out on his chair burbling and waving his glass around. I stood up and said, 'Bye, sir. Thanks for everything.'

'Living in Greece,' Lurch said, 'I will doubtless encounter those Mediterranean storms that break violently over a nearby mountain and after a while move on to another further away, their fury unabated.' I noticed Lurch was smoking one of Johnny's fags. You could tell he wasn't a real smoker.

'No doubt my passing from this school,' Lurch added, 'will come to be seen as a bit like such a storm.'

We said more goodbyes and happy birthdays to Lurch and soon we were back out on the freezing playing fields heading back to school. Maybe because of all the Spanish champagne, I risked lighting up a last smoke. I could see the 1st XV pack heaving at the scrummage machine in the distance, but they were so far away they were almost dots.

It was as we were passing the old swimming pool, when I was just about to put my fag out, that Sperm shot out laughing from behind the changing-rooms looking like a boulder with teeth. He told Johnny to get lost, and marched me off to The Cod's study. The Cod blew his cheeks out and said he felt compelled to make an example of smokers, not least because he suspected I'd been drinking as well, and that as a result I was gated for the rest of term, with no exeats, and that for good measure I would forfeit my House tie too.

Being gated meant you had to carry around a little green book full of dates and times lasting until the end of term. Anyone with a green book was called a Renegade. Some of the coolest bad boys in the year above were Renegades so I didn't mind too much at first. When the other boys were off on exeats you had to take the green book around the school finding masters to sign every two hours to prove you hadn't left school premises.

Luckily, Lurch signed two pages at a time, so I still went to snogging parties. He'd decided to found a school magazine, and made me poetry editor. He said if The Cod ever got suspicious about all his signatures, I could say I was working on the magazine. I think Lurch was just relieved that I hadn't sneaked on him to The Cod.

My job was to write a few poems and get other boys to write the rest. I didn't write any poems and I didn't manage to get anyone else to, either, but Lurch still signed my green book. When the school magazine came out it was very thin and the only poem in it was by Lurch himself, 'by Andrew Heath-Page, with apologies to Walter de la Mare'.

Pridwell was very excited about knowing someone who had a green book and was an official bad boy. He examined all the dates and times and signatures as if he was reading *Wisden*. He bought some DM boots but they never stopped looking new and he still looked like the old Pridwell in his specs.

Then Pridwell said he wanted to take up smoking, so I took him down to the old music room one afternoon. Pridwell had a couple of fags (not inhaling) with me and Johnny but after he'd gone Johnny told me not to bring him again. 'Nothing against Pridwell,' Johnny said. 'But he'll get us all into trouble without meaning to.'

Then Johnny said I should stop acting like a hardened Renegade, because I wasn't one really. 'I mean, it's not as if you're like Beast, is it?' he added.

Beast was a boy called Beast Bentley. His first name was Walter but everyone called him Beast because he was so wild. He was a boarder in my house and was the only other boy in my year with a green book. He was thin and scrawny with woolly black hair and a pointed nose. Everyone teased Beast and as a result he hated everyone and was always attacking them without warning. I felt sorry for Beast. I sat next to him in Chemistry and we cheated together during tests. But whenever I tried to be friendly to him he told me to fuck off.

As Johnny and me left the old music room after Pridwell had gone I told him I hadn't asked to be made a Renegade. But I knew Johnny was right. The next term was Easter term and I wouldn't be gated any more. I would be good. I resolved to get my House tie back, and write some poems for Lurch's magazine, and be nice to Beast.

In the first week of Easter term I was walking down the corridor at night towards the dorm when Beast jumped me from behind. He must have been hiding in the laundry closet half-way up the corridor, because I didn't see him coming until he'd landed on my back. Beast hadn't attacked me before but I'd heard what it was like.

The thing about Beast was that he didn't fight like other boys. He bit you and scratched you and sometimes when you fought back he went quiet and pretended to be dead. Then when you were walking away he would grab the nearest weapon and try to get you from behind. The only way to tame Beast was to pin him down and then really smash him in.

I got Beast in a headlock but he dropped to his knees and wriggled out. I got his arm in a vice but Beast bit my shoulder and clawed my face with his free hand. We rolled off the corridor into the first-years' broken-down Common Room and it was there I finally pinned Beast down. He started sobbing as if I was going to smash him.

'Why d'you do that, Beast?' I said.

''Cause you're a fucking Spac,' Beast said.

I raised my fist but then I remembered my resolution so I got up instead and let him go. He hadn't played dead and his sobs seemed real so I thought it would be all right to.

'That was cool,' Beast said, wiping his tears away.

'What was?'

'Not smashing me in, like all the others do.'

I put my hand out and he shook it. 'You're cool, too, Beast,' I said.

I walked towards the door but before I got there I felt a heavy thud between my shoulder-blades that sent me to the floor. When I turned round on my knees I saw him standing there with a grimy reading lamp with no lampshade and no bulb, poised like a knife.

He pointed at the flex coming out of it and screamed, 'If you call me fucking Beast again I'll ... ELECTRO-FUCKING-CUTE YOU!'

'What should I call you then?' I said.

'*WAL-TER!*' Beast screamed.

After that Walter and me became friendly. His dad had been a business tycoon, but his business crashed and he got ill and died. Walter said his dad would never have let him go to a dump like this school. Walter's whole life at school was devoted to trying to persuade his mum to take him away from it. That was why he was always getting gated and attacking people without warning and sometimes playing dead for so long that the nurse had to come and wheel Walter to the San on the trolley before he 'woke up'.

Walter said he had to persuade his mum because the school would never expel him, however much trouble he got into, because The Cod fancied his mum and wanted his dad's money for the New Chapel fund. So far he hadn't persuaded his mum. Recently Walter had tried signing his letters home with his school number, 'your son. No. 10310', but his mum just wrote back saying he was sweet.

For the first half of Easter term I tried to make my resolutions come true. During evening prep I wrote poems for Lurch. In the end I only finished two. One was about the Sex Pistols and one was about snogging. The second one went,

> 'Of course he's much too young
> To handle the stress and strain.'
> You, me, love, tongue to tongue
> Naïve, brief, teenage pain.

I was imagining The Cod's voice at the start. What had happened in the poem was that I was 16 (I wish) and I'd met a girl at a snogging party and we'd run off and got married for a laugh. Then we'd got caught and I'd been returned to school.

I was taking the poems to Lurch's bungalow but half-way across the playing fields I thought they probably weren't his scene, so I went back to the House and put them in my drawer.

In the first half of term I played for the House at everything – rugby, football, even fives (with Pridwell). Each Monday at Assembly when The Cod gave out House ties, he took out a tie I thought was mine and gave it to some first-year. Pridwell made a chart of what each boy had done to get his tie, and he couldn't understand why I hadn't got mine back. 'It's probably hanging around with Beast that's swung it against you,' Pridwell said.

I stopped trying to get my tie back. I saw less of Johnny and more of Walter. They pulled the old music room down so I started smoking in the bogs with the Renegades from the year above who knew the drummer from the Vapors.

Most of the masters began striking me as mad: the economics master who read *Winnie the Pooh* stories in lessons, and the English master who asked you every week what your favourite word was.

'Wisteria, sir.' I always used the same one.

'Mmm, very good, boy. Very innovative.'

Many of the boarders had been away since they were seven. Unlike them, I knew the surrounding area. I led them to pubs I'd cycled past on the Downs. At first we drank snowballs. They tasted like sweets. The locals were sneering but we were too young to beat up.

That summer in the Colts XI, Pridwell switched from spin to fast bowling and Johnny was captain. But I wasn't there. I was with Walter drinking cider by the River Mole.

I got gated again. Lurch said he couldn't sign any more, because they were on to him. Lurch was very sad about it. Anyone would have thought it was him who was gated. 'Institutions and those who run them,' Lurch said gravely, 'find it difficult to absorb people like us, people of a questioning, rebelling, romantic temperament.' I knew Lurch was really talking about himself, not me, but I nodded, noticing that Lurch had suddenly gone his flustered colour. 'I mean, of course, romantic in the nineteenth-century, not Hollywood, sense,' he added before lurching away.

Things escalated. Walter and me ran away to London. Walter said it was the only thing he hadn't done yet. There would be a huge search and his mum would finally be convinced. But we ran out of money in Soho on the first day. It was after midnight by the time we crept back into school. The next morning, when we got up to face the music, none of the masters had noticed we'd been away.

The June evening of my sixteenth birthday was warm and still with a strange green dappled light that flickered over the playing fields as me and Pridwell bunked off. Walter was in detention so he couldn't come. Pridwell was really pleased I'd asked him. He had his shiny DMs on and tried to spike his hair up to look like a punk, but it soon flattened down into his normal side-parting. I was keen to live up to Pridwell's image of me, so we walked up to the Downs and I drank a pint cocktail of whisky, gin, Vermouth and Coke.

The next afternoon I woke up in the San, covered in sick. The other boys had done their best. They'd taken me to the San hidden in a dustbin, and sworn the nurse to secrecy. But it was to no avail. The Cod's wife had seen me walking back to school in the middle of the road.

I went back to sleep and when I woke up one of the prefects, Mason, was there. He was known as The Vonze because on exeats he tried to look like The Fonze but got it badly wrong. Mason said Pridwell had already been gated by The Cod for half the next term and would have got worse if he hadn't spilled the beans, not only about me and him but about everything else I'd told him – the pub trips and me and Walter's running away and the fags and booze at Lurch's bungalow. 'You are in big, big shit,' The Vonze said.

I drifted off again and this time when I woke it was night and all I could make out in the gloom of the San was the reflection of Pridwell's specs hovering above me. Slowly his mournful face came into focus.

'Hello, Pridwell,' I said.

'I just came to say sorry,' Pridwell stammered. 'I didn't

mean to. The Cod had my dad in his study when I went in. With my dad there I just couldn't . . .'

I told Pridwell it was all right. It wasn't his fault. It was my fault for asking him, and I was sorry about him getting gated and everything. 'Did they take away your House tie?' I asked.

'No. But they said they would if there was any repeat.'

'Well, that's the main thing, then,' I said.

Soon I heard Pridwell's DMs squeaking off down the corridor. The next morning, I was taken straight off to The Cod's study. My school trunk was loaded up outside the door, so I knew what was going to happen.

Auntie Jean was sitting in the study, too. She looked older and more tired. The Cod gave a little speech, trying to put on the charm a bit to Auntie Jean in between lecturing me, but she had a faraway look on her face, and I don't think she was listening much.

I loaded the trunk into the back of the car. I heard a window scrape from high above among the red bricks. Looking up, I recognised the scrawny figure of Walter. He was doing V-signs and shouting out, 'Lucky fucking bastard!' I waved up at him and we drove off through the iron gates.

'I think, John,' Auntie Jean said, 'that it's about time you started looking for a job.'

5

Dolly, Dear

Caroline rang from the paper, regarding the Noel piece. Strangely I didn't bail out of it immediately. Don't know why not. Greed? Fear of Caroline? I'm not used to not needing the money. The first 4-grand instalment would be in the bank at Ipswich by today. I'd take it all out at once, in the new red £50 notes. Never had one of those before.

No, that would only be eighty notes – too thin. It wouldn't be like having 4 grand properly. And imagine trying to pay with a £50 note at the butcher's in Suffolk? The gossip – they'd think you were a drug overlord, or a lottery winner. At all costs mustn't act like a lottery winner. No, I'd get half in fifties, and half in twenties and tens.

I told Caroline that I was going down to Noel's theme park the next day, not expecting to. But I did. It was in the West Country somewhere, Somerset. Drove out in the Dolly – a 2CV, my car. No, it's not some twee name I invented. It's there stencilled on the back: Dolly, in fake art-deco typescript, astride its fake art-deco colours of cream and purple. Frankly, as they say in new Britain, it's an embarrassment: student wheels, easy prey. Lads greet it on Friday nights by shouting obscenities and doing V-signs (well, it's the finger these days). People cut you up the whole time, on sight. Then again, with a known top speed of 55 mph, who wouldn't? The only thing you can do is, when you stop, really hurl the door open and get out looking hard.

Of choice, I admit I'd gravitate more to the Dr Marlsford

saloon. Perhaps a slightly older model. Louchely battered Merc? Don't know nuffin about cars ackshlee; blind spot. And it would have to have a big embarrassing sound system booming out. Ageing white rasta living off royalties, too rich to care. 'Later, man. Mellow.' I could see it. But the Dolly only cost 350 quid.

Stopped off at the bank in Ippo. Hell of a palaver. Faxes exchanged with London. Anyone would think I was a barbarian trying to break down the city walls. Sat there for ages reading mortgage propaganda leaflets. Should have dressed better, shaved. Not 26 any more. Shit – should I have dressed better for Noel? Could be an immediate target for Security.

No fifties when the notes arrived. Looked at me as if I was Martian when I queried the assemblage. He's one of them types that wants those fifties, he is . . . One of them *newfangled* types. Ah, but the twenties and tens looked good, nice fat wad. Rejected the proffered envelope disdainfully in revenge. Stuffed the wad in my jeans pocket casually, white-rasta style.

The M4 was bloody full. Used to be the gateway to idyll, this. How long since I've been out of Suffolk, except to London? Executive saloon-fuckers as far as Swindon. So full, this country. You probably have to go to Cornwall before the suburbs end. All right, exaggeration. Suspicious of the West Country. The male Youth drink cider.

On to the less populous M5 at Bristol. That's a relief. The Dolly was making ominous whining sounds even at 50 mph. Realised this car had had its motorway-spinning days: in this company, it was an anachronism; put it out to pasture. Felt a bit sad about it – very unexpected. A police car appeared in the rear mirror. Mustn't get stopped: tax disc out of date, no MOT; couldn't even get it renewed by bribing Darren, ex-skin who works in the off-licence, born-again Christian, does MOTs on the side. Should use

Darren in some story really. A sign for a town vaguely familiar from the Noel Edmonds leisure-park map came up on the left. Took it.

It was already late afternoon. Swooping country roads and purple heather light on the hills. Real purple, not like the Dolly. It was good to be around hills again, after Suffolk. Find somewhere to stay; go to Noel's place tomorrow. Couldn't find anywhere. Only empty pubs and tatty B & Bs. I seemed to be in a concentration of rural-poor Sky-dish small towns. Not going to stay in an empty pub; couldn't face the intimacy.

Back to the M5 – a huge intersection thirty miles down the road with a Travelodge. Jimmy White recommended Travelodges to me. They leave you alone there. Booked in. Reception had a vista encompassing some fourteen screaming lanes. Paid by cheque in advance. Reception very dubious about accepting a *cheque* – West Country must be more modern, cards-only round here; how long have poor old cheques got left?

Remembered the 4-grand wad just as I was signing the cheque, with the usual deceptively confident flourish (helps calm the nerves). Oh well, one last cheque for the road. As well as the room, I bought four miniatures of brandy and a can of Coke from a dinky glass cabinet behind Reception. Unusual touch. Most welcome. Ascension to the second floor. Passed a franchised fish-and-chip restaurant on the way to the stairs. Examined the laminated menu on the wall. Frozen haddock at three times the usual mark-up. 'Traditional' mushy peas. And there was a *queue*: eager punters, families. The adult-folk eyed me hostilely. What's he up to then, looking at that? Queue-jumper?

I do apologise. But me go in there? Coralled in enemy territory? I think not. Unless, of course, Mr James White is dining tonight.

The stairs, corridor. Usual delay with design-fault bendy

card-key (stick to cheques, man). Quite big room, double bed. They're getting better at this American thing. Doesn't feel like America though, the . . . sense of space missing, however hard they try. Window facing away from the screaming lanes, into a slab of hill. Sea lights down below. Bournemouth? Must be close. 'English Riviera', eh. Night almost there. Purple gone from the hill, but still a chink of pink remaining. Sucked it in. Even so, it doesn't move me, England.

Drank the brandies with the can of Coke on the side. Took an hour. Didn't turn the TV on. Silence, but with crowding thoughts. Went to bed. Put the 4-grand wad under the pillow. Better not forget it in the morning. Biggest tip ever.

Noel's place was in a beautiful estate at the foot of a deep valley. Even periodic poppings-up of the Mr Blobby theme, and similar enemy motifs, could not spoil it. There was a river at the bottom, and post-modern posh gamekeepers doing expert things in the woods, subsuming bewilderment in 'work'. I wonder who owned it before? Dynastic loonies. Bet it was even better then.

I was there early. It was sunny. Not many punters about. Didn't look as though there ever really were. A pervading air of: what exactly are we trying to do? Noel should have got less intelligent staff (like the loonies did). There was a sort of half-hearted zoo as well. A few elephants, bison. No snakes, thank God. One of the gamekeepers was drawing kiddies' names on an elephant in crayon, none too convincedly.

Had another walk round the zoo: found a newly built miniature sunken amphitheatre under an ancient oak tree; a sign announcing some sort of Amazonian ferret, 'allowed to roam in natural freedom'. The amphitheatre was completely empty. Heard a chattering sound; looked up to the tree; glimpsed a flash of ferret teeth, up high among the leaves. Well done, son.

Walked past a bored Mr Blobby balloon-seller and the ubiquitous if underwhelmed face-painting corral towards where I thought the exit was. Apart from the setting, absolutely nothing of interest, personally; certainly nothing to write about. Passed a small church and a graveyard as well. A real church and graveyard. Been there for centuries, before all this. Ten years ago, these graves were unobserved stones on a remote slope. Christ, imagine being buried there now.

Instead of the exit, I found myself in a kind of ante-room. Some sort of retro farm shoppe. Mmm, unexpectedly interesting, looking around. Rows of jars of pickles. Incredibly, each jar label seemed handwritten. This could be the real thing. Picked up a jar and looked at it closely: genuine. These pickles were important. Among their immediate surroundings, their sincerity was actively subversive.

Went back to the door and picked up a retro wooden 'rustic' basket. Piled the pickles in. One of each, and two jars of the hot chilli one: called 'Diabolico: Seriously Hot Pickle'. I could eat three meals a day with this smothered over, no prob. Probably made by the gamekeepers' wives.

To the nakedly state-of-the-art till, tossing in bott. of home-made cherry brandy en route. Quick flourish. Getting cheque-happy. Must stop. Am consciously avoiding breaching the wad now. Why? Dunno. Gotta do some bets. Boring I know, but . . .

Car really struggled to get back up the valley. *Really* struggled. Gripped gear stick all the way up to will it on: gear stick pulls out from dashboard in 2CVs, charming feature, yes? Except when it comes out in your hand. That's happened a few times. Darren fixes temporarily from his odd portable store of junk. When it happens, your immediate prospects depend on what gear you were in last. Reverse – fucked.

And I must ring Caroline to bail out of the Noel piece. It's time. Specially now I've met Mr Blob (papier-mâché version). Turned into the main road. Petrol station up ahead. Pulled in. Took out the wad. Gave the Dolly an unprecedented full tank. Splurged cash out in the shop: lots of Twixes, family-size pack of Fruit Gums, sixty fags, 100-unit phone card. Now that's living. Not strictly gambling maybe. Of course, I'd pay the 12-grand account back. Will I? Past form does not encourage. Don't think about it. At least I'd breached the wad.

Stopped at the green-labelled card-phone in the shop. Nice to be organised enough to use one of these finally. Rang the paper. Didn't ask for Caroline. I'd talk to Steven instead. Deputy editor but he didn't brag about it: genial, unintimidating – if anything, appealingly unconfident. Never actually met him but speak on phone. He's the only male on the desk, poor bastard: ex-writer, once wrote for the *NME*, me and Johnny used to read him at school; now he's early forties, doesn't write any more, had some sort of seize-up. Comrade. He'd understand.

But he wasn't there. Got Caroline instead. Bit my lip and told her straight off I was bailing out of Noel. Waited for the stormy backlash. Didn't come. Caroline seemed quite relieved actually. Well, I suppose if writing about Noel is unfaceable, what must the prospect of editing it be like? Some bullshit about other pieces. Phone down. Only 13 units, that. Seemed a shame not to press on.

Rang Rachel's number at Yellow Jersey Press. The 'private line' she'd given me, that is, not your infested switchboard. Some of us still travel First . . .

'Hello,' Rachel's voice answered, with customary imperiousness . . .

'Oh, hello, Rachel,' I said. 'It's John.'

'Where are you?'

'I'm . . . well, I'm in the, er, West Country.'

'In the West Country?'

'Yes,' I said dumbly. This was a mistake. Just knew.

'I thought you'd be somewhere like Vegas by now,' Rachel said, icy. 'Or Macau.'

Macau, mmm. Made up some shit about a card game in Bristol. Poker. It just came out. Some invented Jimmy-White-associate type has set up this card school (could tell Rachel liked the low-life refs). But he's got more money than sense, see. Going to get fleeced – but only a few people know. Got to set him up, though. That means early losses. Prepared Rachel for plenty of these. Probably a good idea. Thought, what exactly will the accounting procedures be on this 12 grand? Didn't mention this, obviously. Can always say later that the card-school man turned out to be cleverer than we'd all thought.

'Anyway, just thought I'd check in, you know,' I added.

'OK, bye then.' The line clicked.

Jesus, it's relentless. The new brutalism. Maybe I should have tried it.

Found a bunch of Noel expenses in my top pocket when I tried to put the card back in. Took receipts out, chucked 'em. Can afford.

Drove the long drive back to London to meet with Walter. Chewed Fruit Gums exclusively on the left side of my jaw. Last time chewed a Fruit Gum on right a tooth came out with it. Only lost two teeth in all, though. You wouldn't notice kissing. Carol used to like my teeth. Small, white and neat, she said; sweet. Used to lick them when we kissed. You can buy toothpaste with whitener ready-built-in in America.

Bad traff. round Heathrow. Christ, inevitable – the gear stick's come out. At least I was in third. Limped in third in the fucked car all the way to Rodrigo's in Pimlico. Won't make it back to Suffolk, this. Sorry, doll, all sympathy run out. It's goodbye.

Rodrigo's – tapas bar, indifferent food, moderately extortionate. Walter's flat is opposite; only place he goes. His dad left him the flat. Must be worth 300 thou now. Unfortunately for Walter he's remortgaged it 120 per cent at least one and a half times, financing dodgy South London property deals, making him on balance about 200 thou down.

Think Walter will make it as a rich man eventually, though. He wants it. He is an island. All he needs is one working motor from his small fleet of broken-down cars, and the mobile. Drives around talking into it all day, dedicated to becoming rich. It must happen some day. Walter certainly thinks it will. Plus he seems to be getting a bit better at the property. Must be. Until this year he had a day job as a racing journo. Does know his horses. Now he's given the day job up, drives around doing property full-time. Despicable profession, obviously, but friends are friends.

Walter doesn't seem to connect with any of the dozens of people he talks to each day. Doesn't go anywhere in the evenings. Only people he sees socially are me and Graham (who's his lodger anyway). Women don't find him un-attractive; he's a presence, Walter. But he got stung once: wary now and not really interested except for occasional gratuitous sex. Gets escorts in for that by telephone, hundred quid a throw, plus drinks. Even going over to Rodrigo's (25 feet) is a major expedition. I know there is good in Walter.

I was early. Don't want to go round to the flat. Walter and Graham would be lounging about. Neither are really drinkers. Could take drinkless age to get out again. Nipped over to the pub opposite. No chance of Walter being in there; lifetime ban after a parking dispute; so he can't take offence about my not going round; won't know. Sort of thing he takes offence to. Doesn't take a lot, with Walter.

Two large G & Ts in the pub, plus a swift pint for re-hydrative purposes. All in ten minutes. Horrible pub, suburbia-in-London job. So I'm never going back there and I don't care what they think.

Back over to Rodrigo's, calmly order large G & T as if it's the first. Barman believes me – mature Spaniard, type of barman I like; none of your sniffy antipodean dudes, or, worse, English ones. One who understands the noble craft. Shit, listen to yourself. He slyly returns the change from my twenty on a white saucer. Tip-inducer. Bit of a liberty. I mean, it's not America. Craft? Street grafter more like. Leave a quid coin shimmering there anyway. Finish the gin at the bar, then take the follow-up glass of Cava to a table to wait for Walt.

And Graham, no doubt. He does tend to turn up uninvited, Graham. Big bloke, surly-looking at first but actually quite placid. Just sits there next to Walter. Silent, except for very occasional moments when he gruffly confirms exactly something Walter's just said. Walter likes to hint Graham's got gangster connections. Don't believe him.

I wonder if Walter and Graham share escort girls? They talk about it so openly, knowingly. Only thing Graham gets animated about. Doesn't bear thinking. Can't talk anyway.

Walter walked in with Graham in tow. Cracked open a round of nice cold beers then bott. Rioja. Graham silent, but sitting close up to Walter, sort of hovering on his words. They were sitting like that when I first met Graham – ten years ago in a pub in Bristol. Walter used to drive up from London to go to the casino there. Took me up once. Tale of dodgy old roulette wheel; warped, see, with this kind of groove that goes towards 13 Black at three times the normal frequency. Cast-iron certainty. Only a few people know. But those that do, they come from all over Britain to this Bristol wheel.

We'd met Graham in the pub before going on to the casino. Terrible gamblers, the pair of them, still are. And they were sitting together under the pub jukebox, averting their eyes when punters came up to put songs on, then betting on what number would come up. They did this for two whole hours.

And the wheel story turned out to be a dud (Walter wouldn't admit, though; *never* would). Went in skint, came out skinter, as per. And Walter was pissed. He's always had a weakness for casino hospitality; finds the restaurants and bars 'classy'. Drove one of his auction-model cars into a girder on the Clifton suspension bridge on the way back. Car smashed; us, amazingly, untouched. Scarpered before the police arrived. Walked into Bristol. Got the morning train out.

Walter was lecturing me enthusiastically about the Rodrigo's squid that sat before us, in obviously pre-packed rings, large and suspiciously symmetrical, not one tentacle. Prefer baby whole ones myself. What does Walter know about food anyway? *Nada.* I nodded. Forced half a ring down. Tasted decidedly rancid to me. And I was going to have the *riñones*. Better not risk it in this gaff; stick to liquids.

I told Walter and Graham about the 12-grand idea, the three 4-grand instalments. They were not impressed: peanuts. They considered it with some seriousness, though.

After a while Walter said, 'It's obvious. Horses. You don't get receipts gambling, do you?'

'Eh?'

'Well, not unless you want to hang on to them. And that's only losing bets. If you win you give the slip back to get paid, right?' Walter and Graham exchanged knowing glances. Oh, of course, a couple of winners, you two. Forgot.

'And in casinos they don't give you any at all,' Walter went on.

'So?' I said.

'So you nick the money.'

'What, all of it? The whole twelve grand?'

'I would,' Walter said. 'I mean if it's being paid out in such . . . *pathetic* instalments, what's the point? You'd be odds-on to lose it.' True, true.

'Yeah, nick the money. Obvious.' Graham confirmed.

Startling development. I'd been almost there, but not quite. Call me naïve. Of course, there was a moral dimension. Moral dimensions were not to be discussed with Walter and Graham. I laid the nicking-the-money question gently aside, asking Walter instead about the prospect of renting an auction-model car from him, say for a month, as he and Graham hoovered up the rest of the squid *rance* with eager escort-fondling hands.

Turned out Walter had a spare car. Trooped outside and up the road to look at it. Some sort of dirty-linen-coloured discontinued hatchback. Terrible-looking condition, ripped up back seats, wires hanging down beneath the passenger door. 'Oh, don't worry about those,' Walter explained. 'That was only for the electric window.' Had MOT (how does he do it? Stolen MOT books?). Very good runner, according to Walter, been all over the country in it, motorways, everything, cruises at 80 but best not to take it above.

Let's face it, the only way I could go was up. Tried to do a part-exchange deal on it with the Dolly.

'Fuck off, what do I want with that shit-heap?' Walter said pleasantly. No, straight rental. Of course, had it been me, I'd have lent it to him for nothing. I want you to know that, Walt. But he's a money-man. How much do I pay him? No idea. Don't know cars, rentals, prices.

'A hundred and fifty a week?' I offer.

'Oh, tell you what, John,' Walter says. 'I'll do it for you for a hundred. Why not?' I peeled the notes off right there on the pavement, 400 in twenties. He perked up discernibly, then generously offered to drive what remained of the Dolly down to a 'property' of his in Tooting. Safekeeping – a place near the common. 'Never know when you'll be stuck in London in need of thirty quid scrap money, do you?', he added, (unconsciously revealing observation). 'I mean, it's not as if anyone's going to nick it, is it, John?'

Still, a most unusual offer, for Walter. Handed him Dolly keys. So, Tooting, last dwelling place, car heaven. Knew Walter was probably only doing it because he knows he's ripped me off on the hatchback. Don't really care if he has. Got money.

Got into the hatchback with Walter and Graham, off to pub. Walter directs to one in South Ken. Classy. In fact: red-faced businessmen drinkers, a group of Chelsea supporters in football shirts, smattering of au pairs: poor things, lambs for the fire in a place like this; already they're being bought drinks, and accepting. Watch it, darling; England, this.

Stayed till closing time. Beers. Lots of. Lashed them down standing by the swaying bar. Laughter. Toasts to nicking-the-money (but only going along with it) and trip to Vegas. Walter's never been. Clearly considers it a pressing void in his otherwise rigorous adult education. Shit, did I really tell Walter that I'd take him with me? Might regret saying that. Good to see Walter so happy, though.

Sobered up past Chelmsford. Drink-driving must end. Need wheels. Moral regeneration. Sudden strong revulsion to nicking-all-the-money idea. Certainly immoral to nick all. Might be moral to nick some of it, but only if done later on, not gratuitously, and for strong reasons relating to necessary human survival (my own, or loved ones acquired in process. Carol?).

Yellow Jersey Press: subsidiary of international conglomerate. Deal not what it seems, because of 12-grand 'advance' clause, previously discussed. Thus, deal *is* exploitative, and itself immoral. So, no qualms on this front, if it came to it.

Against this, I accepted deal. Also, Rachel's genuine belief that deal is not exploitative should be borne in mind. She is acting in good faith. I therefore have an obligation to act in good faith towards *her*, as far as is possible, given above. Try and protect her job if things go badly wrong, something like that. OK, will try to.

Three acceptable scenarios, then:

1. Gambling goes so well I make more than 12 grand back on bets. Don't write book. Don't nick any money. As soon as get 12 grand clear, pay 'advance' back to publisher. Project just 'unworkable'.

2. Gambling goes well enough that I don't have to nick any money. This means enough money left over to live off while write book. Write book.

3. Bets go badly. Say, 9 or 10 grand down after two and a bit months. Health deteriorates chronically. No real prospect of either winning money back or writing book if I carry on. In this case, nick money as needed for health (moral and physical) and attempt writing book. Put remainder on long-shots in hope of surprise big wins.

BUT, this is important: if DO nick money, MUST write about nicking it in book. Retrieves gd. faith, art. integ. etc. Cld. be consequences, tho'. Pay back nicked money? Shit. No, doesn't matter. MUST DO THIS.

Of these: 2 most preferable; 1 less preferable, if most painless for me – I'd get the blame but at least I'd have paid the money back; 3 least preferable. But even if 3 happened I would have fulfilled my moral obligations to everybody.

Oh, and on a logistical point: ring Walter every day for tips. Don't have to take them. Probably best to at first. Any winning tip of his, he gets 10 per cent.

Good. So that was settled then. Suffolk coming near. Into the hollow before Dedham Vale, up into the swathes of small moonlit fields, pink houses. Always like this bit. Even better coming the other way. Manageable, those fields. Strong moon: lit the pink frames.

Reached down into the doorwell to grab a smoke. Trawled up three packets. Examined them with my fingers on the passenger seat. Jesus, all empty, apart from one fag in one pack. Can I really have smoked 59 since the West Country? Graham had a few. Oh well. Need a break then. Save the last one for when I get home to Red House.

On to the country roads, last seven miles, past the deserted American airfield. See deer there sometimes at night. Supposed to be haunted by fallen airmen. No deer or airmen visible. Just the dead flat all round, icy blue sky reaching to every corner, full of planets. Who needs hills? That big asteroid's not due till 2028. You could see it coming from here, weeks ahead.

Saw the pale brick face of the cottage up ahead. Pulled in crunching on the threadbare gravel. Pig noises, more than usual. Heavier motor, see, lads, woke you all up. Plus, I should advise you, am carrying approx. 3,400 in pocket. OK, 3-3 maybe. Another four coming in three weeks!

It's not the money, though. It's this 'past' thing, knew it was a good idea. Can feel it working already; restoring cells.

Yeah, and what about the 700 that's already gone? Admit to that? . . . No. Dispersable but necessary expenses. All part of essential preparation. Have to write about the rest, though.

Got out and stood, lit up a beautiful fag, then went in and ascended to my starry chamber.

6

The Dirt Track

Some of what Lurch said must have sunk in, because soon I was travelling. Auntie Jean told me that the trust Mum had set up had £15,000 in it and that I would get it when I was 25. Since this was a long way off I started work as a clerk in a company making door locks. It was owned by some racehorse owners who were friends of the Greaveses. All I had to do was write addresses on batches of envelopes, then wait looking out of the window at the company car park until the next batch of envelopes was put on my desk.

The caretaker was an ex-jockey named Pat Gilbody. I remembered his face from the gallops at Newmarket. He had a wizened face even then, when he was young. All the other jockeys called him 'gargoyle' and said he was touched, from making the weight. He never rode a Derby horse.

Pat Gilbody had started at the lock company a year before me but he was still very keen. All day I watched him hiding in his hut in the car park waiting for shoppers to try and use the company spaces. He waited for them to leave their cars and then rushed out almost licking his lips and put his clamp on the wheels. When they came back he pointed to the sign and charged them £20. He only had one clamp so he could only do one car at a time. He still managed to clamp five cars that first day, including a couple of old people and a woman with two kids wailing in a double-pushchair. Pat didn't care. He was ruthless.

On the second day I don't know how many cars Pat

clamped in total because I went out for my lunch hour and never came back. Auntie Jean said she'd done all she could do. She spoke to someone from the Trust on the phone and the next day I was given £500 in £10 notes in an envelope. Auntie Jean explained that it was an advance on my Trust money. 'And you better make the most of it because you're not getting any more for another eight years,' she said sternly as she handed it over to me in the car.

She looked a bit upset as she said it. I pretended not to notice and said thanks. I was glad she didn't let her feelings break through. She had enough on her plate, with Julian and Stuart about to come home from boarding-school for the holidays, not to mention the Greaveses' horses, and Nobbin (Noggin having died of old age).

Auntie Jean sighed and then said, 'You have our number, don't you, John?'

'Yes, Auntie Jean.'

'Well, there we are.'

We sat in silence until we reached the station. As I held the car door Auntie Jean said it was time for me to start calling her Jean and not Auntie.

I caught a train to London and then one from London to Newhaven and at Newhaven I got the ferry to Dieppe. I knew about Dieppe because there was a school trip there which me and Walter were barred from. Johnny and Pridwell told me all about it. In Dieppe wine was 50p a bottle and cider was even less. When it was time to go back Sperm had to carry six boys including Grainger back on to the ferry one by one. Then they came round and started a fight with some boys from another school in the ferry disco and Sperm had to break that up too.

The concrete jetty at Dieppe stretched miles into the sea. Clusters of black rocks jutted out into the breakers beneath the jetty like hands beckoning. Beyond the grey pier I could see Dieppe in the distance, and the wooded coastline on either side.

Soon we docked. I went to a shop and bought a bottle of cider. It was just as cheap as Johnny said. I took the bottle and went to a quiet part of the quay. I gave a few toasts to Johnny and Walter and Lurch and Pridwell. I felt nice and dizzy as I walked to a main road and started to hitch.

After a week I'd hitched to Nantes. From Nantes I went down the coast until I reached Biarritz. At night I stayed in youth hostels or sometimes cheap hotels. The dormitories in the hostels were like school except more comfortable.

I had no trouble hitching apart from a blond man with body-builder's arms who picked me up on a country road. After a while he put his hand on my knee so I told him to fuck off. He got angry and swerved the car about and flung my bag on the back seat so that my clothes spilled out. He skidded to a halt and ordered me out and tried to drive off with my clothes.

I grabbed most of them back and then picked up a rock from the side of the road and chucked it at his back light. He stopped again and stared at me silently in his wing mirror so I started acting like Walter did during his attacks, lumping up and down and shouting and putting on wild faces. We stayed like that for what seemed like ages, him sitting staring and me lumping up and down in the road. Then he threw his cigarette out of the window and screeched off again.

At Biarritz I got a job in a no-star hotel run by a half-blind old woman named Madame Dupree. She had a three-legged dog called Matot. Together they were quite a sight. My job was to put wallpaper up in the six rooms, including on the ceilings to cover the cracks, so that she'd qualify for a star. I was there a month and didn't see one guest. The wallpaper looked terrible after I put it up, with air pockets like pillows bulging out and the edges hanging down. But

Madame Dupree didn't seem to mind. I don't think she could see it.

Each evening we ate in the basement. Matot had the food that Madame Dupree had prepared for the guests. She and I ate slices of tripe or ancient pâté that she kept in labelled jars in a cupboard. Some of the jars went back to 1968 so I steered her towards the more modern ones when she was in there fumbling around.

Every morning and evening I took Matot for a walk on the vast beach at the foot of the town where the black waves were as high as houses. At first there was usually only us and a few surfers in wetsuits, and two thin old Englishwomen wearing lipstick and hats with black lace, who Madame Dupree said had lived in Biarritz for years, and who sat on the promenade bench above the beach cradling tiny yapping dogs.

Then May came and the sea turned blue. The first holiday-makers arrived on the beach. During the evening walks I went body-surfing while Matot hobbled about excitedly on the sand sniffing people.

At night prostitutes began lounging on the streets round the hotel. From my window I watched the younger ones getting into cars or walking into the other no-star hotels with men. Some of the old ones were still there when I went outside to lock up. One always winked at me. She was big and stocky and wore an orange wig. Sometimes she called me over but I just smiled and shrugged.

Then one night when I was locking up she was out there on her own. This time when she called out I went over. I gave her thirty francs and followed her up the steps of the next hotel. On the way up she said her name was Sonya, but I didn't think it was. I thought I recognised her face from the bakery counter.

As soon as she was in the room she hitched up her skirt and bent over on the bed. But I couldn't do it. I just stood there with my trousers down. After a bit she sighed and turned round and put her hands down my pants. She had thick wrists and chubby pink hands that smelled of disinfectant and sex.

Her hands worked quickly and efficiently as if she was kneading dough. After she'd finished she said, '*Voilà, c'est pas grave, heh?*' The smell seemed to cling to me for days, no matter how many times I went body-surfing to try and wash it off. Matot was very curious and stuck closer to me than usual on our walks wagging his tail.

After the inspector refused to give our hotel a star for the summer, Madame Dupree said she couldn't afford to keep me any more. On the day of my departure she opened a farewell bottle of champagne (putting some in Matot's bowl) and gave me a leaving bonus. She got quite tearful about it, saying how much she'd miss all my work, even though by then the wallpaper was hanging down from the bedroom ceilings in damp strips like suspended forests.

I kissed Madame Dupree goodbye on a leathery cheek and gave Matot a last pat. He was so out of it on the champagne he almost keeled over. Then I walked from the gloom of the basement up into the light of the street, past the warm hum of the bakery, back towards the main road.

I hitched into Spain and spent two days standing on a burning motorway waiting for a lift. It was strange. The more I waited there in the scorching sun the happier I felt. Finally I walked back to a town and got on a train. The train was going across Spain, back into France, and then into Italy. I was supposed to get off before the first border. But on the train I became feverish. I was deliriously happy as the border went past. Then I fell into a deep sleep full of bursting dreams.

I was lying in a tray on the bakery counter. Madame Dupree and Sonya were there, looking at me in orange wigs. Then they pushed the tray into the oven. The smoke darkened . . . but then it cleared again, into a waveless lagoon. I could see Matot in the distance on a beach, as I lay back in the liquid blue.

When I awoke, the train was standing at a station in Italy. I grabbed my bag and scrabbled off. I walked through the cool of an empty old station with a high stone roof, and outside into a square. No one asked for my ticket. I don't even know what town it was. I drank from a water fountain and followed a sign to the port down a hill. I bought a ticket on a ferry to Greece called *The Ionian*. I stayed all day in the green shade of the deck and all night watching the wine-dark sea.

It was early morning when we came into Piraeus, with only *The Ionian* moving among the sleeping hulls of empty ferries, and the lingering trace of fuel in the air mixing with the smell of the fresh sea. I walked across the quay to a kiosk selling newspapers. I bought some smokes and an English-language paper called the *Athens Post*. I looked at the date on the paper and realised that it was five days since I'd left Biarritz and that it was my seventeenth birthday.

I was down to my last £100 by then. In the back of the *Athens Post* I read an advertisement for a job. It said: 'Writer needs willing assistant. Some research skills. Contact Mr Edwin Duplessis.' I rang the number and an American man answered. I got the job and it was there that I met Mr Duplessis's daughter, Carol.

She wasn't his real daughter. She was half Apache and half Spanish and had been adopted by the Duplessises when she was a baby in Detroit. She was 15 years old with bronze skin and very blue eyes. She had black hair and lips that made two tiny dimples under her nose when she smiled, and she was the most beautiful woman I'd ever seen.

Mr Duplessis wasn't a real writer, either. He just wanted

to be one. He'd been a successful businessman in Detroit, in toys. But all his success in business had just been the planning stage for moving to Greece and becoming a writer. His wife was called Judy and she still lived at their old house in Detroit. They weren't divorced or anything. It was just that Mrs Duplessis didn't like Greece much, and thought that it was a matter of getting Mr Duplessis's plan to be a writer out of his system. Then she thought he would go back to business in Detroit.

'That's really what she thinks!' Mr Duplessis said quite often, incredulously.

He and Carol and a bad-tempered black kitten named Nobel lived in a tall thin house on a mountain called Pendeli outside Athens. On one side you could see the start of the city, and on the other nothing but miles and miles of deep-green pine forests stretching down to the sea at Marathon. There was nothing on Pendeli except for the house and a farmhouse further up the dirt track, and a church half-way up the mountain full of icons and candles that were lit by the shepherds.

Mr Duplessis had chosen the house because he'd read about Mount Pendeli in a book. The mountain was the home of Pan. He was invisible, but you could tell he was there by a line cutting through the grass underneath the pine trees like a sharp rush of wind, even when there was no wind or the wind was blowing in the other direction.

Mr Duplessis said he hadn't actually detected Pan's presence yet, but that he hoped to soon, and that anyway just being there on Mount Pendeli meant he could put his writing plan into action in a way that he never could have done in Detroit. 'No Pan, no plan, huh?' he joked.

Overall there was a six-year plan divided into three two-year sub-plans, one for each of his first three books. At the end of the six years his writing would be famous throughout the world, although he admitted it would probably take longer to go down as a great – probably another four-year plan at least. He was looking at ten years in total.

That was why he'd named the kitten Nobel. Even after the first six years, he'd still have to call out Nobel's name. And every time he did, he'd remember that there were still things to achieve, and another plan to do. ''Cause that dumb cat is going to look me right back in the eyes as if to say, "Ed, you're the one who called me this goddam silly name, and you ain't lived up to it yet." And you know, John, it's those kind of things that keep you going.'

Mainly my job was looking after the paperwork for all the plans, plus the card index that Mr Duplessis used to store his diary entries in, for his memoirs. But really I didn't have very much to do. I think he just liked having someone around. At first I stayed in Athens at the YMCA, but then Mr Duplessis said it was silly making all those bus journeys, and I might as well move in to the spare room next to his office, as long as I didn't mind doing a little extra work sometimes, like jotting down his dreams in the mornings if he'd had some that were good material.

But after I'd moved in Mr Duplessis never asked me to, and soon I realised that jotting down dreams was just something he thought writers should do and that he'd probably read in another book. In fact, by the end of most mornings I'd finished all the paperwork, even after stringing it out. So I did other things instead, like watering the thin sprouts of grass in the rocky yard which Mr Duplessis was trying to grow into a lawn, or retrieving Nobel from some tree, or sometimes going down to the American Club on Mr Duplessis's scooter to buy his favourite packs of sliced turkey and cans of iced tea.

I wasn't allowed to read any of Mr Duplessis's book yet, but I knew he was going at a terrific pace. He told me he was averaging 2,500 words a day. 'There've been a few days I've dipped to two point two,' he said. 'But you get right back on track with a couple of two-sevens.' All I knew was that his book was called *Back in Time for Breakfast*, and that it was about a toy manufacturer and this toy he'd made that went out at night doing terrible things, and that nobody found out about it until it was too late.

'Of course, it's allegorical,' Mr Duplessis always said.

Even when it was finished nobody else would be allowed to see it until the New Year when Ted Kleinbeck came over from Florida. Ted Kleinbeck was an old lawyer friend of Mr Duplessis who'd once worked in publishing and would know what to do. 'We've got to put all the legal stuff in place,' Mr Duplessis said. 'Y'know, protect the title, all that jazz. Until Ted's seen it and until that book is fully protected, *no one* is going to get to open it up.'

Mr Duplessis seemed fond of Carol but because of all his writing he didn't see her much. Every morning she walked to the end of the dirt track to catch the bus to the American school. She walked in fast jerky movements with her head down. The only time she looked up was when she walked past Mr Duplessis's green Volvo and snatched a glance at her reflection wrinkling her nose.

The next time I saw her each day was when she came back down the track after school at four. She went straight to her room on the top floor and played terrible Led Zeppelin records for hour after hour. I'd tried to start a conversation up with her once about the Vapors and the Clash but she said she'd never heard of them. 'John, you're boring me, OK?'

From her room there was a staircase on to the roof. Thick metal spikes came out of the flat roof, like they did on most houses in Athens, in case the person living there wanted to add another floor. Mr Duplessis had painted the whole roof silver, including the spikes, as the first stage of a solar heating plan. But he'd abandoned it soon afterwards, because it might have distracted him from his writing plan, which was the main one after all. If you walked up high on Pendeli and looked down, you could see specks of the silver roof glinting among the trees.

Sometimes Carol took her speakers up on to the roof and sunbathed listening to Led Zeppelin, and once I saw her dancing topless except for the coloured scarves she always wore, with her tiny breasts heaving in a strange unrhythmical dance as she flailed her arms and shook her head.

I decided Carol lived in her own world and didn't let anyone in. Even Mr Duplessis couldn't get in. Of course I wanted to get in, but it seemed very unlikely.

The only time Carol sat with us in the evenings was the one evening a week when there were episodes of *Dallas* and *The Love Boat* on television with Greek sub-titles. They were very old episodes which Mr Duplessis had seen before in Detroit. He loved watching them again and sat there slurping his iced tea with a wry expression, occasionally telling me what was about to happen.

Carol didn't like them at all. She perched on the arm of the sofa making tut-tutting sounds and impatiently swinging her legs. Then about half-way through she flounced out saying how stupid they were and how stupid we were for watching them. Every week she was there for the start of *Dallas* just to have her disgust confirmed.

Usually Mr Duplessis seemed too engrossed to notice, but once after Carol had flounced out he put his glass down hard and raised his hand into the gloomy pine-scented air between us and the television. His hand sort of quivered there for an instant, with its palm cupped, as if it was trying to hold on to an invisible object. 'You know, Carol's real intelligent,' Mr Duplessis said. 'But it was the same back in Detroit. I guess I thought that bringing her here she could meet some people but, I dunno . . .' His hand went down and after a pause he said: 'Take a look at JR's face when he sees who's on the horse.'

One Saturday morning when Mr Duplessis was out on Pendeli Carol appeared in the doorway of the garage where I was trying to put the scooter back together. She'd wrapped one of her scarves round her head like a wedding veil. The summer was ending and the light was less harsh. The garage had no door and as she stood in the doorway the sun filtered through the scarf in a soft shadow, making her face look glowing and grave like the portraits of Mary in the Pendeli church.

'So what's my dad paying you?' Carol said coolly.

'A thousand drax a day,' I said. That was about seven pounds.

'You should have asked him for more. Dad would have paid.'

'I don't mind,' I said.

'Dad thinks he can buy anything.'

I said nothing.

'He thinks he can buy being a writer but he can't,' Carol said.

I kept my head down, tinkering with the scooter, waiting for Carol to get bored and go away. She was pacing slowly round the garage humming 'Stairway to Heaven'. Then she slipped on a bolt from the scooter and went sprawling to the garage floor with a yelp. Dirt and oil were all over her clothes and her scarves. 'Oh my God,' Carol said, sitting up. 'I'm so clumsy. I'm always doing things like that.'

Carol started to laugh, and I laughed too, as if I was floating, and Carol said that what we really should do was go down to this beach at Marathon, so she could clean up, and go for the last swim of the summer, as long as I could put the scooter back together.

'It's called Skinias beach,' she added as she walked back out of the doorway. 'It's not a great beach but it's the nearest one. You pronounce it "skinny ass".'

I put the scooter back together as fast as I could. I drove down the snaking black Marathon road, through the pine forest and past the old marble quarry with Carol's fingertips on my hips. We swam in the pale shallows of Skinias beach until the wind got up and clouds turned the water grey. I summoned all my courage and kissed Carol as we lay drying on the sand. Carol kissed me back, and the rusting cans and skidding rubbish left on the beach from the summer merged into a haze. Then it started to rain and we got back on the scooter, and as we turned on to the dirt track towards the house Carol leant forward close against my back and shouted, 'Don't think this means I'm an easy lay!'

After that Carol let me in. Now we were a team and we didn't let anyone else in. I don't know whether Carol was an easy lay because I'd never had a lay with anyone else and neither had Carol. All I know is that we started doing it all the time. We did it in the forest and in the ruins of the marble factory and once on the silver roof, but only once because Nobel was always up there and wouldn't move. When we did it I felt my body was hers and hers was mine, and our single body was pure, and I felt ashamed of the days of passing round porn mags at school, and watching the strip show in Soho with Walter and the thick smell of the bakery woman's hands. Now they were all a dead dream.

In the autumn storms broke over Pendeli and I thought of how Lurch would have liked it. So I wrote to him giving Mr Duplessis's address, telling him what things were like and that occasionally I had a nightmare in which I was back in the broken-down dorm, and that he had to get out.

And Lurch wrote back in his spidery black italic ink, saying, 'What a surprise! Pleasant almost. A letter that contains such a finely balanced mixture of compliment and adverse criticism that it is difficult to know how to reply.

Anyway, now you are no longer here. You have travelled in the true sense. The past is past and I believe that no one should hold the past against himself or against others.' The new boys he was teaching, Lurch said, were 'even more unimaginative than usual', adding, 'how many of them write poetry?'

It was strange thinking of Johnny and Walter and Pridwell being in their last year, being prefects (though not Walter of course) and walking on the quad. So I wrote to them too. Walter wrote back first. It was a short scrawled note that said: 'Dear Fucker, You'd be amazed what's happening here. My study is a fucking fortress. No one gets in – not prefects, Spacs, The Cod, no one. Everyone is fucking terrified of me! Your friend, Walter.' I didn't really believe him, I have to say.

Then Pridwell wrote saying he'd rescued my poems about snogging and the Sex Pistols when Sperm and some prefects came to take away my drawer as 'evidence'. Pridwell gave the poems to Lurch to put in his magazine. Lurch was almost delirious, according to Pridwell. But then when Lurch gave a draft of the magazine to The Cod for a read-through, The Cod told him to take my poems out because it was 'obvious' that I must have copied them 'from some pop record'. Lurch was furious but he couldn't do anything because he'd already been in big shit from the bungalow incident with me and Johnny – 'to my everlasting shame,' Pridwell added.

By the time Johnny wrote back Lurch had left the school. Sperm caught a first-year called Dawling coming back from Lurch's bungalow and Dawling said Lurch had propositioned him. Almost everyone including The Cod believed Dawling, and by the next morning Lurch had resigned 'on health grounds'. When Dawling found out what had happened to Lurch he started blubbing, saying he'd made the whole thing up to get out of trouble, and that it was Sperm who'd first put the idea about propositioning in his head. But hardly anyone believed Dawling this time and anyway it was too late. That was the story according to Johnny, who always told the truth.

Johnny said he'd seen Lurch twice afterwards walking on the Downs. 'The first time I saw him he was walking towards Epsom,' Johnny wrote. 'I called out "hello, sir" and he called back "hello, Loathsome". The second time I saw him really clearly. I noticed he was in a bad way. He was staggering, John, either ill or just pissed. He didn't stop.'

The New Year came and Ted Kleinbeck arrived. Mr Duplessis was out shopping for the book-celebration dinner he'd decided to have, so I waited with Ted Kleinbeck in the study. He was a large genial man with a knowing smile. However, I soon realised that one thing Ted Kleinbeck knew nothing about was Mr Duplessis's book and that he thought he'd just come for a holiday.

Mr Duplessis had only been back a minute when he was thrusting the great stacked block of *Back in Time for Breakfast* into Ted Kleinbeck's reluctant hands.

Then Mr Duplessis strode out of the study saying, 'Take your time, Ted, I'll be gone the rest of the day.' Shortly afterwards, I saw him disappearing into the forest wearing his walking boots and the serene expression of a soon-to-be-confirmed genius.

Ted Kleinbeck sat in Mr Duplessis's special leather writing chair slowly turning the pages. Hours passed. I got Ted Kleinbeck coffees. I heard Carol coming in from school, the reverberation from her hi-fi starting. Then I heard her hands on the new piano playing 'Yesterday'. Mr Duplessis had bought her the piano after Carol said she wanted to be a musician. All she ever played was 'Yesterday'. I thought of her hand moving up my leg. Normally I'd finished work by this time.

Ted Kleinbeck's brow furrowed and he rubbed his neck. He grew more and more exasperated. Finally he put down *Back in Time for Breakfast* and began pacing the room anxiously.

'Why is it always me?' he said. 'It's been thirty-eight years since I was in publishing. Still they come to me with their books. Friends, relations, even the mailman did it once. And you've got to let them down gently of course. Tell them there's a lot of promise. Tell them all they did was get a little ahead of the curve. Tell them what they did was write a third book instead of a first book, that the publishers aren't ready. What you've got to do is make their failures seem noble, you see. And yet . . . *and yet!* Still they come with their *terrible* books . . .'

Ted Kleinbeck sat back down on the leather writing chair, squeezing the top of his nose with a large hand. 'I mean, Edwin is one of the good guys. I've known Edwin a long time. But this is too much. You know what I'm going to do this time?' He paused grimly. 'I'm going to tell Edwin the *truth*.'

It was a Friday night so Carol and I went out while Ted Kleinbeck told Mr Duplessis the truth over the celebration dinner. I had my own motorbike by then, an old East German MZ 125 with '1965 Balkan Rally' written on the petrol cap. It wasn't really mine. I paid 2,000 drax a month to a mustachioed customs officer at a port near Marathon. He hired out all the impounded bikes as a sideline. I had to deliver it back the following July in time for the inventory.

Every Friday night we rode down to Athens on the MZ. No one wore helmets. Mr Duplessis made me buy one for Carol, an orange one, but she never put it on. In winter the centre of Athens changed from the dusty bowl of the summer into a magical city. At night the illuminated Parthenon threw pools of shadow and yellow light on to the teeming squares.

That Friday night we went to a place called Bar Theatre. It was a tiny bar up a side-street with a blue and pink flashing piano on a sign. As soon as Carol saw it she said we had to go in. Inside there were a few wooden tables, a piano and bar. The only other people there were a Greek girl wearing a satin dressing-gown and high heels, and a middle-aged woman behind the bar with dyed blonde hair who said her name was Mimi and spoke French.

I knew it was a clip joint straight away but Carol didn't. She just said, 'I love this place already.' We sat down and ordered drinks. Mimi brought the drinks to the table but refused to let us pay. Carol played 'Yesterday' on the piano with her orange helmet beside her on the piano chair, and Mimi and the Greek girl sang along and clapped.

We always went to Bar Theatre after that. Sometimes there was a different girl at the table but Mimi was always there. She refused to take a drachma for our drinks, and always eyed us with the same strange look, and whenever we came in she looked up and said, '*Ah, les amoureuses.*'

On Saturdays Carol slept in till twelve. Mr Duplessis had tried to wage a campaign to get her up earlier but he'd long abandoned it. While she slept I got on the MZ and went down to Athens on my own. I felt as though my life had become a film. The streets were a film set that I walked on Saturday mornings, full of people arguing and cars blaring their horns, and wailing radios and the smell of pastry and cheese, and the faint smell of mothballs from the priests and old crones passing by on the pavements dressed in black.

Sometimes on the way back I would stop at a run-down suburb called Marousi. There was a snack bar that sold cheap beer. I drank the beer until I was nearly drunk, and flicked through the copies of *NME* and *Rolling Stone* that I stole for Carol from the kiosk selling foreign papers on Kolonaki Square. No one ever caught me. Then I got back on the MZ with nothing in my mind except the headiness of the beer and the anticipation of the next scene.

And once on a whim travelling back from Amourroussi I decided to try and find a back way through to Pendeli across country, so I turned off the Marathon road earlier than usual, up a steep white track. I passed through empty fenced-off plots that no one had built on yet, and the rutted track made the wheels of the bike twist and shudder. A motley pack of thin stray dogs came chasing out from a plot, snapping at the wheels. There were loads of strays along the dirt tracks. You could always outrun them because they were starving and weak. But a strong headwind buffeted the bike, and I didn't know the turns of the track, so the dogs kept coming back alongside just when I thought I'd lost them.

The track darkened and I realised I'd passed under the lip of Pendeli. In the distance there was a grassy bank where Carol and I had done it once. Suddenly I felt a new wind on my back, forcing me through the headwind. Then the wind lifted from my back, and everything was calm except for a line cutting through the grass ahead like an invisible razor. It was quite distinct, and then it was gone.

For an instant I felt scared. But then a joy gripped me, so strong I had to shout it out. I stood up on the worn pedals of the MZ and let the bike idle until the dogs had almost caught up. 'I'm so happy!' I screamed at the dogs. 'I'm so happy and so lucky!'

After Ted Kleinbeck went back to Florida Mr Duplessis said he'd decided to write a different book. 'It's like Ted said,' he told me. 'With *Breakfast* I got ahead of the curve. You see, it's more like a third book than a first one. I guess I've got to get back to the curve and kind of ride along it till the readers are ready.' So I asked Mr Duplessis what he needed to get back to the curve, and he sighed and said, 'Material, John. Yes, material.'

I became Mr Duplessis's material-gatherer. I went down to Athens with a notebook but I soon realised my Greek wasn't up to it. I went to the American Club and made notes there about the American women lying on loungers on the baked terrace, and the Pan-Am airline pilots having races in the pool.

At first Mr Duplessis was excited but then he said he was getting ahead of the curve again. His daily word average went down from 1,000 to 500 to 200 to nought. He stopped writing his memoir cards. He started going on material-gathering trips himself. He went to the Peloponnese and to Mount Olympus to try and find the main Gods, but he never did.

Spring came and no rain fell. The stream on Pendeli dried up as if it was late summer, and the dirt-track grass was parched to tinder by the first week of May. It was still cool up among the green pines, but I had to keep the sprinkler going to keep Mr Duplessis's lawn alive.

Once when we were inspecting the lawn I mentioned the masters playing croquet on the quad (it was Lurch's idea; he said croquet was the civilised form of rugby, but the croquet club didn't catch on) and Mr Duplessis snapped his fingers eagerly and said, 'Now this is a great angle for a book.' This book, he said, would be set entirely in England at a boys' boarding-school, 'but with an American sensibility that articulates the repression better'.

For a week Mr Duplessis quizzed me about all the details of the school, but then he got bored and said he had a new angle. He bought a video recorder and never went on material-gathering trips any more. He recorded all the episodes of *Dallas* and *Love Boat* and sat in his chair watching them, taking notes. The American Club opened a video-hire shop and sometimes I got Mr Duplessis two videos a day.

Carol said it was embarrassing to see her dad like that but Mr Duplessis seemed all right to me. He was trying to get somewhere he increasingly suspected he couldn't get to. But he was very thorough and he wasn't going to give up until he was sure.

By then Carol had decided not to be a musician. She was going to be an actress instead. She auditioned for Desdemona in the American School play. She walked around the roof at night practising her lines and I sat with Nobel on the silver ledge being Othello. She didn't get the part but it didn't put her off at all. She said the people who decided were 'real jerks' anyway. She knew all Desdemona's lines perfectly. She kept on speaking them on the roof, and when she was on the back of the MZ, and sometimes in Bar Theatre too.

It was later in May that the first forest fires started, down near Marathon. During the day military planes swooped down over Pendeli carrying water. More fires flared up along the coast and the planes put them out quickly, except for one that raged all night. Carol and I watched from the roof as the distant orange tongues flicked the sky.

At the American Club everyone said it was the Anarchist arsonists again. The *Athens Post* was full of news of fires around Athens, and a map showing how a pincer movement by the arsonists could seal off the city with a ring of fire. But Mr Duplessis laughed wryly and said they were all being paranoid, and that it was a combination of the dry spring and people throwing cigarettes out of car windows.

Carol and I went down to swim at Skinias beach and there was charcoal floating in the shallows. She'd decided to stop sunbathing, because it was vanity and evil. So between swims we sat wrapped in towels in the shade of a half-built house, looking out at the sea and the burnt tree stumps, and the pale roots exposed like bones.

We did it in the porch of the half-built house and the rain came down, just like it had done the first time we went to Skinias. It was beautiful riding back with a rainbow over

Pendeli. The rain kept on for a couple of days. The fires died out and the planes stopped coming, and after that the talk of arsonists evaporated for a while.

Then one hot Saturday I was coming back from Marousi with my head full of beer when the road seemed to explode just past the Marathon turn. The air burned my throat like hot ash and smoke raced across the road in swirling gusts. Beneath Pendeli the smoke got thicker. The fire seemed to be spreading very quickly. Goats, dogs and tortoises were coming out of the smoking thickets to take cover in the road. I saw an old goatherd beating a snake with a burning stick, and the terrible crackling sound of the fire came in and out of earshot as if it was circling me.

When I reached the house the green Volvo was outside with all the doors open. The Duplessises' belongings were crammed inside with the scooter strapped to the roof. The fire was about a mile away but already black wafers of ash were skidding through the air. I parked the MZ and saw Carol sitting idly dangling her legs from the boot of the car. She still looked sleepy.

'The house looks funny, doesn't it?' she said. I noticed that the furniture and the rugs had been piled on to the balcony. The sprinkler was on top of the balcony rail, sprinkling all the things.

'Dad's been watering the house,' Carol explained. 'He's on the roof. Nobel won't come down.'

I went up to the roof. Mr Duplessis was on his knees on the ledge, holding out an upturned rake with both hands. Nobel was perched high up on one of the metal roof-spikes looking defiant. Mr Duplessis was trying to dislodge Nobel into the cradle of rake but Nobel wasn't moving. 'Come on, kitty,' Mr Duplessis was saying soothingly. 'Kitty-kitty-kitty-kih-teee.'

'Mr Duplessis,' I said. 'Don't you think we should be going?' Intermittently the ash wafers were bombing on to our heads. They were getting bigger and hotter.

'I don't want to tip him over the wrong way,' Mr Duplessis said. 'He's too far up the spike. I can't get any leverage with this thing.'

He handed me the rake. I couldn't get Nobel down either. Mr Duplessis shouted, 'Will you come down here, you dumb fucking motherfucking goddam cat!' But Nobel didn't move.

Finally Mr Duplessis said, 'Get the sprinkler.'

I got the sprinkler. I sprinkled the roof and the spikes. Then I lodged the sprinkler so that it poured down on Nobel in a steady rain. Nobel's whiskers twitched as thin channels of water formed on his oily fur. Nothing would move him. 'At least he's got a chance this way,' Mr Duplessis said as we left the roof.

Quickly we shoved the sodden rugs and furniture from the balcony into the main room and closed all the doors. Mr Duplessis drove off with Carol in the Volvo towards Marathon while I followed on the MZ. We booked in to a small hotel and in the evening Carol and I watched *Last Tango in Paris* at an open-air cinema full of tittering crones, while in the distance Mr Duplessis drank ouzo at a café on the seafront, his face tilted happily up towards the café lights, as if a great weight had been lifted from him.

The next morning we went back to Pendeli. Practically all the pines had been burnt down on the Athens side. The fire had stopped just short of the house and the only damage was some singeing at the back. I went into the study and started to tidy up, but I could tell Mr Duplessis wouldn't be using it any more and that he'd already decided to go back to Detroit. Through the window the lawn looked lusher than ever, what with all the sprinkling. Nobel re-emerged to roll about on it in the afternoon, and Mr Duplessis went up and rubbed Nobel's chest and said, 'Well, Nobel, I guess yesterday you gave me the sign.'

On Carol's last night before leaving for the US, we went to Bar Theatre and then to a park on a hill overlooking the Parthenon. It was tiny and dark and tucked away among some old houses. You could see the whole of Athens through the gap at one end. We often used to stop there on the way back, to kiss and to tell each other stories, and it was in the park in the winter that we'd first said officially we were in love.

But we agreed it was impossible to keep going out when we lived on different continents, because one of us was bound to fall in love with someone else sooner or later, and that would only make things worse for the other. So we did it in the park and kissed for the last time and agreed we were now split up, but that we'd never forget each other and that maybe in a few years we could meet up again and be friends.

Carol said she was planning to leave Detroit and go and live in New Orleans as soon as she finished school. 'When I think of New Orleans I think of Bar Theatre spread over a whole city,' she said. 'Plus I want to play Blanche in *A Streetcar Named Desire* one day, so I have to see what it's really like.'

'I'm going to be a writer,' I said.

Carol said, 'That's cool. I think you'll be a lot better writer than Dad. Then when you're a famous writer and I'm a famous actress you can write me a play.'

We got back on the MZ. Pendeli looked strange and lunar in the dark with all the trees gone, and the rushing air smelled sweet with burnt pine. I turned up the dirt track and trained the headlamp beam on the empty white earth, looking out for the shadows of stray dogs. Carol hugged me tightly as we freewheeled down to the house – an uncharacteristic gesture of affection for her.

'John!' she shouted.

'Yes.'

'Do you think Jim is going to miss my pussy?' Jim was

Carol's embarrassing name for my cock.

'Yes,' I said.

And I didn't really know what to say after that.

So the next day I said goodbye to Carol and Mr Duplessis, and rode down to Marathon to give the MZ back to the mustachioed customs officer. Then I hitched back to Athens and bought a ticket to England on the Magic Bus. I didn't know where to go at first. The school term had ended and everyone had left. I rang Johnny's house from Victoria Station but no one was there. I didn't have a number for Walter. Finally I got hold of Pridwell and he said to come and stay. He lived near Epsom even though he'd been a boarder. Pridwell said his dad was away on church business in Africa and I could stay all summer at his place if I liked.

Pridwell was driving by then and he picked me up from the station in his dad's Fiesta, proudly waving a cigarette out of the window and blinking excitedly behind his specs. He told me Johnny had failed all his exams and gone into the army, and that no one knew where Walter had gone. We went to a pub and I stood behind Pridwell all night at the fruit machine as he tried out his unbeatable system. We were drunk by the time the pub closed. We drove to school in a blur and tried to break into the pool for a swim. Then Sperm ran out shouting from the Masters' flats with his chest heaving, and we ran off giggling at the thought of him keeping watch even then.

The next day I felt bad, because it was wrong to go back. I spent the rest of the summer with Pridwell watching the spinning fruit-machine wheels. At weekends we went to parties in the Fiesta, at neat houses in cul-de-sacs, with girls with hard sticky lips who smelled of chewing gum and still kept teddies on their beds, and boys who said they knew someone who was 'starting on 14K'.

But I told myself there was still so much time ahead — when you thought about it, it was dazzling. On a bus one day the conductor mimicked my Greek mannerisms, and I soon lost them. Sometimes I thought of Carol, but I always tried not to.

7

The Fridge

Found a small old fridge in the stable. Quite good nick, just lots of cobwebs. Cleaned it up with a hose. Rubbed it down with an old horse blanket. Looks nice. Bloody heavy, though. Half carried and half rolled it into the cottage and through to the study. Put a plug on it – took ages, not sure about plugs. Used the one from the long-knackered record player. Plugged fridge in. Didn't blow up. Humming sound. Works! Great. Always needed an extra fridge.

Went out to the new hatchback. Drove through the crisp morning fields down to the dual carriageway, pleasantly unpopulous as usual; thence to Ippo. Have decided all driving must be done a.m., to avoid d.d. This to be my great preparatory expedition. Get everything in. Then I would be ready to do Rachel's work.

Entered the city walls – bungalows – keeping assiduously to the 30 mph speed limit (actually have no choice; everyone does round here). First to Supergrape, East Anglian booze-supermarket chain. Used to go there *a lot* when first moved to Suffolk. Ages ago – staff won't remember. Can walk in as a paragon of sobriety. Supergrape staff: typical sneery young English New Wine dudes. Well, they think they are. That's why I go to Darren. Rather die than sneer, Darren would. Genuinely unjudgemental about the extent to which people want to abuse themselves. You could go in ten times a day, boozer's death-pustules sprouting out of your face, and he'd be exactly, genuinely, the same bloke. 'All right, John?' Their choice, innit. But he hasn't got anywhere near the same range, it's true.

Minimum purchase of one wine case or equivalent at Supergrape. This guarantees exclusively m-class winos. You go round with a shopping trolley to make you feel breezy. Took a trolley, chucked in mid-range whites and reds, plus two botts of the mighty £7.49 Lebanese, Musar, its noble blood drawn from the shrapnelled vines: treat for the first big winner. Deserve it. Case of 24-bott. German Pils, solid ancient label: look good in new fridge. Gin botts and case of tonic – both own label, let's not go mad. Bacardi? Why not? Cokes. No Cava stocked: un-bloody-believable. Paid. £157.60. Cash.

One of the would-be dudes helped me out to the hatchback with the loaded boxes. I tried to make a bit of convo. (Pang of shame?) Got these relatives coming over, you see. That's why I'm buying all this stuff. Thought I'd anaesthetise everyone to soften the blow, y'know. Huh. Still, looking at this stuff, I can't quite believe that we're going to get through it all.

'I'm sure you'll find a way, sir,' the dude said, turning insolently back towards Supergrape. Was that a stressed *you'll*? Cheeky little fucking runt.

Listen, mate, wanna know the truth? This lot is *nothing* to a geezer like me. Not careful, I'll come back and drink you dry. Break in in the middle of the night, drain every bottle, no prob. Walk out whistling. Then where would your range be, eh? Didn't say that. Just got in the car.

Next stop, FranCo's, the barber. That's what it says on the sign. Essential prep; feel clean, sharp. Feel, anyway. Bit of a wait by the hair-strewn floor. Read provided copy of *Penthouse*, unseeing. Old-style barber, FranCo, Durexes laid out by the mirrors, for his hombres.

Never really got porn. Specially not the soft stuff like this. Tried it of course; been down to the hard kernel, in uncontrollable urges. But it's never delivered. Don't know why not. Such purification with Carol: probably never got over it. Left me and porn with a too-strong sense of . . . mutual degradation.

Women openly getting into it now. That decided it: stopped trying. Not on principle. Just seeing the types of women who said they like it, on TV. Not 'liked', sorry, 'used'. Oh yes, my husband and I *use it* regularly. Obviously we keep it well out of the children's reach until such time as we do use it.

Oh, you do, do you? That's controlled urges, then. Knew I couldn't hang around with this new lot watching too. I mean, they were *pragmatists*, bloody *winners*.

'Hello, meester . . .'

Strange noise. Never mind. Anyway, total opposites as well, incidentally. To male porn addicts. In the worst stages of their porn addiction, males are usually completely . . .

'Meester, *excusa* . . .'

What? Yes: completely and utterly in their worst state of *out*-of-control fuckedupness. Definite losers (my school). So there's a big clash coming there, eh . . .

Suddenly found my *Penthouse* being taken gently away . . .

'The chair is ready, sir.'

Shit, must have 'gone off' . . .

'Sorry, FranCo,' I said.

'Is all right, sir. Don't worry. When you got a *Penthouse* in your 'and, I know is sometimes difficult to think of nothing else.'

Asked FranCo for a No. 2 shearing job, suedehead on top. He doesn't like doing them, proud cutter that he is. But, gotta keep ruthlessly getting back. Early mid-80s: my time. Always had suedeheads then. White socks, DM shoes and fake Crombies: Madness look. Populist *yet* rebel. Still looked like a student, even though I wasn't. Didn't mind: softer edge OK, like Terry Hall from the Special a.k.a.

At least it was an *English* look, not like current 70s 'Philly' retro (Huggy Bear would turn in g., if were dead), assorted baggy jackers and whiggers. White rastas are different of course.

Talked football with the swarthy FranCo. Who doesn't these days? Acceptable with FranCo; he was talking about it in primordial times, long B.C. (before commerce). 'Oh yeah, sir, Munchister Unided.' Despite Man U allegiance, his place a shrine to great wise ex-Ipswich Town manager Bobby Robson. Framed photographs crowd round mirrors: one of FranCo with arm respectfully round sage Sir Bobby. It is never 'Bobby' with FranCo, always 'Mr Robson'. True un-retro noble worship. I am touched when he talks.

Brings on a good flashback: a cricket match at school, on day of Ipswich v. Arsenal Cup Final, 197? Pridwell smuggled mini-transistor radio on to field – typical Pridwell ingenuity and planning. Prid. Arsenal fan, as was Johnny H. Myself, Chelsea. Always considered The Arse as natural enemy. Still bent furtively round transistor at end of overs with Johnny and Pridders, though. Johnny was captain. Had to keep our leader buoyed. Remember tremendous late flurry of goals being transmitted via sign language through the covers. Almost unbearable tension. Unfortunately, destroyed cricket concentration. Lost by nine wickets.

Opposition wasn't interested in hearing about it at tea. Proper major toff public school. Only talked rugger. That's what we decided anyway.

Left FranCo's. Drove out to an arcade on the Ippo outskirts. Last stop: Barry's Thrift Shop. As usual in suburban areas, a viciously possessive parking zone. Had to park about 3/4 mile away. Clouds darkening overhead.

Barry's looks like a charity shop at first sight: a few lines of manky old clothes on hangers; the odd pile of torn books; poignant lost tongs of once-proud cutlery all mixed up in old steel mugs.

In fact, in the back room lies the biggest collection of fenced clothing and shoes – most still immaculately encased by original shop wrappers and boxes – in existence this side of the black Thames. Incredible prices. Ten per cent of retail on av. Dunno how he gets them. Barry wouldn't tell you: wizened-before-his-time cockney, always holding yellow tape-measure in one hand; old boxing-type uneducated bullshitter-sage. You listen just in case he's the real thing; true slum prophet. Don't think so as much as I used to, though. Still, he's about the only white cockney I've ever met who doesn't constantly and sneeringly take the piss. Regularly holds down No. 2 spot on my ADVANTAGES OF LOCALITY list, behind Darren. Could even have been challenging for No. 1 if he wasn't a bit, well, weird.

Very careful, Barry is. When you enter his face fixes into a sort of rigid but ultra-alert contortion, nose sniffing the air for undercover coppers. Remembers everything. Knows you've been in before, and what you bought. But it might have been some undercover 'lulling' operation, right? So you always have to go through the same routine. Browse through the charity stuff for a respectable period, then ask him something along the lines of, 'Haven't got anything else, have you, by any chance?' Doesn't seem remotely copper-proof to me, but it's code enough for Barry. Don't think he'd really care actually, if he got nicked. The shop's not what he is; just what he does. Necessary burden. Prophet, see. Glad to be relieved of it.

I discovered Barry's by accident. Needed a suit one day. Passing the arcade. Started trying on some of the manky suits. Already decided against purchase. Just out of politeness, I'd said idly that when he got some more in, I'd definitely be down to get one. And Barry had shot me this hawklike glance. Within seconds he'd disappeared into the back room and returned with a 250-quid new Next suit (30) and a 40-quid Pair of unscratched M & S brogues (8).

Exact fits can be a problem. With Barry's bounteous yet, in legit. retailer's terms, limited stock, it's not surprising. At those prices, who cares? And if anyone can get you near, Barry can. Always measures you up with the yellow tape before he goes into the back room. Expert hands, lightning quick but the research is exhaustive. Dying breed: sweatshop raised; may not be a prophet, but yes, there is wisdom in those hands. Does minor alterations on site as well.

No punter ever gets in the back room. No browsing there. And Barry doesn't want you going in too much. Once went in two weeks running: he didn't like it. All that cash passing between the same two pairs of hands: vulgar, unnecessary. I could tell that's what he'd thought. Went in three months later and he couldn't have been more obliging (after I'd done the routine, naturally).

Think that's really when I started crossing the line, when I became a regular at Barry's. The Bacardi binge was just a confirmative, physical twist of the knife: because I started looking at people coming out of Next or M & S in Ippo, with their bags, thinking, what mugs: I can get that jacket for 175 less, *mugs*. Which they weren't of course. They just don't want to go into Barry's squalid premises. Don't want to enter Barry's world; our world. They can afford not to, just about; 'just about's' still enough. But once you've crossed that line you can't cope with just-abouts. You're into all or nothings, but pretending they're neither, and soon genuinely not caring whether they are or not. Deluded gambler's aesthetic: that's Barry and me (no, not me, surely).

Went in, did the routine. Barry disappears nimbly into back room. Returns laden with astonishing bargains even by his standards.

Bought a beautiful dark green suit, bit big round waist, but Barry says he can fix OK by moving side-button

('You've lost weight, son. Been down the gym, have we?'). Must be worth 350 min.; all mine for 35. Pair of 100 Italian ankle-boots, walnut, unfortunate but still acceptable buckle. Turned them over to look at soles – important, current shoes knackered, gonna be wearing these till they crack – examine: virgin pure. Barry virtually gives me these for *eight quid*.

Then he does a sudden look upwards as if he's just remembered something really special. Scampers into the back room. Jesus, Baz, I'm not a mug, spare me these salesman's touches. Comes back holding a spanking old but completely unworn Crombie. Real beaut. Must have been worth 500 new, today's prices. Barry says it's worth 600 unworn second-hand – understandable realms of fiction – but it's mine for 40. How did he know? Prophet after all? Took it, obviously.

Few trimmings: three tailored Jermyn St shirts for a fiver; three disgusting ties – don't wear ties, but they're Barry's trademark freebies, he puts them into your bag at the end, with a munificent crooked smile, so you have to accept them as honourable gifts.

At some stage during all this I tell Baz about 12-grand book. Must stop doing that. He's not overly impressed. Thought he would be, more. Coming to conclusion that only people who are impressed are Rachel and, increasingly, me.

Leafed off the readies: 88. Cash-only in Barry's, manifestly. After I'd paid I said I might as well change into it all: took the blue-and-white-striped Jermyn and then put on the rest. Barry stood guard between two rails of crap suits, a human shield watching the door. B. put my old clothes in an Asda bag and gave it to me. I said goodbye gruffly, because that's what you do with Barry.

Walked down the pavement by the arcade and it started to rain. Shit, can't get rained on in these threads. Who sells umbrellas? Don't get umbrella shops. Baggage shops, isn't it? No baggage shops round here. Could go back to Barry's. Are you joking? After five minutes? Never be able to go there again.

Finally made it to the hatchback. Not feeling too good. But brazen out vomit-urge. Can't vom. when things looking so up. Sit in stationary car thinking about umbrellas to distract. The Youth don't don't use 'em any more. Prefer wandering around in retro anoraks, rain splashing off slimy hoods. Put hoods up even when not raining. Put no cred. in umbrellas. Wouldn't be seen dead. Misplaced, that: Madness often carried umbrellas, partic. Suggs, and they had cred. to spare (despite later unwanted fringe NF following).

Urge went. Felt 'up' again.

Stopped off at the great dual-carriageway supermarket on way back. Own-brand Cava botts, 200 fags, papers (lots of, as per, but also *Racing Post*) and, oh yes, snacks. Must buy: make you feel civilised, good *meze* atmos. Crisps, normal and ridged ones, up-market cheese balls, olives (canned like Lurch's). Tossed in some extortionate dips and a bag of pistachios in honour of the late, unlamented Mr Jimmy Gruber.

Payment: cheque. Thought that was pretty generous of someone carrying 3.05 grand in his jeans pocket. Jesus shit! Not wearing jeans any more! Where the fuck's the wad! Scrabbled down into Asda bag on floor by checkout. Ah. Wad present and correct. Transferred to suit pocket as surreptitiously as possible. Discernible increase in respec' from middle-aged checkout yokel due to new threads and immac. Crombie.

Woman in front paid by cheque as well. Good to be back in the tolerant land of cheques.

Weather brightened as I passed the airfield. So much achieved and it's only midday . . . Beautiful rainbow looped over Pig City. Luck halo, got to be. Passed the Colonel and his wife, my neighbours, as I turned down Red House Lane. They were out gardening as usual. Nice people. Must be late 70s, he prob. early 80s. She an undoubtable ex-stunner; no, not ex, still is in my (respec'ful) eyes.

The Colonel's a former Japanese POW. God knows what he went through; wouldn't dream of telling. Stoical, his generation, unlike mine, spilling the *habas* at every opportunity. Lovely garden full of herbs and flowers, as kempt as mine is un.

They're in No. 1, Red House Farm Cottages. I'm in No. 2. It's only fair. Deference to the Colonel. There's no No. 3, only the fields and pigs.

The Col. has a tremendous but strictly unflaunted sense of public service and remembrance. Saw him at the airfield once, putting cut flowers on airmen's graves.

Think he saw me. Never said anything. Don't mention the war.

Would like to honour my own fallen comrades. Stanley? Difficult in a silent invisible war. Can't find the graves, hear the entombed voices. Plus they still look living when they're dead.

Colonel would frown at that. Would think we're bloody lucky. Probably are. You can only live in your own time.

Waved. They waved back with their shears.

Unloaded in study, put the German Pils botts. in the new fridge. Looked exceptional. Shame light inside doesn't work: an illuminated fridge full of booze, ajar in the dark night, is there anything more alluring?

Spent hour reading *Racing Post* before ringing Walter for tip. Big race at York. Got to be as knowledgeable as poss. Give a tipster a mug: lazy tipster. Go through all form etc, trainer bullshit, columns. 'Champion Tipster Henry Rix.' He looks a bit smug. All in all, favourite looks a cert. Bosra Sham.

Phoned Walter. Got a tip: Desert King in the big one. Down at 6-1 in the paper.

'What about this, what was it, Bosra Sham?' I said. Decide I want Walter to think I'm a mug, to test his commitment.

'No! Fucking nag.'

'Oh, I thought that was the one the trainer said was the best horse he'd ever had,' I added, quoting accurately from the *Post*.

'No!' Walter lied. I happen to know he reads it every morning, every word. 'Very opposable, this Bosra Sham. And no value even if you fancy it, which I fucking don't.'

'So why this Desert King then?'

'At sixes, John, Desert King represents outstanding value in a four-horse race,' Walter averred, rather indignantly.

I asked him how much. He said 500. I was thinking more like 70.

'Five hundred, Walter?'

'I would. At *least*. Might as well lump on. You don't want to piss about with fritterers, John.'

Told Walter to put a 100 win-bet on. This news received by Walter as if it were the greatest frittering offence ever perpetrated by Mankind. With the spurned air of a wounded elder, Walter put phone down to put my bet on with his one accessible telephone account with small-time dodgy bookie's. Rang back sorrowfully to confirm bet placed.

Don't feel ready for lump-ons yet. Must get Switch card for 12 grand so can open own dodgy telephone account and avoid staking arguments with Walter. Can't go putting a 100 bet on in U-Bet. They wouldn't believe you.

An hour to go before Desert King victory (OK, *appearance*). Rang Rachel and asked casually for Switch card. She completely unconcerned, agreed immediately. Own SWITCH! First result of the day. Went to other room to turn TV racing on. Instead, moved TV to study. Why didn't I think of that before? Turned TV on. Worked!

Horses trotting out for an earlier race. Ah yes, always preferred the Flat. Watched the sinewy glide. Genetically planned million-dollar babies. Only two-year-olds in this one: mere nippers.

Some sort of classical-music accompaniment on the TV. That's new – corny but, I admit it, I was milked. Stood there for a minute watching the noble exploited beasts, real tears welling up in my eyes. Didn't let them pop out, though. Got to save tears for tragedy or writing.

Turned and went to the fridge. Cracked open nicely chilled German Pils. Put two chairs together. Looked around. Fridge, fags, TV, electric typewriter, biro, list-books, gin: all within reach. Shit: I'm ready. Could get used to this. And despite near-vom. attack, old Marlsford's drugs seemed overall to be kicking in nicely.

Reclined with the beer watching the beasts. Began what I would later recall as 'the one week of organisation'.

8

New Orleans

I was 22 when I joined the paper. At first I worked on the night desk, sitting up with the old sub-editors who knew the *Oxford Dictionary for Writers and Editors* off by heart. They were wise and cynical. Most of them were ex-reporters who'd had their day, or had never had it and never left the subs' desk, or had left to write novels that had never been published, and so had come back.

Most of them were within a couple of years of retirement age and on the verge of getting the newspaper pension that they all called the 'Golden Nugget'.

The editor was a silver-haired avuncular man named Tony Bamber. He liked horses and drinking and cigars but he kept them under control. Above all Tony liked his secretary, Angela. She was 35. She was plumpish with ginger hair and dressed in twin-sets and pearls, and looked like 1950s London secretaries looked in films. In fact she was from the North, Lincoln, and spoke in a blunt, wide accent. She was ferociously efficient and commanded the respect and fear of the subs' desk. There was nothing retro or modish about the way she dressed – it was authentic. The secretaries on other desks made fun of her immaculacy but never to her face.

As far as anyone knew, Tony had never made an overt pass at Angela. It went beyond fancying. It was devotion, love, even though Tony knew that it would always be spurned. Often he took Angela out for lunch when he should have been schmoozing with management. On

Tony's days off, some of the subs tried to draw Angela into jokey conversation about Tony's attentions, and never succeeded. She didn't love Tony, but she wouldn't hear a word against him.

Though Tony was responsible for carrying out the cuts that made the subs' hours longer and their perks less, they forgave him because he was a real newspaper man and because it was all management's fault really, and because the Golden Nugget was so close it wasn't worth making a fuss. When Tony had to announce more cuts he came out from his office and sat on the desk. 'Well, boys, more bad news,' he always began, and the old subs nodded acceptingly, because Tony loosened his tie and took off his jacket, and tipped his ash into the plastic cups from the vending machine just like they did, making it easier to accept, even though they had no choice.

'What more can I say?' Tony usually ended. 'We all know the way the wind is blowing.' And the old subs gave a final grim nod to show that they did, and that they'd forgiven Tony again.

The only people the subs never forgave were the reporters. They sighed and slowly shook their heads as they subbed the copy. Sometimes they closed their eyes for seconds at a time, as if it was all too much. When the reporters came in for meetings in Tony's office, giving little waves and saying hellos as they walked past the subs' desk, the subs slyly rolled their eyes at each other and pretended they hadn't heard.

The most hated reporter was Dean Bucknall ('Deano'). Most of the quotes he put in his copy were generally thought to have been made up. He was a tall, unathletic cockney in his thirties who had had no journalistic training. He was known among the subs for getting 'zenith' and 'nadir' mixed up. Deano claimed many sexual conquests on assignments, though no one believed him. Angela objected to Deano as well, but even despite this Tony Bamber always backed him. 'I know Deano's a bad man,' Tony would say. 'But he always delivers on time.'

Apart from Deano, the most ridiculed figure on the desk was a photographer named Stanley Denham ('Stanno'; I was 'Jonno', of course). Stanno was 33 but he looked much younger, mid-twenties at most. I was amazed when he told me his age; 33 seemed so old. He had a thin face with smooth, gaunt skin, and long hair that he sometimes tied up with a rubber band.

The subs and the reporters derided everything about Stanno: his pony-tail; the way he talked about proving photography was art; his attempts to be cool. There was a story among the subs about Stanno standing by the juke-box in the local pub, the Mason's Arms, scratching an imaginary record with his hands. 'The Great White Rapper', they called him, and this was often shortened to GWR as an alternative to Stanno.

But though I went to the Mason's when Stanley was there, I never saw him doing that, and knew that he never would. I agreed with the subs about Deano, but I thought they were wrong about Stan. I didn't think he was trying to be cool: I thought he genuinely was. All the younger photographers on the picture desk tried to look like him, whilst deriding him almost as much as the subs.

Each night on the desk the copy poured through our fingers. I knew I was learning, but I didn't think I'd stay in newspapers long. Soon I would leave to become a real writer.

I did leave for a bit, but found after I'd bought a new electric typewriter that I had nothing to say. So I went back to the paper, this time as a reporter, replacing Deano, who to general astonishment had been recruited by another paper at exorbitant expense.

Tony Bamber put me and Stanley together as a team, calling us 'his boys', and for two years we travelled all over the place together on stories, often abroad. As well as doing the stories, Stanley and I used these trips as opportunities to go on wild sprees, fuelled by our cash advances on expenses. Stanley was more into drugs than me, but he was equally into drink. Neither of us was proud of these sprees, but they usually seemed to happen. Sometimes they happened with such frequency that we ended up owing the paper more in cash advances than we had earned from the stories.

When we weren't abroad, much to the disgust of the old subs, we were driving around in the two new company Saabs that Tony, in his wise benevolence, had decided we must have use of.

Stanley and I bought separate basement flats near to each other in Battersea. Unfortunately we bought the poky rooms at the height of the mid-80s property boom, and almost as soon we had set foot in them, their value halved. But this didn't make much difference to me, and in general I couldn't believe my luck. Nor could Stanley.

Unlike me, Stan had been born very poor. Like me, he had been chucked out of school – several, and for more serious offences – and had also been in some trouble with the police before he discovered the Art of photography.

As long as we delivered, Tony did not mind what he called our 'cavortings'. He seemed rather to like the thought of them, as if fondly remembering cavortings of his own. Thus he indulged us. In Tony's affections, we bowed only to his raging love for Angela. In return, we did everything Tony told us to without question, and tried our best to deliver on time.

Often on free Saturdays Stanley and I walked over from Battersea to Stamford Bridge to watch Chelsea. Being 33, he'd been a fan for ten years more than me, and claimed to have actually been present in Athens for the great '71 Cup Winners' victory against Real (unlikely).

There was never any difficulty getting in. Chelsea were

bouncing between first and second divisions. Half the ground was empty. We stood in the Shed End. It only cost about £7. We usually went to a different spot on the terraces for each half, either down to the right among the family men and oldsters with their gallows humour, or over to the left among the seething NF Casuals chanting 'One Man Went to Mow' – obscene version – with 50p's clenched between their fists in case the trouble went off. There was a strange phase when the Casuals threw celery on to the pitch.

We saw many humiliations, Grimsby 2–3 being the worst. I minded, but not too much. I watched the games in a trance, sucking in the frenetic action, the primitive nearness of the Casuals and the dilapidated grandeur all at the same time. They may be your team and you will support them from birth to grave, but beyond that absolute, you went for your own reasons.

When Chelsea scored we danced about and took swigs from Stanley's whisky flask. Between goals – long periods – Stanley was more vociferous. Sometimes he joined in the 'One Man Went to Mow' chants with knowledgeable conviction. I could tell he didn't really know the words. Then again, they don't give out song sheets.

Afterwards we walked back over Battersea Bridge moaning about players, but still glad we'd gone.

I had always planned that on my 25th birthday, when I received the £15,000 trust fund, I would go off on some worldwide search for Carol, beginning in New Orleans. But instead I frittered away the money within eight months of getting it. Mainly I spent it with Stanley in assorted venues. Walter was also around, during one of those intervals of friendship before some terrible bust-up. So quite a bit went idly on blackjack in the low-end Soho casinos that Walter then favoured.

Then within a few days of exhausting the £15,000, there was a story about muggers targeting British tourists in New

Orleans' French Quarter, and immediately I knew I had to use it as a pretext to go and find Carol after all.

When I asked him, Tony wasn't keen.

'I don't see it for us, Jonno,' he said. 'It's been done.'

But Tony didn't want to disappoint me, either. So as a financial compromise he said I could go for three days, 'but no Stanno. We'll use a local snapper.'

At the airport, to my dismay, I saw Dean Bucknall standing at the check-in counter, resplendent in ugly new super-journalist clothes. Naturally he was on my flight. He was making a doomed and humiliating attempt to get an upgrade into Club, and used my arrival as proof of his renown throughout the airport world. I greeted him as warmly as was possible.

Soon, at Deano's behest, I was sitting next to him at the back of Economy. He wasn't doing the muggers story ('been done') but a story about a former MP and a religious group called the Shriners. The biggest ever Shriner convention was being held in New Orleans. I feigned sleep for most of the way to avoid further conversation.

About twenty minutes before landing, Deano took off his wedding ring and said, 'Change into the away strip, eh.' But after I informed him we were only going down to change at Houston, he put it back on again. I noticed Deano had the annoying habit of scratching his balls every thirty seconds or so.

At New Orleans things got worse. Because of the Shriner and other conventions, there seemed to be only one hotel room left in the whole city. After we'd checked in around midnight, Deano announced that he had no intention of going to bed, but was going out 'on the razzle' in Bourbon Street. I didn't want to be woken later by a razzled Deano, so reluctantly agreed to accompany him.

We hadn't even reached Bourbon Street when Deano

dived into the nearest available premises, a run-down hostess bar called Desire's in a side-street opposite the hotel. Even by Soho standards it was grim, though thankfully the drinks were both cheaper and real.

Old hostesses lounged boredly around a few scattered customers. Most of the hostesses were out of it either on booze or drugs or both. But Deano was happy enough. He'd collared one with a blonde perm and jaded but still noticeably muscle-toned skin, of the sort you get only from years of training. She'd probably been an athlete or a gymnast before whatever happened to lead her here. Soon she'd got Deano dutifully peeling off notes from his advance on expenses. I looked at his hand and saw he was in the away strip again.

I sat on a stool by the sticky bar-top and looked out at the side-street. It was raining on to the black alien pavement. I finished my drink and, without interrupting his conversation with the athlete, indicated to Deano over her shoulder that I'd see him later.

However, Deano, as befits his professional reputation as a deliverer, is not a man to get rid of easily. I'd just turned into Bourbon Street when up he came behind me, looking slightly hurt and scratching his crotch.

'Yeah, was a bit of a dive,' he explained.

We walked the length of Bourbon Street and then started back up again. Despite being the central tourist zone there weren't many tourists out on a night like this. Nor any visible Shriners, for that matter. According to Deano, they wore fezes and drove about on mopeds.

Occasionally as we walked, pan-handlers came up with their hands out muttering entreaties. Twice a dope-pusher emerged from a side-street to walk beside us hustling for a deal, then dropped back and disappeared smoothly off the main drag. Deano was alarmed but I assured him fancifully that they wouldn't allow muggers in the tourist zone.

I remembered that Tony had made a rueful comment to me about having gone to New Orleans once, and that I had immediately recognised this as a reference to his legendary 'six-day bender' with a sportswriter named Harry Webb, one of his old muckers, at the time of the Ali–Spinks fight in 1976.

I watched my shoes beside Deano's going up the drizzly tourist zone and wished I'd never had this stupid idea in the first place. Then Deano's shoes veered urgently off to the left and into another clip-joint. This one was called Big O's. He must have earmarked it on the way down. We walked in and almost immediately I saw Carol.

She was dancing on a stage wearing nothing but a kind of small white toggle between her legs, the sort that I'd noticed had also been regulation in Desire's. The dance was of the usual US clip-joint sort, revolving around a floor-to-ceiling gleaming metal pole, providing innuendo moves as well as showing off the toggled essentials to open effect as they went round.

I glimpsed her through a glass partition in the corridor as we went through to the main club. Carol's pole-work did not seem very good. But the jerky dance movements as she went through the routine were unquestionably her own. Her hair was cut shorter, to shoulder length, and her hips and mouth seemed fuller in an elegant way. Her little breasts looked just the same.

Deano was practically galloping into the club. I put my head down as I passed the end of the glass partition and walked bowed to where Deano had sat facing the stage, at a distance of some twenty feet. We were in the middle between the stage and an area where a few girls on tables were dancing close up to men, and where no doubt you could get really fleeced. In the stage area, ten or twelve more men were corralled leaning on a long plastic-covered arm-rail, drunkenly offering up dollar bills which Carol occasionally paused to collect with her teeth.

I put my head down, looking at the dim-lit carpet while Deano ordered drinks. I didn't dare look up again. I felt shocked, a shock compounded by exhaustion from the flight, and fleetingly I wished I could evaluate this development, at least when it wasn't 6 a.m. my time.

I looked up. Carol's set was ending. She couldn't put any more bills in her teeth so she and the men were stuffing them underneath the cord round her waist that held up her toggle. As each man put a bill in her cord Carol gave him a fake wide-eyed look as if to say he shouldn't be so cheeky. She actually seemed happy in a trance-like way.

'Jesus Christ,' I let out.

'Yeah, gorgeous that one,' Deano said. 'Touch of the Hiawathas. Can't dance but, fuck, I . . .' Deano added that he'd like to give her one.

I ignored Deano and tried to think. Strangely I was shocked more by the fact of finding Carol than by what she was doing. Now I had found her I didn't know what to do or why I had tried to find her. I wished I was back in London just talking about Carol to Stanley; or, if I had to be in New Orleans, that I was here with Stanley and not bloody Deano.

Carol exited the stage and disappeared behind the bar. A few more dancers did their acts and also disappeared. Then some of them reappeared as hostesses in our section wearing négligés, hustling for table-dances. This seemed to be the system. Carol had not reappeared from behind the bar yet, but I was sure she would.

To make matters worse, Deano had clocked the system as well. Uncharacteristically he'd waved away several hostesses, and made it known that he was waiting for 'one'. I was sure this would be Carol. I was now sitting with my head almost between my knees, getting nearer and nearer the frayed carpet. The only thing I knew was that I had to get out of this crouched position, since a confrontation seemed unavoidable.

I straightened and a waitress came up. The waitresses were distinct from hostesses. They wore faded bunny-girl uniforms but were not in the market for table-dances, and went about the drinks-carrying with a breeziness that set them apart from the intense pseudo-engagement between the dancer-hostesses and the men.

'Rum-and-Coke please,' I told her. I didn't normally drink these but the sweetness seemed a good idea.

'You mean a Cuba Libre, sir?'

'Yes.'

'Do you want me to get you a girl to talk to, sir?'

'No, it's OK.'

'OK, hon.'

I tipped her $5. Deano said, 'That's a bit generous, isn't it?'

Carol emerged from behind the bar and began making a bee-line for our table. I sat rigidly staring at her, resolving to communicate something with my eyes once she got in range, without knowing at all what they would be communicating. Instead, she ignored my gaze and went straight up to Deano.

'Hi, what's your name?' Carol said.

'Dean.'

'Wanna table-dance, Dean?'

'How much?' Deano said, momentarily dropping his lascivious manner and adopting the practised look of a serious negotiator.

'Twenty-five dollars,' Carol said.

Deano passed over the notes unquestioningly and stood up, already facing the table-dancing area. Carol put a hand on his knee as he got up, and squeezed it. I couldn't look any more.

I picked up my rum-and-Coke and sipped it with fake insouciance. My whole skeleton seemed locked except for the hinge of my elbow letting my hand reach the glass. I felt as if everyone in the club was looking at me, and recognised the hateful feeling of my face blushing.

Then I heard Carol's voice say, 'Hey, Dean, what's your friend's name?'

'Oh, that's Jonno,' he said enthusiastically, if also impatiently.

'Well, *Jonno*,' Carol said, with no hint of recognition. 'Do you wanna come and see some pussy too?'

I found myself trooping off behind them to the table-dancing section. We sat round a small table while Carol climbed on, took off her négligé, tossed it to Deano and did the dance. I watched as little as I could and stared downwards. At the end of the dance she asked if we wanted a 'special' dance.

'How much?' Deano said.

'Fifty.'

I had no doubt Deano would be on for it. Apparently, though, he now required a good-faith contribution from me.

'Come on, Jonno, it's only twenty-five each.'

I delved coldly into my pocket and handed him the money.

Half-way through the new, more explicit dance Carol stopped and asked me why I wasn't watching. 'Dunno . . .' I said. Christ, couldn't even speak.

Deano had begun shoving extra dollars under Carol's cord, in the appreciatively expert manner of someone who knows a good one when he sees it.

At the end of the dance, Carol squeezed his leg again, further up, and asked him to promise that he'd stick around to watch her next set. Maybe they could have another 'special' dance afterwards. Deano promised dutifully and heartily, handing Carol her négligé back.

She disappeared behind the bar to prepare for her set.

Deano and I went back to our seats in the bar-hostess area. I ordered a rum-and-Coke from a waitress, drank it quickly and ordered another, tipping extravagantly and temporarily diverting Deano's attention from the stage.

'Steady on, Jonno,' he said before turning his head back.

I was paralysed. Deano, in the meantime, was getting his second wind. He was talking about getting Carol back to the hotel for a private session later.

'I don't know about that, Deano,' I managed.

He told me they all did it, that he knew when he was 'in there', and that it would only cost a couple of hundred dollars between us. 'Trust me,' he added.

Carol re-emerged from the bar on to the stage. Deano said we should go up front. I followed him dumbly towards the red plastic arm-rail. We leant on it side by side. Deano was already exchanging jocular comments with the other men in the corral. His journo contacts-book was legendary, and I could see why.

Carol began her dance. About half-way through she saw me there and looked at me with her old eyes for the first time. She came over, leant down and kissed me full on the mouth. I felt her tongue and responded greedily, like a starving dog who'd finally made it back to his old master.

After a second she pulled back and then bent her face towards my ear.

'My God, John, it *is* you,' she said. 'What the fuck are you doing here?'

'I dunno . . .'

'Tomorrow I finish early. Meet me outside at ten.'

She sashayed back and continued her dance. The whole exchange had lasted only a few seconds. I recoiled from the arm-rail flooded with shock and love. Already Deano was leading a response among the other men, pointing his finger above my head and making faces.

'Jesus Christ, Jonno!' he exclaimed. 'You're in there.'

9

The One Week of Organisation

Got slightly bored just sitting there waiting for Desert King's victory. Turned to the pile of unread newspapers. Buy at least five every day, plus five weekly periodicals, more monthly, and several free-sheets. Properly read about 5 per cent of material contained therein; just the essentials: obituaries, letters, my articles and, recently, those of my new comrade in the silent war, the tolerance-fatigued Tom Layburn.

Speed-read the rest, flicking through the pages every few seconds, except on trains, out of consideration for fellow passengers.

Also have on constantly at least three radios in different rooms in cottage. Different stations. Great fan of new low-end talk station. Strictly no TV until 8 p.m., for necessary avoidance of mind-numbing temptation. Shit! Got the TV racing on! Oh well, that's work.

Anyway, no TV till 8. Then regularly watch till 3 or 4 a.m., well into the complete trash and ancient Open Univ. progs. Stagger upstairs wrecked and go to sleep listening to sound of low-end talk station or occasionally, if am in mood for Greece-inspired melancholia, the World Service. This is my daily routine.

Thus am bloody well informed about range of high and low subjects, local and international, with constant updates through most hours of both day and night. Rarely have use for any of said info except in the more boring lists.

Am told such info-gathering and constant wilful bombardment by all available media – excepting daytime TV – is common syndrome among booze-addicts as means of creating illusion of rigour through what are really hours and hours of completely idle dissolution. Of course, in my case it was all research.

Talking of research, picked up phone and rang Rachel. Told her about Desert King. First bet and everything. Got to involve them, you know, these editors. Though not too much.

She sounded strangely outraged that I was saying I hadn't put a bet on before.

'I thought you said you were playing poker with Jimmy White and some West Country mafia types,' she explained.

Oh, yes. That. Forgot about that.

'Yeah, yeah, I did that,' I said impatiently. 'I meant, *bet* bets. Y'know, horses.'

'You can't just bet on horses. I want varied material,' Rachel said sternly. Christ, is there no pleasing some people? Gave assurances about doing non-horse bets.

'How did it go in the West Country anyway, John? I hope you won. You said you were going to.'

No respite. Convo with Rachel like a tightening noose.

'No, bad, I'm afraid,' I said.

'You lost?'

'Yes.' Well, I would have done if I didn't win, wouldn't I, darling? No draws in gambling.

'How much did you lose, John?' Jesus, like being back at school.

'Er, about seven hundred,' I said.

'What!'

'No, eight hundred actually, now I remember.'

'But, but, how did you . . . *feel*?'

'It happens,' I said, with what I judged to be the air of a practised poker hombre. 'The guy turned out to be cleverer than we'd all thought.'

Put phone down as soon as poss. No good telling her about essential prep. Wouldn't understand.

Began reading obits and speed-reading rest. Classical music. Looked up and there was Desert King trotting out. Not too sure about Desert, at first glance. Bosra Sham looks a bit tasty. TV pundits all predicting Bosra Sham will piss home.

Chucked the papers on the floor by the great mountains of past papers and gave it my undivided.

Three furlongs out and we are going to win, Desert and me. Jockey is beautifully positioned just in behind BS. But BS is starting to labour. Desert is practically cantering; easily going the best; a couple of other nags about to drop back. No, mustn't start talking like Walter: noble beasts.

Desert jockey icy still. Probably under instructions to track BS and jump her on the run-in. Won't even have to wait that long now. Easier job than expected.

No whip, just hands and heels. Beautiful horsemanship. Mind you, it's easy when you're riding a Ferrari.

Comes up on BS's shoulder. Jesus, he's going to *glide* past; not even a reminder. What's 6-1 × 100 less Walter's 10 per cent commission? Should have had the 500 on. Sat back to glory in the last furlong and three-quarters none the less. Then . . .

Oh my God. Mystery horse, ———?, suddenly emerges and romps past both of 'em on outside. There's no catching ———? now. DK still annihilates BS for second, though. Even-money favourite: I think not. BS: too right!

Terrific run from Desert. Well done, Walter. Knew he was committed. Couldn't ask for a better run than that at sixes, ever. Unless it won of course.

Picked up the phone and rang W. Offered him effusive congratulations before asking him for a tip in the next.

'Oh,' Walter said. 'I thought you'd be pissed off.'

'No, no. Marvellous.'

'Good, John. Good.' A new tone of respect entered Walter's voice, and I knew that in his mind I had passed the 'non-mug' test: the ability, like him, to accept constant losses with equanimity.

Put down phone and it rang immediately. Rachel.

'Oh my God, John. I just watched the race on the office television. I feel so sorry for you. First the West Country and now this . . .'

Didn't bear thinking about. Gave Rachel a reasoned explanation of 6-1 shots, value and the gambler aesthetic. Could tell from the silence at the end of the line that she thought I was a nutter.

'OK, bye then.'

Addressed the desk between races. Meticulously entered each horse's name, price and amount staked on the bets list. 'Amount Won' column on far right of page. Kept phone line open with W. for easy flow of tips. No winners but cld. see why Walter tipped them. Value runs all the way. Two thirds and another second. 100 on the nose each time. Great.

After each loser, wrote out cheque for amount lost to Walter on outsized hombre Yellow Jersey Business Account cheques in nice fat new cheque-book sent by Rachel. I, sole signatory. Beautiful. Legit. cheques!

Do suspect, though, that cheque-book idea is covert plan by Rach. to mould final form of book. Also prob. monitoring exercise. She dropped ref. to sort of glossary section at the back, exhaustive run-down of bets etc, additional info; plus some idea of italic para in each chapter detailing current diminution of 12-grand account. Must be a touch of the Pridwells in Rachel. Endearing.

Looked down at immac. bets list: could easily do it. But no. Of course, must entirely resist on grounds of artist. integ.

Wonder what the fuck Pridwell's doing these days. Bet he's doing well.

And WHERE'S THE BLOODY SWITCH CARD anyway?

York meeting ended. Turned TV off. Sat down drinking another German Pils and examined Yellow Jersey cheques made out to Walter. Put folded cheques in an envelope and addressed to Pimlico in usual shameful inelegant left-handed scrawl (pens designed for right-handers; they got everything; pragmatists).

Got up and immediately my gaze settled on a tiny loose stamp among the newspaper mountains. Unbelievable. Never usually happens. That kind of day.

Walked up the road to the post-box. Waved to the gardening Colonel and his beautiful wife on the way back. Beginnings of lovely Eng. country summer evening.

Phone ringing when I got back in. Please let it not be R. with more refs to low-life W-Country poker games. Know I made it up in first place but: it was just one of my little jokes, my dear, don't you see? Have another Mint Julep, poor thing, and stop being so silly.

Wasn't R. It was Walter. Big tip for evening meeting at Kempton. Ten minutes' time. Horse called Mantles Star. 11-8 fav. but all the other noble beasts were complete nags. Would absolutely piss home. Must be a lump-on, Walter said.

Mmm, *evening* meeting, eh? Detected slightly blasé tone in W.'s voice. Could be getting carried away? Why not.

'How much?'

'Five hundred,' Walter said. 'I would.'

'I'll do two hundred.'

Even Walter could not disguise his admiration at this up-turn.

Race not on TV. Had to rely on W. monitoring on his mobile via some dodgy 0891 race line.

Rang me back approx. twelve mins later. Mantles Star lost by a neck. Was pissing home but got touched off on the line by some nag. Must have had a virus that just caught up with him in the final few steps. No other explanation, W. said.

Didn't give him the pleasure of sounding remotely disappointed. Didn't feel remotely disappointed, in fact (not even the next morning, when after buying papers found that W. had somewhat exaggerated narrowness of winning distance).

Instead asked Walter in cruel muggish sympathetic tone how much he'd lost on Desert King.

'Oh, I won on that race, actually,' Walter says.

'Eh?'

'Yeah, laid Bosra Sham, didn't I?'

Laid? Bit of a technical term for me in still recent epoch of 5p e-w Heinzes. Searched memory for what it meant. Didn't let on to W. Ah yes, laying off: bookmaker transfers betting liability by making same or similar bet with other bookie or insider punter like W.

'How much?' I ask idly.

'Only five hundred. Bookie I know. Should have taken more.'

'Bloody hell, Walter, you could have cut me in.'

'I thought you said you quite fancied Bosra Sham,' he says, indignantly.

True. Tight bastard, though. No. Mustn't spoil mood. Just a money man. Part of his charm.

Put phone down. Ah, end of an excellent first working day. Wrote out new cheque, updated immac. bets list and admired it for a while. Worked out I was now approx.

£700 down, not counting essential prep . . .

All tax paid up front of course. Only mugs turn down opportunity to lose more money on each bet.

[Note to Rachel: plse. ensure above para. is retained. Promised W. I wld. include to protect him from poss. legal ramfctns. of special 'tax-free' bets arrangement w. dodgy bookie on my behalf. Hope this is ok – J.]

Glut of big Flat meetings that week. TV racing every day. Phone line practically burning up with Walter tips. Must admit 'Amount Won' column looking a bit forlorn after two days and still no winners. Did occur that at this rate I could go through the whole 12 grand in the next eight days. Almost all value runs, though. Patience.

Walter cheques; envelopes; walks to post-box. Drinking much less. German Pils only, even in eves. No wine, let alone gins or Cubas. Colonel giving me a few quizzical looks. Not used to seeing me out and about looking so breezy.

First winner on third day: My Emma, 125 e-w at 7-1. 250 bet. Elegant little horse. Classy. Strong feeling about her as I watched her mincing round the paddock; almost love. Absolutely glided nobly home. Christ, that's over a grand. Dancing round study shouting out exhortations of love to My Emma at top of voice.

Gotta say it: gambler-aesthetic theory is fine, but sometimes winning is so much better.

'And it wasn't even being aimed at this race,' Walter informed me almost immediately on his mobile. 'Being laid out for the Arc, this My Emma is.'

'Jesus, Walter. We've got to get on ante-post for the Arc. Now. Five hundred. No, a grand.'

As I outlined these rashly escalating figures, I sensed Walter and I had never been closer.

'No, John,' he said in a shrewd lowered tone. 'Wait for the Paris-Mutuel on the day. Frogs don't rate the English horses. Go off at a big price.' Truly, the man is a wise elder.

Went into kitchen to celebrate with bottle of shrapnelled Lebanese Musar. Just opened it when someone knocked on front door. *Visitor?* Unusual. Peered through mist of hovering flies outside side window to check it out.

Oh Christ. Bloody Mr Potter. Chairman of local Neighbourhood Watch, in which take no part on principle. Pragmatist vigilante group. Laughable. Apart from principle, nothing to watch round here anyway. Hasn't been a proper crime for eleven years. Then again, that was a murder.

Doesn't deter Potter. Writes monthly newsletter detailing non-crimes. Always ends letter: 'despite this, residents are advised to maintain their usual vigilance, since in other parts of the country crime rates are rising alarmingly'. Always has to deliver it by hand. Don't think even the Col. reads it, and you couldn't get a more public-spirited gent than the Col.

Goes beyond realms of ultra-pragmatism, this Potter. Mad. Still enemy. Had to be fronted up.

Opened door holding opened bottle of Musar with fag clenched between teeth, just to confirm his worst fears. He handed me newsletter. Put it straight in outside letter-box dismissively (always do read it, tho'; retrieve later).

Potter said something about *another* of my tiles about to fall off roof. Could be dangerous if someone passing. Bloody nerve. Ignored it. He returned hostile glare gamely. In fact with interest. Almost real hatred. That's a bit strong. Thank God he couldn't fight. Could he?

Went to close door. Potter said, 'Erm, is there anything I should know about?'

'Well, I've just won on a horse, if that's any help,' I said.

'Oh . . . have you?' Potter said, edging back. 'Well then.'

He practically scarpered out of front garden. Wished he'd slow down so a tile could fall on his head (something in it for him: he survives; I get done for attempted manslaughter and he's got a crime to put in his newsletter.

Drank glorious Musar nectar in study and followed up after deserved nap with Cava bott. during late-night crap TV. Won't even have to nick the money. No. Not going to nick money anyway. Write book. Yes. Well, probably be able to pay the 12 grand back in a couple of weeks at this rate and won't have to.

Beaut. clear blue planet-full night sky so kept curtains open and lay back on bed staring at it. Open curtains produced fleeting bad Angela flashback but pretended it hadn't happened. World Service tonight, I think.

Because of increased booze intake, no jitters that night, just sweet melancholic sleep.

Previous two nights, due to decreased exclus. German Pils intake, some minor jitters dreams, inc. a few snakes. Buoyant mood carried through into sleep and so was able, in so many words, to tell them to piss off.

However, interesting development. Incredible what they throw at you when you're asleep, the enemy. On second night snakes preceded by advanced guard of new characters – Vonzes: exact lookalikes of the great Fonze; you only know they're not really him when they open their mouths to speak; terrible, evil breath; but by then they will have led you unwittingly into the snake lair.

As I said, though, snakes were no problem, so survived easily. And found out that if you touch a piece of unvarnished wood with the nail of either little finger, the Vonzes disappear. Since bedroom is made up of rows of exposed knackered wooden beams, will be easy. Just reach up. Next time, will have the Vonzes well sussed.

Woke up rested and not-too-bad hungover on fourth day feeling ready for 500 lump-on bet. Luckily Walter had just the thing.

'Coastal Bluff. I honestly reckon this one is going to piss home, John. At 13-2 it represents exceptional value.'

'Any dangers, Walter?'

'None. The only one I feared was Danetime and that's just pulled out. All the rest are nags.'

'Really?'

'I'd go a grand.' I bet you would, Walt, if only you had it.

'I'll stick with five hundred.'

'Suit yourself.'

When W. rang back a few minutes later with his usual confirmation call I knew something was up from his unusually friendly manner.

'Done you a favour, John.'

'What?' Sensed what was coming when he said that.

'Put you on for seven fifty.'

'You can't do that.'

'I just did.' W. sniggered. He found this genuinely amusing. When he finds things amusing he can be at his most dangerous and volatile.

'Well, if it loses you can pay the extra two hundred and fifty,' I said.

'I can't afford that!' Ah, so the truth comes out. Walter not so amused now.

'I did it for you, John. Thought you'd be bloody grateful when it comes in.'

'It hasn't come in yet.'

'Jesus Christ, want the results in advance, do you?'

No arguing with this logic. Don't want argument. Do deal with W. whereby he only gets paid his commiss. on 500 if it comes in. W. accepts without argument, confirming my view that it remains insufficient penalty for his immoral action. Starts sniggering again. Can tell he still thinks it's a cracking joke.

While waiting for Coastal Bluff victory, go out in hatchback to garage shop for papers, fags and Cokes for quick surge in blood-sugar levels. Unusual road-work congestion on dual-carriageway by shop, and hatchback starts feeling strangely hot. Going to put petrol in but can't remember whether unleaded or not. Must ring Walter about it. Wld never forgive me if I wrecked one of his cars. Him wrecking them is a different matter.

Before leaving shop, surprise myself with speculative car-knowledge efficiency by successfully putting water in what seemed to be the radiator nozzle. Car fine on way back. Really am becoming incredibly organised in everything I do. It's all discipline. Back exclus. on G. Pils today, for instance. Discipline.

'No, just the normal bog-standard shit,' Walter said helpfully, about the petrol. Also confirmed rear back plastic nozzle on right of engine was indeed radiator.

'Oh, should be fine, then,' he observed. 'Never had any trouble with that car. Go anywhere in it.'

Walter then made joke: 'Oh and John, you know this Coastal Bluff? Put you on for another two fifty, all right?' Walter's voice disintegrating with hilarity. Ha ha. Better bloody not have done.

Put TV racing on. Settled at desk w. papers. Oh good, final Test match vs Aussies starting tomorrow. Have that on the radio while I'm watching the racing. Busy day at the office coming up.

Just started reading obit. about fallen brigadier when phone rings. Rachel. Do they ever let you work in peace? Walter probably trying to get through already. Sprint race. Going to keep mobile phone line open throughout due to magnitude of stake. Not that care of course. Must keep convo short.

'Oh, hello, John,' Rachel says. Ominous tone. 'I thought you might be there. There's something we really must talk about.'

Deflect her by saying I've got this huge bet just coming on. Coastal Bluff. A grand. Don't know why I said that. Must stop. There again, could be true (better not be).

Rachel both appalled and fascinated. A whole thousand? Asks me how I feel again. Standard TV-interviewer question. Some people object to it. Personally I quite like being asked how I feel. Doesn't happen every day, does it?

'Dunno, really,' I reply. Light a further gambler-style fag

loudly. Agree to talk after race. Says she's going to watch it on the office TV. Oh God . . .

W. straight back on. Already they're going behind stalls. W. my personal commentator informs me that our horseman is in purple today. Stalls snap open. Only 6f. Follow purple flash with eyes. Nicely prominent early. Have to be in these mad dashes. Lightning-fast sprinting beasts. None of your long-range tacticians.

Already past half-way. Purple flash exactly where should be. Poised to . . . Jesus H. It's going to as well. Already moving ahead, into extra gear. Only the silence of Walter's rigid concentration at the other end of the line. Dropped phone, leaving it hanging. Stood up . . .

Into last furlong. Almost there. Christ, it really is pi . . . Remembered Desert. Shot quick glance around. Nothing coming. *Nothing*. It is there, virtually. What's 500 × 13-2? Several Gs, and then . . .

Something bloody strange is happening. Something flashing around Coastal's nose, dangling about. Peer at TV. Oh my God, it's the bloody bridle! Bridle's come off. Jockey clinging to Coastal's mane.

Line yards away. Still leading, but they're catching him with every stride. Gonna catch him . . .? Yes. No. No!

Yes. They did. I think.

Stewards call for a photo. Pick up phone.

'Unbelievable, John,' Walter says. 'Never happened before in the history of racing.'

'Ah, sweet Jesus,' is all I can manage. Our greatest moment sabotaged, poor Coastal and me. And Walter. That was the one. Never get a tip like it again.

Watch several replays with phone line open.

'What do you reckon?' I say.

'Touched off on the line.'

Wait several minutes for decision. Dead heat announced. What do they pay out on dead heats? Half odds? Even

Walter doesn't know. Couldn't see it myself. They probably gave Coastal a share of the spoils out of sympathy.

'John,' Walter concludes gravely before putting down phone. 'I want you to know that you have just been swindled out of several thousand pounds.'

To my surprise, realise that former buoyancy has been fully restored and that I don't mind at all. Seem to have out-non-mugged the great non-mug. Incredible.

Walter back (mournfully): 'It's even worse than I thought. Half the stake. Plus a 15p-in-the-pound deduction for Danetime being a non-runner.'

I say: 'Oh well, still get over a grand and a half, won't we?'

W: 'John, it's legalised cheating.'

Felt great. Living again. Only had one G. Pils. No stupid nutter lists. Only the one immac. one that was entirely legitimate. Wanted to open up window and shout: 'Hello! I'm back with you! Organised!' Didn't, though, because of the flies.

Plus got first chunks of past back. Got Walter back. Soon be ready to go and get Johnny and Carol. Then could go on with rest of life. No melancholy, past-fixation, lists, snakes, jitters, too excessive booze consumption (but some), wilful media bombardment. Silent war? Dunno. Have to think about the war. Seems true even sober.

Just go on, survive, organised. No prob. Easy.

Rachel rang. Answered her in mellow tone of gratitude for her contribution to letting me go on. Seemed to work immediately.

'Oh, hello, John, I was going to ring up and try and be cross with you, but now I don't know if I can.'

'What is it? Tell me.'

'It's just that you're always on this number when I call, and you always seem to be watching racing on TV. I'd always imagined that you would actually be *there*.'

Said mellowly, 'I *am* there.'

'Yes, I can tell that.'

'Well, I am. Put on lots of bets. Must have gone through about three grand already. If Coastal's bridle hadn't broken I would have been virtually up overall.'

'Yes, I saw that. Apparently it doesn't happen often.'

'Oh no. Hardly ever, Rachel. Amazing horsemanship, hanging on to the mane like that. Loads of material.'

'Yes. So you will be getting out more, John, and putting bets on other things than horses.'

'Of course.' Gave Rachel litany of prospective non-horse lump-ons and excursions: 100 bet on England v. Aussies in Test at value 4-1 – going down to the Oval of course; 250 on Barcelona in upcoming Euro match against Newcastle – exceptional value at 6-4, seemed a certainty, Barca.

'Will you be going to Newcastle?' Rachel said.

'Er, probably not. Playing blackjack that night. London casino. Friend of mine.'

'Oh good. Is it another friend of Jimmy White's? You've got to get him in.'

'No, but similar.' Lit loud fag.

Rachel said, 'Which day are you going to be at Lord's? We're going to be there on Saturday.'

'We'? Must be boyfriend.

'Oh, shame,' I said. 'I'm not going down till Monday. Denouement, you know.' Should be over by then. Dead rubber and the Aussies wanting to go home. Bloody good value bet, that.

Rachel seemed pleased. Said it was good she'd rung me. She felt a lot better now.

Put phone down. See? Be yourself. Forget all this wise-guy stuff.

Picked phone up again immediately and phoned Walter on mobile to put on said bets. Barca 250 a bit steep but did it anyway. W. tried to persuade me out of England 100 bet.

Ignored him. Just trying insincere wise-elder scepticism to atone for Coastal Bluff 750.

'Suit yourself, John,' he concluded. Knows s.f.a. about cricket.

Yet another day pleasurably survived. Shut down study. Went out for a walk. Thought about walking to pub. Decided against. Only bloke who's ever there talks mainly about snakes. And he's younger than me. Relative nipper. Tragic.

Walked up road instead. Usual wave to Col. shearing in twilight. I'll be able to talk to him again soon, in that casual, fluent and polite way, about individual objects – plants, dogs, houses etc, not people or wars – the way he likes. Used to be able to do but . . . haven't been able to, last few months. Will soon.

Patted dog as I walked back. Not actually theirs: belongs to tragic white-trash fam. at broken-down farm at top of hill. Veritable mangled trailer-park of junk out the front. Just let the dog wander round the lanes.

Colonel's wife feeds it sometimes. Funny-looking little dog: never had one myself. This one looks like small black straggly carpet on legs. Bloody followed me back to cott. after I patted it. Col. shouted out: 'Looks like you've got a new friend!' Well, that's a start to me and Col.'s convo relat.

Dog sat on doorstep as if it was going in. Told it to piss off. Felt a bit guilty seeing it slink away. But spent two years trying to bite my legs off on MZ, dogs.

Cld. murder eve. cocktail but don't. Discipline, man. And great day at work. Go to bed early. Bad jitters. What the fuck? Detox supposed to only take three days. Wake up in crying dawn with serene sense of relief and achievement and go down to study.

Take weekend off. Deserve it. Watch and listen to cricket instead. Run out of G. Pils. Don't replenish. Minrl watr or nothing. Eng. win after terrific action. I win 400. Marvellous. Must be virtually up ovrll.

Rach. rings to congrat. So happy. Touching and sweet.

Put all non-horse bets down in immac. and legit. list book.

Next morn. get up for work. Almost thru this. Drinking. Bin at it a few years. Eight?

Letter from hosp.: endoscopy apptmnt. Put hose down gullet. Worse than enema. Fuck that. Fuck you. Don't need nothin'. Do it on own, thanks.

Fold apptmnt card into aeroplane like old Penguin wrappers. Aim at bin from dist. of at least five feet. Flies straight in. Pisses home. See.

Study. Phone. First call of day. Normal clients presum. – Walt? Rach?

No. Bldy Marlsford.

M: 'fraid tests have come back rather as feared. One ray of sunshine though. No hep. Great. Something like that.

Fuckin' angry. Stood up. Dizzy. Shakes. Get air.

Walk out of cott. and lean on hatchback in socks. Door closed. Locked out. Fuckin' marv.

Kicked door hard. Again. Put hand through window by door. Open-palm. Shld have used fist. Clean. Avoids main art.

Bldy pane. Bld all round wrist. Go ahead and open door. Fuck it. Stagg. back and lean on htchbck. Look at wrst bld comg. Too far to gt to Ipp. if gt main art.

Htchbck keys inside. No pan.: calm, man. Hpns, Hppns. Glance over twds Col. hse. Their htchbck gone. Sht. Nw cn't evn d. in arms of Col.'s wife.

OK. Art. OK. Cmg bck, back. Slwly. Rch thru bldy pane and go in. Wlk to stud. drippg bld. Stnch w. nwpaprs & immac. bet-list bk.

Later, I felt better. I examined my wrist. There was no serious damage. I changed out of the bloody clothes, showered and put on my new green suit. I drank a couple of Cuba Libres in the sitting-room of the cottage, packed a small bag, and put the Yellow Jersey cheque-book into the pocket of the suit. Then I went upstairs, did my teeth, hung the suit up and went to bed.

10

New Orleans (cont.)

After meeting Carol in Big O's I spent the whole of the next day with Deano. I just wanted to get through to ten o'clock as innocuously as possible. In the morning Deano rented a flashy mugger-attracting sports car. We drove around the centre of New Orleans in it, wearing ridiculous new sunglasses (Deano's big reflective ones being far the worst).

Although they evidently didn't come out at night, being good men, it was true that the city was full of Shriners. At almost every intersection there were two or three of them pulled up beside us, wearing fezzes and inexpertly revving their rented mopeds. Intermittently, Deano told me more about this story he was doing, but I wasn't listening and he was only half-hearted about it anyway.

Carol's kiss hovered over the atmosphere in the sports car. Deano was clearly fascinated by it from a clip-joint-user standpoint. I was also fascinated, of course, but from a different and doom-fearing point of view.

I wondered whether it was possible that Carol had not really looked at me with her old eyes, and that she had just looked at me as some difficult punter, with an untold wad in his pocket ready to unfurl. But no, I reasoned as we drove about, there was what she said – 'My God, John, it *is* you.' She definitely said it. That proved she remembered and that it was true.

After a couple of hours of driving around, Deano pulled into a petrol station. We were out by the airport somewhere and the neighbourhood seemed bleak and probably dangerous. Deano did the filling-up and went to pay. While he was in the kiosk a young black guy came up to the car window.

I realised immediately that he was the pump-attendant from his semi-uniformed clothes. He began asking how much fuel I wanted. I began explaining that we'd filled up ourselves.

But from Deano's vantage point he obviously thought I was being accosted by a mugger. He came charging out and went right up to the pump-attendant, almost chest to chest, with Deano sort of elevating himself from his heels.

'No trouble, OK, man?' Deano said tersely. The word 'man' sounded ridiculous coming out of Deano's mouth. The pump-attendant wandered off.

Deano got in the car and we drove away. Despite the absurdity of the situation, I was touched by Deano's misguided display of physical courage and thought, it's people like Deano who win wars. I offered up half the petrol money and he snaffled it into his increasingly rumpled linen jacket.

We went back to the hotel. It turned out the drive-around had constituted Deano's whole research. He began to write his piece on a portable Tandy. I'd been given one of them once by Angela but had never worked out how to use it.

Not wanting to disturb him, I went out on foot to get the material for my own piece.

About three hours later I was back. It was still only mid-afternoon and the day was hot. I was surprised by my efficiency: I'd been to the police station and got some quotes about the muggings from some junior lackey, met up with the local snapper and examined some murky alleged bloodstains on pavements.

With a few more quotes I'd have enough material to

write the piece. But that could wait. On the way back to the hotel I bought a bottle of Bacardi and some Coke. I hadn't drunk in the afternoons since the Greek days in Marousi, but had a strange compulsive thirst as the clock ticked by slowly.

I set the bottles down in the room next to a plastic bucket full of ice from the machine, and poured one and then another. Deano didn't have any. He gave me a slightly disapproving look. Strictly a work-hard-play-hard man, Deano.

He'd finished his Shriner piece and was admiring it on the Tandy. In the process of writing it, he'd stripped down to some orange underwear, a too-small designer vest and black socks. So, I reflected, it was true that Deano did make his quotes up.

We went out on to the balcony on the first floor. I drank the icy rum-and-Cokes while Deano paced around the balcony, proudly reading out his made-up Shriner quotes from the Tandy and scratching his orange underwear.

At ten I was stationed outside Big O's on the other side of Bourbon Street. Minutes passed and a few Shriners went by in fezzes. There was some sort of knick-knack shop next to Big O's. An old woman manning it gave me a smile as she was closing up. That was a good sign. At least I didn't look like a clip-joint-haunting mugger or perv, as I'd increasingly begun to fear.

Then Carol came out. She was wearing a pair of jeans and an old green raincoat, with a small rucksack dangling from one hand – you need something to carry the toggle and négligé around in. I felt myself swaying slightly. At first I thought it was all the rum-and-Cokes, but then I thought it was probably a real 'swoon'.

She came straight over and collected me in her slipstream, and we headed off south down Bourbon Street. Another possibility that had recurred throughout the day with

Deano was that in these first few steps she would tell me to fuck off. But she didn't seem to regret anything.

Impulsively I put my hand round Carol's arm. She looked briefly startled, but then accepted it. I felt a sense of being unable to control anything I did.

'Carol, can I stay with you tonight?' It came out with an undertow of starving-dog desperation.

'Sure, John,' Carol said jauntily, as if it was obvious that I'd be staying. Suddenly, I knew my Deano days were over. Deano seemed a generic term for the last few years.

Carol guided us both into a bar where she knew a few people. It was full of the type of white m-class grunge kids who would get on anyone's nerves. At 25 I felt like an elder statesman. Ganja fumes drifted across the air, to the obvious pride of the clientele.

We stayed there about an hour. Carol bought me drinks – trendy 'shots' of artificially coloured spirits – and cigarettes from the machine. She searched through my wallet looking for photographs of undeclared wife, kids etc. I asked her if she had a boyfriend. She said no.

The music made conversation impossible. I was relieved. With all the shots added to the rum I was now entering an advanced stage of drunkenness. There was a pool table in a separate room in the bar. Carol said I should play, since sometimes we used to go to this billiard hall in Athens. I played one game with a goateed young grunge-type. I'd played with Stanley quite a lot but never this pissed. The pockets were bigger but the balls mushroomed into drunken double-balls when I took aim.

Thankfully the grunge-type couldn't play at all. I beat him but I certainly wasn't up to facing other challengers, so I walked back under the deafening beat to Carol, who was watching in her raincoat. She seemed delighted by all this and handed me another coloured shot, which I drank down, and then we left with our arms entwined.

We went to numerous other bars and walked further and further away from the tourist zone. Somewhere along the way Carol picked up a joint, which we smoked as we walked and which I passed back to Carol in the nonchalant manner of a practised dope-fiend. I was now completely wrecked.

We went to a last bar containing under-age grunge drinkers with skateboards. Then Carol insisted that we go and walk by the river so we left.

We went up a dark path. I could smell the river was near. Despite being wrecked and lovelorn, I felt a childish excitement at being near a new river and wondered what fish you could catch. We stopped at an old abandoned wharf. The Mississippi stretched out into the distance. It was more like a sea than a river. I stumbled down a slope to inspect the water. It seemed actively black. God knows what monster fish lurked in there. I went back up the slope and kissed Carol. I clung on to her for dear life.

'You know why I kissed you in the club like that?' Carol said.

'No.'

'So I'd know if I still loved you.'

I wanted to say, 'And?' but I wasn't sure I could form the word, so instead I kissed her again. Then we walked on up the path back towards Bourbon Street, picked up a cab and went to Carol's apartment.

Her place was on the lower ground floor of a building facing the streetcar tracks. As we went down the steps she said she'd just moved in. She'd only been in New Orleans doing the clip-joint job for seven days. For all the years in between she'd been in Michigan. I couldn't even attempt to evaluate this statement. I didn't know whether it was good or bad, irrelevant or fateful, and I didn't care.

The apartment was bare except for a few things scattered around. The only decorative adornment was a string of

Christmas lights that Carol had put across the wall above her bed, even though it was summer.

She turned the lights on, we got into the bed and somehow I managed to perform the Act. During it I felt an almost unbearable love and, finally, emptiness. It was as if I had poured my entire self forlornly into another being.

It was mid-morning when I woke and got up. Carol was still fast asleep. On past form, it would be some considerable time before she stirred.

I grabbed my jacket and took Carol's key from the table. As I walked up the sunlit steps I felt as though I was floating. I carried on floating through the main door to have a look around outside.

Across the road from Carol's apartment, there was an all-purpose shop with a line of pay-phones down one side. I went over and rang Angela on the free number, to find out how many words I had to file on the mugger piece.

'Twelve hundred,' Angela's voice said in its Lincoln tones. We chatted for a while, even though Angela, Lincoln and the paper seemed a million miles away in my new floating world.

While we were chatting a young black guy with crack-head eyes came up, hovered closely, and put his hand in my jacket pocket. I had nothing in there. My packet of fags was on top of the telephone. I picked up the box and offered one to him. He took two out, putting one in his mouth, eyeing me suspiciously.

'Light?' I added. He nodded, so I lit his fag.

'Check you, man,' he said, before walking off.

'Who was that?' Angela asked from down the phone line. 'Not some floozie I hope, Jonno.'

'No, Angela.' I said goodbye and hung up.

I walked back across to the streetcar tracks in no doubt that if I hadn't been floating I would have just been mugged by the black guy.

I got on a passing wooden streetcar. It was empty when I got on, and when it filled up it was entirely with tourists and a few moped-less Shriners.

In the centre of town I searched around for a bookshop, with the idea of giving Carol a copy of *Lolita* as a present. I found the main bookshop but the American version of *Lolita* had a horrible shiny cover so I bought her *Under the Volcano* instead.

It was one o'clock when I got back. Carol had just got up and was doing her teeth. I gave her the book.

'Tonight you must meet Jim Gruber, John,' she said.

'Who's he?'

'Jim's this old guy who runs the club.'

'Jim,' I said, warily hoping the teenage dick reference wouldn't occur to her.

'I know,' Carol said. 'And what's funny is he really is a complete dick.'

It wasn't that funny, but we laughed for ages anyway.

I'd been interested in boxing when I first knew Carol and this, apparently, was why I must meet Jim Gruber. As well as owning Big O's, he managed some fighters. He also owned a hotel called the Orleanna. He had a fighter staying with him at the moment called Derek Jay. 'Derek is real big and Jim is sure he's going to be champ,' Carol explained. That weekend she was going down to Mexico, Cancún, where Jim and Derek were setting up some fight, and I must come of course.

I told Carol that I couldn't come to Cancún because I had to go back to London and the paper, but that I'd be coming straight back to New Orleans in a few days. It was a shame: I'd always wanted to go to the Yucatán peninsula. The great asteroid that destroyed the dinosaurs was thought to have landed there in 65 million BC.

I didn't know the details of how I could finance my new life with Carol in New Orleans yet, but I was sure I could work out some plan with Stanley back in London.

Carol left for work with her rucksack around four. She was doing an early shift again and would be finished by ten. We would meet at Big O's and then go to the Orleanna Hotel with Jim Gruber and Derek Jay for a few drinks.

Carol said I should come early so I could watch her set again. She was planning a few new moves; and it was great that the club was letting her use her own Led Zep tape to dance to. I realised that in the sick dream I hadn't noticed, thank God.

I kissed her goodbye. She seemed genuinely delighted with her recent employment in the sex industry. The innocence of her enthusiasm moved me and I swooned a bit again.

I began the rest of the afternoon by examining the things in her apartment. There wasn't much there. On top of the fridge I found a letter Carol had started, saying, 'Dear David, I am here in New Orleans getting my head together . . .' Apart from *Under the Volcano* I only found one book: *In Chanting Forest* by Sonya Cone. In the bathroom I noticed a tube of toothpaste for sensitive teeth. I'd forgotten Carol used that special stuff.

I walked back across to the shop opposite keeping a lookout for the crack-head, bought some Bacardi and Cokes and returned to the apartment. Amazingly, even in Carol's rented fridge there was an ice-dispenser. I sat down with my drink thinking, it really is heaven, this country.

When I was wrecked enough I wrote Carol a not-bad poem about her and New Orleans. I titled it 'This Sad Thing'. Rereading it, I realised I should have got the Shriners in somewhere. But I decided to give it to Carol anyway.

I was in position in Big O's at nine, in the bar-hostess section. Thankfully there was no sign of Deano. This time I looked at the stage, taking a professional interest in the dancers as they came on and off. There was a XXX-rated one who was introduced as 'Rosa'. Carol was introduced as 'Carol'.

Occasional hostesses came and sat down next to me hustling for table-dances and then left. Carol kept a cold eye on them. She always was viciously jealous, Carol.

At around 9.30 an old white guy and a huge black guy came in proprietorially. Various hostesses cooed around them and it was evident that these were Messrs Jim Gruber and Derek Jay the fighter.

They sat down in a hastily arranged VIP section by the bar. Jim Gruber talked incessantly. Derek Jay just nodded solemnly. Gruber was a ridiculous-looking figure, about 60, with dyed jet-black hair moulded in a faintly Elvis-inspired way and wearing a shiny grey suit. He could only have been involved in clip-joint-owning and boxing.

Soon after ten Carol emerged from behind the bar wearing her raincoat garb. She introduced me to Gruber and Derek Jay and we shook hands, Gruber giving me a two-handed mafioso-style clasping. Derek Jay had massive hands but his grip was surprisingly tentative, as if he was unsure if I was some hombre friend of Gruber's that he had to be careful around.

A wiry mustachioed Magnum type called Frank came out of a booth and shook hands slyly with everyone. He was the DJ and general MC whose voice introduced the girls' names on stage. Carol thanked him effusively for letting her use the Led Zep tape. Frank shrugged generously.

Carol appeared to think this post-work mingling was normal, but I could tell Gruber was edgy about it. Despite Deano's optimistic beliefs, I'd thought it a fantasy-preserving maxim of clip-joints that punters should never see the hostesses in anything but their pleasing toggled states. After a couple of minutes, Gruber hustled us all out into two cabs, and thence to the bar at the Orleanna Hotel.

The bar was a dim, red-lit, slightly dilapidated place. Gruber referred to himself as 'Jimmy' and to Carol as 'hon'. He wise-cracked and speechified about a range of subjects, ate pistachios from a bowl and spat the shells back into the same bowl. He was drinking a strange green concoction topped up by a worried Asiatic barman, which finally I identified as vodka-and-grenadine.

I drank rum-and-Cokes and Carol bourbon-and-Cokes. She was certainly knocking back a few.

Gruber and I talked boxing for a while and then Derek Jay joined us toweringly but uncertainly and we all discussed his recently decided-upon ring moniker. This was to be: Derek 'Big O' Jay.

'I'm happy, man,' Derek said in a American-tinged Jamaican accent.

He told me his mother lived in London. He made references to several epic amateur fights he'd had there but I didn't believe him: I followed the boxing scene quite closely and had never heard of Derek. Seemed a nice enough bloke, though.

We stayed an hour. It was obvious that Carol was Gruber's new 'No. 1' girl. At the end, Gruber invited me to come to Cancún. There was another English guy, a boxing guy called Ronnie who was a 'great, great guy', coming down. I said again why I couldn't. Gruber said it was no problem. He was only going down to talk business with Ronnie anyway. Derek's fight in Cancún wasn't till the next weekend, and I could come down then.

'My treat, Johnny!' he added.

Carol and I left and went to a few grunge bars. Because of her occupation, looks, and recent arrival in New Orleans, she seemed to be regarded as some sort of novelty grunge-affiliated sex expert. At one bar, a girl came up and excitedly gave Carol a ring with a phallus engraved on it. Carol then reached into her rucksack, pulled out a pair of handcuffs, and showed them to the giggling grunge-girl.

'What were those for?' I asked Carol when the grunge-girl had gone.

'Oh, I could do this thing with you, John. But it wouldn't be fair. It's not your kind of thing.'

'What kind of thing?'

'It's a real jerk-off thing anyway. I just do it with some of my friends.'

'Which friends?'

'My friends in the club of course.'

I was now getting wrecked again. I sat there while Carol went off to score some more dope, developing a theory about the changing facial skin of people in love. For years I'd been in bars with Stanley with all the women giving Stanley the eye and not me. Looking back, this must be because, although Stanley was not conventionally good-looking, he was permanently in love with everyone, whatever they thought of him, which gave his skin a permanent loving sheen. Since I'd fallen back in love with Carol, I'd noticed several women giving me the eye. This must have been because my facial skin had changed, too, physically advertising my floating state.

I went up to order another drink. While I was at the bar, a woman in her mid-twenties came over and started a conversation. She was in New Orleans for a convention, but not the Shriner one. She was attractive, college-educated and, as far as one could tell, available: all in all, what Deano would term perfect wife material.

However, before the convo could really get underway, Carol returned with the dope, clocking the perfect wife with a vicious stare. I followed Carol to the bogs at the back of the bar, where she wanted to show me 'something really cool'. Once we got there she rolled up a joint and showed me how to do a blow-back. I knew how to do one already but pretended I didn't. I enjoyed the taste of her

143

lips a lot more than the sensation of the blow-back.

We got a cab to go back to Carol's apartment. It stopped at some lights and three drunken jocks who recognised Carol from Big O's tried to jump in, but she deterred them easily by feigning sleep, so I didn't have to get involved beyond telling them to fuck off.

At the apartment she sprang back to life under the Christmas lights and informed me of the ground-rules for tonight's Act. We were clearly going to draw upon the full repertoire of her recently acquired knowledge. Afterwards Carol fell immediately into a deep sleep. It was my last night before going back. I forced away my own sleep and watched her for a long time.

At 8 a.m. I woke in panic. I'd completely forgotten to write up the muggers piece. It was 1 p.m. in London: past deadline. Jesus shit. All my stuff was still in the hotel room. I grabbed a pen and some paper and sat in Carol's bathroom writing the 1200 words, making up the quotes Deano-style.

It took me an hour and a half. Carol had no phone. I rushed over the road to the shop pay-phone. The crack-head was lounging in the vicinity but there was no alternative.

I put over the copy and then got through to Angela. Her tone was grave. She said Tony wanted to speak to me in precisely one hour's time.

I went back to the apartment. Despite the early hour Carol got up to say goodbye. She gave me a poem she'd written. Apparently it was in return for 'This Sad Thing'.

Hers was a few lines long and was called 'My Forest'. It seemed to be a fairly explicit ode to her libido.

'It's an allegory,' Carol said, lighting one of her menthol fags. Christ, I thought, it runs in the family. She's written her third poem instead of her first and gotten ahead of the curve.

'How is Mr Duplessis anyway?' I enquired.

'Oh, I guess Dad's fine. I haven't spoken to him or Mom for six years. I'm trying to find my Indian father.'

I pocketed 'My Forest', said goodbye and floated up the steps towards the streetcar track and my final ever encounter with Deano.

The Brief Laying Down of Arms

I lay there under the knackered beams of the cottage listening to the late-night low-end talk station, trying to work out what was going on.

Under booze and prob. for other reasons had long ago developed fixation with past. Common syndrome. But recent cycle of benders and withdrawal attempts now seemed to have produced an almost psychotic approach to the present.

Almost like adult autism: self-absorbed ultra sense of reality quickened by wise-guy cockneyesque-one-liner thoughts; mind seemed to be moving at twice normal speed, but within stunted set of recurring references, like fruit-machine only ringing up same combinations of oranges and lemons but at lightning speed.

Slowed down now. Feel much better after the two Cubas. Window/blood incident must have snapped me out of it. No more benders. No more withdrawals either. No real need. Damage done. Just go back to the old calming steady drip. Try and run again soon. Need that. Balance.

Found I wasn't fearing sleep for the first time in ages. Didn't go off yet. Savoured calm listening to radio voices and thinking about bets.

Rachel was right. Had to get out of that study. Get out of the cot. Glad I did the week of organisation, though. Must be just, with so much frenetic phone and TV action in a confined space, mind started going that bit too fast. Whizzing. Fruit machine exploded.

Big heavyweight fight coming up in Atlantic City in a couple of weeks. Lewis v. Golota. Go to that. Sea air, dilapidated boardwalk grandeur, constant mugger-danger in streets behind boardwalk: my kind of place.

No, complete shit-hole, actually, A.C. Called 'The Sewer by the Sea' even by residents. Shame the fight isn't in Vegas. Could do with another visit. Wonder where the hell Carol is?

Slow down. You're doing it again.

Strong fancy for Golota. Saw him spar once. Might even have been against Lewis? Iron-chinned Pole. Mean. Dirty, too. Lewis won't like that. Bloody good boxer, Lewis. Underestimated. But he won't like it.

Plus Lewis'll be a big favourite. Should get twos or threes for Golota. Value bet. Think he can win.

Already told Walter. Over the years, in between bust-ups, W.'s never gone against me in boxing bets. Always says he'll have a little fritter, and then lumps on far more recklessly than I do.

Yes, that's what I'll do. Take the second 4-grand instalment and go out a week early. Play blackjack in the boardwalk casinos and suck in the big-fight atmos in the decrepit town.

I was just drifting off to sleep well into early hours when something on the radio pulled me round. Reports coming in that Princess Di had been in a car crash in Paris. Nothing serious, apparently, walked away from scene totally unhurt. Jesus, big story, still.

Leant on pillow listening for twenty mins, wondering how low-rent talk stn host would deal with sudden change of tone from normal late-night convo bullshit. Needed delicate handling, this. Partic. interested because this host always sounded completely plastered on air. One of my favourites. Now bit worried for him.

Listened: immac. performance by host. Caller reassurance, retention of dignity, awareness of wider ramfctns, not phoney either: altogether, perfect pitch. Well done.

Dropped back down on pillow and was just drifting off again when he said that Princess Di had died.

A minute passed and I started crying; sudden. No, weeping. Emptying everything out. Couldn't believe it. I mean it was terrible obviously. I'd have expected myself to have been sad. But the truth is, I didn't even like her when she was alive. Didn't actively dislike her. Certainly not an enemy. Just didn't really like her. Didn't really take an interest in the royals. Irrelevant to the war.

I carried on weeping; couldn't stop. Why now? Guilt? No, don't think so. Something bigger.

Don't remember stopping. Must have cried myself to sleep. Next morning, drove into the town and felt a pall of mourning hanging over the hedgerows. Wept again in the car, unable to tip them back.

Parked and sat in the car until the tears stopped and then went into the Co-op for some fags and beers. Everyone in there seemed the same as me. Saw Potter the Neighbourhood Watch man walking round with his basket, red-rimmed eyes. I didn't glare at him for once. Nodded and he nodded back.

At the checkout, got the really vicious one. Just passed the stuff through gently this time, even looked at me and said 'Thanks' when I gave her the dough. Said 'Thanks' back.

Drove up to the surgery to pick up latest supply of drugs. Saw Marlsford hovering at the back of the dispensary getting something, ashen.

Unbelievable. Drove home and sat in sitting-room watching the news coverage. Crowds coming out everywhere bearing flowers. No bets. Gave Walter quick call. Feared this call. Thought Walter might make jokes about the mug flower-bearers.

But he didn't. He was unusually subdued. No offers of tips. Would never *say*, Walter. Never bleed outside. Most outwardly unsentimental person I've met. But he was moved, I could tell. Christ, even Walter.

Sat watching the TV cov. for hours and hours, and then days, drinking dark beers and crying, as the coffin was carried back from France to the empty windswept airfield, to begin the slow procession.

Voyeurism? Crossed my mind. But knew it wasn't. That's when I knew what it was:

It was a laying down of arms.

In her coffin lay all our invisible dead. For the first time in the silent war we could bury them, entwined with her.

Thus we laid down our arms for the period of mourning. And as we did so, watching each other across her coffin, we saw in our enemies' and strangers' suffering our own, and for a brief time could acknowledge the equal mortality of our human skins.

Watched the funeral march: the bitter tears of adults and the children's sweet terrible grief.

Watched the hearse recede up a dual-carriageway strewn with flowers.

Then the dead were buried and the period of mourning finished. We picked up our arms and resumed war footing immediately.

As the silent war began again, I turned off the sitting-room TV, wiped away my tears and rang Walter for a tip.

12

Cancún

I took the streetcar and rang Tony from a safe pay-phone in the middle of a mall. He gave me a terrible bollocking about missing the deadline. I took it stoically of course, only making up a few bits of mitigating bullshit. He was absolutely right. Then I walked up the road to Deano's hotel.

Deano was lying on the bed in his orange underwear with a Walkman on. Phil Collins no doubt. Seeing me, he looked unusually angry.

'Jonno,' he spat. 'Where the *fuck* have you been?'

'Eh?'

'I've had Tony Bamber ringing up half the night, going mad, and that fucking Angela as well . . .'

'What did you tell them?'

'I told them you were with some bird.'

'You didn't.'

'I bloody did.'

'Shit.'

'Totally fucking unprofessional, Jonno, totally fuc . . . that table-dancer, was it?'

'Yes.'

'Jesus fucking Christ,' Deano said disgustedly.

I pointed out Deano's not uncentral role in going to Big O's, and that as the plotter of 200-dollar private sessions with table-dancers, he was not in a position to give moral lectures. When this had little effect, I told him the truth. There was no real need to, but I just thought, sod it.

'Christ, I didn't know you fucking knew her,' Deano said. Personally I couldn't see what difference it made, but evidently it made one to Deano. He stood there concernedly scratching his nuts.

'Yeah, well,' I mumbled.

'Fucking Ada. Hope I haven't landed you in the shit, Jonno.'

I told Deano not to worry and said goodbye to him. I got in a cab and travelled to the airport in the pale light, feeling I had crossed some sort of line.

Once back at the paper, I went and saw Tony. There was no mention of what Deano had said. I knew I was pushing it, but I asked Tony for a week's holiday. To my surprise, he agreed readily. Absurdly, he seemed to feel some guilt at the savagery of the bollocking he'd given me.

'Go and take a break, Jonno,' he said. 'It's probably why it happened. I know you and Stanno have been hard at it all year.' Stanley was away on some assignment. I still hadn't worked out the financial details, but I was back in New Orleans within four days, just after Carol's weekend in Cancún.

She was discernibly more subdued when I saw her again. She clung to me in the apartment all the time. She was also drinking more – a stream of bourbon-and-Cokes – and was no longer interested in phallic rings. Something very bad must have happened when she was in Cancún with Gruber. But Carol insisted nothing had. She said she was actively looking forward to going again at the weekend.

That Friday we flew down to Mexico. Gruber and co. were already down there; in fact I don't think they'd come back. Complimentary Mexican champagne all the way. Gruber was paying for everything – flight, accommodation, everything except walking-around money.

I looked out at the passing sky and wondered what possible motives there could be for him paying for me. International press coverage of Derek Jay? Highly unlikely. Surveillance of Carol's friends? No point. Surveillance of Carol and her friends from secret perv-onlooker standpoint? Jesus H. Christ . . . Still didn't think so, though.

Carol perked up on the plane. She read my 'This Sad Thing' poem aloud in a happy if inappropriate tone.

We stayed in a place on the beach called Capitaine Laroche, quite a few miles outside Cancún. Derek Jay's fight was the next day, in some bullring. We all had cabanas on the beach: Carol and me; Gruber; Derek Jay and his trainer; Ronnie the 'great guy' Englishman.

Also floating around was Rosa the especially raunchy table-dancer. I think she was in Ronnie's cabana.

The first time I met Ronnie was in the Capitaine Laroche reception as Carol and I checked in. He was a stunted bear-like cockney with low-life interests in Florida that Gruber wanted a piece of. At reception, he informed me about the size of Mexican coins. They enthralled him. He took some out of his pocket.

'Look!' he said. 'See how big they are? Fucking incredible!'

He held a coin up to my face and I agreed friendlily that it was indeed large.

He turned away to show someone else and Carol said, 'I forgot to tell you, Ronnie is a *real* jerk.'

That evening we all ate together on a sunken terrace, by a swamp on the other side from the sea. The food was old-style French with a few Mexican side-effects. Carol didn't eat anything but the drinks flowed, served by young practised Mexican waiters who each wore a red flower in a buttonhole of their white shirts. They checked the rest of us for where, apart from Gruber, the money lay.

Gruber held forth about his 70s days in a mafioso's Vegas

hotel called The Aladdin, and then about a famous *haute-cuisine* restaurant in New Orleans called Antoine's. He described to Ronnie his privileged knowledge of the secret Antoine's recipe for Oysters Rockefeller. Ronnie was all eager attention, but it seemed to be going a bit over his head.

The table-dancer Rosa sat between Gruber and Ronnie making flirting sounds. She was a bit younger than Carol, probably only 20 or 21, but she was a real pro.

We sat further down the table. Ronnie tried a long-range conversation with Carol but she ignored him. In fact, she ignored everyone apart from me and, when unavoidable, Gruber.

To everyone I voiced the subject of the 65 million BC asteroid but no one except Ronnie was interested.

The next morning while Carol slept I went swimming and then lay on the white sand facing the cabana. I saw a huge lizard marching slowly out of the swamp and wondered about the snake population. Carol woke up but didn't join me because she said sunbathing was vanity and evil. Oh yeah, forgot about that.

I was coming out of the dream and felt very uneasy about Carol and me being in this place with these people.

In the late afternoon, after Gruber and Ronnie had returned fruitlessly from marlin-fishing, we all went off to the bullring for Derek Jay's fight in a convoy of rented VW Beetles.

It was still light when we got there. The fights had been going on since mid-afternoon and most of the crowd seemed drunk. There was a moat round the inside of the stadium and in parts of the moat were stacked crates of Chivas Regal bottles, Coke bottles and boxes of ice, all being mixed and handed up in plastic glasses.

I bought Carol and me several. A part of me wanted to be a restraining influence. The other part of me wanted to get back into the intoxicating dream by becoming as wrecked as I had been in New Orleans.

We walked around the infield with the drinks, wolf whistles being aimed by sections of the crowd at the unresponsive Carol.

Darkness fell and Derek came on. He was wearing his new purple robe with 'Big O Jay' written on the back. He was easily beaten on points by a squat Mexican who looked like a cab driver who'd just wandered in from the rank. I felt sorry for Derek. He was crying as he left the ring, but fair play to the cabbie.

Afterwards Rosa got in the ring wearing one of Derek's cornermen's jackets and not much else. She did a cameo of her table-dancing routine which the drunk crowd wholly appreciated.

Gruber didn't care about Derek's defeat. I could tell business with Ronnie had gone well. Ronnie spat at the turf and made a throat-cutting gesture with his hand, to say Derek hadn't been worth anything anyway.

The next afternoon we all flew back to New Orleans and straight from the airport reassembled in the bar at the Orleanna. I was desperate to get away by then, but Carol seemed to be in a booze-induced genuine trance.

In the red-lit bar Gruber spewed pistachio shells accurately into the white bowl and speechified about the categories of Big O's chicks, ending up with the story of Iris the Alpine Milkmaid from Cincinnati:

So that leaves us with the final 5 per cent category. And to me, these are really the ones. And don't think I'm gonna start talkin' about strippers who do it for kicks 'cause that is all bullshit strictly for the jerk-offs. In fact in all the years I been in the business I only ever hearda that happenin' one time and that was with a real fuckin' crazy who was the wife of a guy who ran one of the clubs they got in Houston. And this crazy bitch was a fuckin' grandmother pushin' 50 who had cosmetic surgery. Face, tits, ass, pussy, she had it everywhere. Her old man let her strip in the club for kicks and 'course she was fuckin' all the clients and it was a complete fuckin' disaster, broke their marriage up.

No, the 5 per cent I'm talkin' about, which is the growth area in my opinion, is the 5 per cent who wanna raise some dough short-term to put themselves through college or somethin'. And they look around and they see that for what you gotta do and for the hours, strippin' is just about the best dough out there. And 'cause they're only going into it like in the short term these chicks really tend to hustle the jerk-offs and I noticed that they go a little hotter in their act, know what I mean? 'cause they got this sort of attitude which stems from the fact that maybe they think that they are a little superior to the run-of-the-mill fuckupskis and the Polacks and addicts and assorted refugees and 'course the jerk-offs, and that they ain't really part of the scene. So they have this kinda, kinda . . . contempt, yeah, contempt, see, like the rest of us are some bunch of fuckin' jokers.

It's like with Iris the Alpine Milkmaid from Cincinnati. Any of you remember Iris? Well, Iris was in this category. She needed six or seven Gs to go on some kinda writin' course and relocate to New York or some other complete bullshit she believed in at the time. This is when she started. So I said sure honey 'cause she was nice-lookin' with these huge jugs even though she had on these kinda arty clothes which in my experience tend to mark out the grade-A stuck-up bitches. And she said how long would it take to make the six Gs? and I said, well, if you really hustle and give

155

the jerk-offs somethin' special then you could do it in two and a half months, but are you sure this is somethin' you wanna do, honey? And she said in this cold voice of hers, what is something special? So I said to her, the thing about the jerk-offs is what you may think is a sexy act ain't necessarily what they gonna think is a sexy act. I said, you ever seen a porn movie, honey? And she said no. So I said, well, that's where most of the jerk-offs borrowed their imaginations from, so why don't you go down to the end there and see Frank – you know, Frank the DJ – and if you ask him nicely I am sure he will show you a porno tape of which he has a fuckin' huge collection and is probably the world's expert on porno as well as bein' a low-down sleazeball who thinks I don't know he's been dealin' big H to the chicks for years as well as loan-sharkin' for which he regularly gets interest in the form of blow-jobs.

So this Iris turns up to work the next night and I cannot believe my fuckin' eyes 'cause here she is dressed in this Alpine get-up, this big heavy short dress with sorta straps on it and a blonde wig tied in these little pig-tails and these huge jugs are hangin' outta the dress and between the jugs is this bell, a fuckin' bell for Chrissakes, which is one of the bells you might see round the neck of a cow so they can't get lost. And I am thinkin' the only thing she ain't doin' is yodellin' or whatever the thing is they do in the fuckin' Alps and I get hold of Frank and ask him what the fuck is goin' on. And Frank says to me, *Alpine Milkmaids* is one of the top-sellin' pornos of all time and he thinks this Iris is gonna be a big hit with the jerk-offs.

And, y'know, Iris is a big hit. Within a month and a half I think she passes the six-G mark easy. And 'cause she's only doin' it short-term she moves in here at the Orleanna and I give her a room on the first floor for 200 bucks a week. And one day Willie Ng the barman here, he went up there at midday carryin' her breakfast tray and he must have been in a fuckin' trance as usual and used his pass key 'stead of knockin' and kinda busted in there and there was Iris gettin' dressed and she had virtually nothin' on and Jeez did she get mad. She slung Willie Ng out and splattered the breakfast everywhere and then a few minutes later came stormin' down here demandin' apologies and undertakings and other complete bullshit just 'cause Willie Ng had seen her jugs and maybe caught a glimpse of a coupla pubes. Now let me remind you, these very same jugs and very same pubes complete with Alpine trimmings were available for public inspection every night!

'Cept, you know what? The fuckin' joke was on her. 'Cause one thing I learnt about these short-term chicks is they ain't so short-term as what they think. You know why? 'Cause these 5 per cent in this category, havin' no additional overheads like the big H and some half-breed kid to raise like the projects chicks, they get to like the dough. And 'cause they like the dough they get lazy. And pretty soon they forget all the arty complete bullshit idea they was supposedly savin' for and they basically do nothin' 'cept get up in the afternoon and go to the mall and buy some nice clothes and some jewellery which maybe they can't afford but it don't matter, 'cause all they gotta do is go to the club for a few hours for a few days a week and hustle their pussies and, guess what! they paid for it all. And this is a nice lazy lifestyle.

So Iris says she's gonna stay two months and she stays two years. Here I am turning over a coupla hundred strippers a year so this is some kind of record.

In the end I had to fire Iris on account she got a little too lazy and she started gettin' fat and she wasn't gettin' no younger neither. She musta been pushin' 25 and as you know the jerk-offs like fresh pussy these days and 23, 24 is really the limit and if you go to them clubs over in Houston you ain't gonna find no girls over 22.

So I had to tell Iris to take a hike and suddenly life ain't so funny for Miss Stuck-Up Bitch the buddin' fuckin' Shakespeare who ain't writin' no plays and maybe wishes she coulda got off her fat ass a little sooner 'cause the last I heard, it was Frank the DJ who told me, Frank saw her sittin' in Desire's, which as you know is a louse-pit hell-hole where all the terminally fucked-up fuckedupskis go before they die and you wouldn't wanna touch the glasses let alone the chicks, and she was still wearin' the stupid fuckin' Alpine get-up and the bell and the blonde wig, you know, with the pig-tails? well, the wig has now gotten a little dirty over the years and in fact according to Frank, Iris did not look too clever at all and when he says 'Hi, Iris' she just looks at him with that dumb glazed look fighters get when they're old, like with the shiny eyes? Anyway like I said I don't got to give a fuck and all I was doin' was tellin' you how the categories work of these chicks. But I gotta give that Iris credit where it's due 'cause in the two years while she lasted she was a real fuckin' pro.

It was a grotesque story but Ronnie laughed fondly as if it was a familiar nursery rhyme. From behind the bar, Willie Ng embarrassedly topped up Gruber's glass of vodka-and-grenadine.

Carol said, 'John, can you get me another bourbon-and-Coke?'

I got Carol the drink and thought about what I could do.

This scene was vicious, dependency-instigating and much too low-life even for my tastes.

'Carol?' I said when we got back to the apartment. 'How much money do you generally make a day?'

'Oh, thirty bucks, maybe twenty-five most days.'

'Christ, that must have been a real bonanza with me and Deano.'

'Yeah, sorry about that, *Jonno,*' Carol said in a terrible fake English accent.

That night I held her sleeping booze-sodden body under the Christmas lights. You got used to the lights after a while. I looked up into their haze and recognised our pressing need for a cash reserve. You couldn't start a new life in America without stake money. I'd have to go back to London again and raise a few grand.

In my semi-wrecked state, this did not appear to present much of a problem. People did it all the time, didn't they? Raise a few Gs? Should only take a week, maybe two. Easy. And if it came to the worst, I could always sell the Saab on the side. Well, maybe not. Biggest ever advance on expenses, that would be . . .

At midday when Carol got up I told her I was going back again and she was not happy.

'How many goddam days?' she said.

'I dunno. Two, three, maybe a week. As long as it takes to get the money together.'

'A *week.* Fuck you, John. I had a boyfriend before you came.'

'So did I. A girlfriend I mean,' I lied.

'Well, fuck her too.'

'Carol, it's no problem,' I reassured her. 'It's only a few grand.'

To confirm my solvency, I had a phone installed in the apartment that afternoon. It was amazingly simple compared to England. I could have ordered ten lines and they'd have done it. As a bonus, my credit card went through.

I went over to the crack-head shop and bought some provisions for Carol while she tried out the new phone, generally by calling Directory Assistance in various cities in search of her Indian father.

I called a cab for the airport and got my stuff together while Carol sulked and drank Bacardi-and-Cokes from my stash. She had got very thin. I don't think she'd eaten for a few days. She hadn't taken in that she was a week away from her liberation and the new life.

The cab arrived. Carol kissed me perfunctorily. I walked out on to the street, a window opened and Carol shouted, 'John!'

'Yes!'

'You are coming back, aren't you?'

'Of course I am!'

In London the sky over Battersea Park was heavy and close. Immediately it bore my own self-delusion down on me. I knew that I had never been good at getting money except by extreme luck or inheritance.

I rang Carol regularly on the new phone for two days. She sounded bad. She said I had to come out straight away and if I didn't I would have betrayed her. I reassured her again.

On the third day I walked round the park under the hemmed-in sky, past the boating pond, running track and the remains of the old funfair, and had an idea: I could go to one of Walter's low-end Soho casinos where they let you cash two cheques a day. And then after I'd cashed two cheques for seven days running I'd have . . . shit, only £700.

After one week when I rang Carol the line was dead. I got a number for the apartment building and the caretaker said Miss Duplessis had moved out: no forwarding address.

I was working as normal at the paper. Weeks went by. It was seven weeks before I got back out. I had to ask Tony for another week's holiday. He was highly suspicious. He only gave me three days off.

'Not thinking of going back to New Orleans, are we, Jonno? Dangerous things happen there, you know.'

I shrugged at the bizarreness of this suggestion.

Tony added, 'I'm not giving you more, because you'd miss the Christmas party. I'm putting on a terrific spread this year. Make sure you're there.'

I got into New Orleans late. I had £1,000 cash for the new life – half from overdraft and half from a late spree of low-end casino cheque-cashing. I booked into the old Deano hotel and then went to Big O's: nothing.

On the way out of Big O's, Frank the DJ was coming in up the stairs holding several packs of fags for his late shift. He greeted me in his smooth Magnum manner and asked what was happening. I told Frank and Frank said he had a policy of only going out with table-dancers himself, so he knew the problem.

'Some of these chicks, man, they just fly off. Nothin' we can do.'

Frank said he might hear something and, unprecedentedly for a low-lifer, gave me his home phone number. I pocketed it and walked down Bourbon Street past the pan-handlers, going into every grunge, tourist and locals bar. I bought some dope from a swooping drug-pusher, imagining I was scoring it for Carol, then got back to the hotel and found out it was oregano.

I tried out Frank's number and it was real: Frank's voice overlaid with smoochy 'mood' music. I slept, woke up late and walked to Carol's old apartment. I stood outside facing the shop and it was as if everything had already turned to stone.

I missed a few streetcars, missed her, thought: I'll never see her again.

Walked back into the Ancient Athens area, out on to the path to the river. Stumbled down the slope to the water. Tried to get the picture back. But the river was clear, so I went away . . . I went straight from Heathrow to the Christmas party.

13

(Black)

Had kept study door closed throughout period of mourning and the brief laying down of arms. But after period was over, seemed almost sacrilegious to work in sitting-room so moved TV back in.

Today, went out to stable and dug around junk. Found piece of disgusting hard green plastic with perforations. Seemed perfect fly-shield. Amazing what you can find in that stable.

Now leave front door on latch all day to avoid lock-outs. Hope Potter comes round and finds out.

Went back to study and opened window. Opened the fuckin' window, man! Lightning quickly pressed new green fly-shield against cool air-rushing frame and fixed with drawing pins from desk. Ingenious.

Stood back. A few of the bastards were still getting in, but not as many as when the window was open without the shield.

Hardly ever use the study these days. Only for the TV racing, really. Started branching out beyond Walter tips. Had a couple of winners of my own. Informed Walter of course, in passing. Get feeling he's started rationing the tips in revenge. Envy.

Est. that I am approx.

£3,900 down.

No prob. Already got next 4 grand instal. out from Ippo. Thin elegant wad entirely in red fifties. Hatchback got *very* hot in traff. Rachel doesn't seem to call any more. Probably found another author. Not bothered. Relieved in fact.

What was it Gary Glitter said? 'The teenyboppers, they get fickle and they leave you.'

Coastal Bluff ran again and both W. and me positively lumped on. Think W. may even have rustled up own stake equal to my 12-grand-rich (well, 8) 500. Excptnl val. at 7s. Came nowhere. Doesn't matter. Be 14s next time.

Started backing this horse called Croft Pool in freelance capacity. Backed it twice already. 25 e-w both times. Wld have gone more but hd to put bets on in U-Bet. Don't want to be too flash with the wise pensioners present.

Reminds me, WHERE IS THE BLOODY SWITCH CARD? Can't go into battle unarmed, babe.

W. thinks it's a nag, this Croft Pool. Just hasn't read the form back far enough of course. Big early-season win, *very* disappointing form since. Sense a coup. 50-1 last outing.

Must stay with Croft Pool. Even when you're 100-1, bloody insulting, I'll still be with you, Croft.

Watched Newcastle–Barca match that evening. That 250 on Barca to win. Dead cert. Barca 2 down within first fifteen mins. Thought they did exceptionally well coming back to lose 2-3. It's only 250.

Switched over to watch Booker Prize ceremony. Had a 100 on outsider of field: Mick Jackson. Bookies know s.f.a. about it. Pure publicity-value stunt odds.

Ah, but *I* know. Had tip-off from lit. maf. source. Tremendous value at sixes, Mick Jackson. Would have backed him each way as well but they don't pay out on places in the Booker.

Mixed and drained two deluxe-model G & Ts while waiting for Mick Jackson victory. Moved on to Cuba Libre freshener just before Mick went up to collect on my behalf.

Shit, what? They've bloody gone and given it to the favourite! Unbelievable. Classy filly, mind you. Sort of a human My Emma. Don't know what happened to Mick Jackson. Probably had a virus.

Drank Cuba. Went upstairs and tuned in to World Service.

Went down by train to London casino with Walter next evening. Blackjack. Essential prep. for Atlantic City gambling trip in two days' time. Walter knows I'm going for Lewis–Golota fight. Have feeling he thinks I'm coming back and then going with him to Vegas later.

Must tell him it isn't going to happen. He won't mind. Hasn't mentioned it. Probably be too busy on mobile doing huge deals. Probably forgotten.

Meet W. on steps of semi-plush tower-block West End hotel. Enter by casino door carrying 1-grand stake money in green-suit pock. Hand over Crombie reluct. to smarm. Latin staff while W. signs in and then we ascend to bar to discuss tactics for 1-grand loss.

Hombre barman waves away proffered payment for two Bloody Marys as if we are far too important to have to pay. Unimpressed. Still leaves them with £995 profit. Notice everyone else coming in gets exact same treatment.

'I prefer this place to the Soho ones,' Walter muses. 'It's got a bit more class, John, you know?'

Look through glass screen at casino floor down below. Less a floor than a carpet remnant. Cramped room with a few huddled tables and one roulette wheel, no doubt w. extort. minimum-bet table limits. Vegas gambler wld laugh his head off looking at that.

Unwisely, offer W. watered-down version of this observation.

'Oh well, be able to see it for myself soon,' W. says. 'How long are we going for? A week? Two?'

Pretend not to hear. Instead fumble in pock. for grand notes. Give W. half in fifties. He will gamble half my stake.

Plan is to sit at same table and for W. to card-count: attritional prof-gambler specialised art; prior knowledge of likely remaining cards enables you to lump on stakes before certain hands. They chuck you out if they suspect, tight bastards.

Can't do it myself. W. claims to be semi-expert. He will make covert signal when it is time to lump on stakes. Signal to be quick restacking manoeuvre of one pile of his chips with his hand.

We finished Bloodies and descended, taking places on the emptier of two b-j tables, joined only by hombre youngish Lebanese guy. Extort. £25 minmm bet table limit. *And* given only £25 chips by croupier when cashed in. Noticed W. has started off with two chips as his basic pre-lump-on stake. Thought: this shouldn't take long. I go with one chip.

Played impecc. attritnl b-j for an hour or so and managed to claw our remaining presence at the table. Me slightly ahead; W. levels. Bloody boring, though. Might as well do a day job. Know W. in partic. is not temperamentally suited to this kind of work for much longer.

Last few mins he has started making a few silly comments and sniggering. Dangerous. Usually prelude to frontal assaults.

Still seems to be concentrating on cards, tho'. Not making too many restacking signs. When he does, bloody obvious. Purses lips, glances about, then at me, and generally looks incredibly suspicious. No actor, this boy.

They must have seen. Must have concluded he doesn't know what he's doing when it comes to crd-counting.

Think they're probably right.

Croupiers revolve again and we get faded ex-beauty lookalike of that singer, whatsername? 'Lilac Wine', did some nice torch songs once as well. Shit . . . Elkie Brooks! Felt kick from W. on foot-rail. Missed restacking sign, it seems.

Next five mins W. executes whole rash of these accompanied by sniggers. I follow incr. dubious and our chip piles go down swingeingly.

W. now abandoning covert sign entirely and saying things out loud.

'John, think I feel a lump-on coming,' W. says, collapsing on to diminishing chip pile in mirth.

I, not amused. Nor is Elkie Brooks. Lebanese guy also finds it all hilarious and starts joining in. In new anarchic spirit of b-j comradeship with W., Leb. guy announces he has lost fifteen grand at this table in last two days. Seems cheerful enough about it. Looks like can afford. Perfect combo.

Decide I've had enough of this and remove myself and chips to next table, leaving W. to squander the other half of my money. Address new table with pure air of proper gambler and lose all remaining chips within mins due to ultra-cruel run of tens and aces by House.

Get up and practically manhandle still-sniggering W. from adjacent table, at same time returning his three remaining £25 chips to their rightful owner. Knew at this point we should go. You can do quite a lot with 75 quid in real life.

Instead, walked the tiny distance over cramped floor to roulette table. Croupiers had revolved again and I was once more in the hands of the sour-faced beauty, Miss Brooks. Actually, from standing-up vantage over roulette wheel, didn't look as much like her as I first thought.

Couldn't remember my old roulette numbers. Scattered the three chips randomly over boxes. Watched little white football going round shiny new and definitely ungrooved wheel.

As it was going, remembered old numbers: 13 Black, of course; 27 Red as No. 2; Zero as a fall-back position. Combinations of, when flush. Oh well, too late now.

Came up 13 Black. Always happens when you're not on.

Paused to watch Elkie snaffle my chips, then walked out with now recovering W. to fetch Crombie.

V. bad prep. for A.C. Totally cleaned out of 1-grand stake in less than hour and a half, excluding comped-Bloodies drinking time.

Poor gambling perf. Sick materialistic disregard for gambler aesthetic. You're not supposed to chuck it away. Supposed to *lose* it.

14

The Christmas Party

The Christmas party was a typical Tony-organised affair in the West End. Lashings of premium-label booze and shell-fish on ice, along with a few trays of Tony's favourite pickled herrings for his personal use. Tony himself was walking around being mine host, filling up everyone's glass from a bottle of lethal-proofage schnapps.

'Ah, the errant Jonno!' he announced when I came in. It was already ten o'clock and the casualties were evident. Tony thrust a glass into my hand and filled it more than once.

I could see all his old muckers were there, inc. Harry Webb and Don Short the sportswriters from the legendary N.O. six-day Ali–Spinks bender. Even Angela seemed unusually tipsy, though still obviously immaculate, with a fresh hair-do that must have taken an hour to set under some salon's tin helmet.

In between circulating, Tony made devoted forays back to tend to her glass.

Got wrecked rapidly. Stanley wasn't there because he didn't 'do Christmas parties'. No doubt loving everybody somewhere else with his permanently exuding skin. Hardly seeing anything of Stan these days.

Deano hadn't been invited, thank God. Thought he might have been.

Talked to Angela about how she missed aspects of the North – realised she was *very* tipsy; Tony should stop re-fills – then to Harry Webb and Don Short about old fights.

After a while, realised I was talking complete bullshit to everybody. But everybody else seemed drunkenly to be doing the same.

Shit, seemed to have drawn attention to myself. Was conscious of general hubbub about casinos, references to my gambling spree after getting £15,000 trust money. Of course I'd told everyone about it at the time.

Schnapps-fuelled suggestions about mass visit that night to low-end Soho casino after the Christmas party was over. Went along with it all happily.

Angela looked through my pockets as a joke. Found both 1,000 new-life cash and Carol's 'My Forest' poem, which was still lying crumpled in top pocket. She waved wad around and read poem out loud saucily to a few hovering casualties. Knew something was wrong about it but too wrecked to evaluate. Just seized both back as soon as I could.

'Was that from one of your floozies, then?' Angela said.

Tony had observed this little display and shook his head at me from across the room, mouthing 'Jonno' gravely. Though he had been chucking back the schnapps, Tony retained a residual journo hyper-alertness. Constitution of an ox, he had.

Remembered where I'd just been and felt an almost debilitating sadness. Decided to go. Casino idea a non-runner anyway. Couldn't get them all in on my membership.

Slunk off. Encountered Angela on the stairs. She was putting on a fur coat and leaving too. She had a chastened air about her. She said Tony had given her too much to drink and now she needed something to eat, but she didn't want to go and eat somewhere on her own.

I said I'd come with her. Angela appeared to be sobering up already and probably what I needed was some good northern sanity.

Drunk-drove up to Islington where her pad was, parked the Saab and went into an old-style Italian tratt. with the phallic pepper-grinders. Angela ordered jugfuls more wine. Clear she had no intention of sobering up, though she really should do.

Listened wreckedly to her animated convo which seemed to revolve almost entirely around sex. It was only after about ten mins that I realised Angela was trying to seduce me. Just seemed too incredible to be thinkable, as I first thought it. Why now? After all those innumerable conversations about wordages?

Decided that in N.O. my own facial skin must have picked up an echo of the love-glow. I was appalled, none the less.

'My favourite film scene is the one in *10*,' Angela was saying. 'You know, Jonno, where Dudley Moore or is it Julie Andrews, anyway they're looking through the telescope at the hippies, and one of the men hippies comes up behind the girl hippy on the pool table and just, well, you know, *takes* her from behind . . .'

'Oh yeah, I know that scene,' I said, as if we were just debating it on *Film '79*.

'Do you, Jonno? And you know what? It always reminds me of a camping holiday I went on, in Belgium. I didn't know the campsite showers were *unisex*. I went in for my shower and then this *man* came in and started washing his *thing*, and I must say it seemed to be getting rather big . . .'

Jesus shit. Despite all known warning signals, I found myself getting uncontrollably aroused.

Angela was now on to the subject of the pepper-grinders, making the obvious ref., and hanging her immaculately coiffured head out towards me over a grinder.

I kissed her. Couldn't believe it. In a restaurant, apart from anything! Pure-lust greedy tongue kiss. Starving-dog but for different superficial reason.

Paid the bill and left still in the grip of the uncontrollable urge. Galloped to the Saab feeling like Deano but blocking out any poss. evaluations. Pause while Ang. asked me to lay out fur coat lengthways on back seat before she got in the front. Her special coat: didn't want it getting crumpled sitting on it.

Was in process of laying down coat lengthways when felt Ang. pressing against me from behind. Turned and collapsed together on to back seat. Rolled around heavy-petting for approx. fifteen minutes. Sensed people walking past looking in. Had closed back door with foot at the start.

Would have gone on rolling around for longer except for group of young white NF types stopping at the window and drumming on it, leering. Islington: probably Arse fans.

This incident brought Angela round. She made sure coat was properly smoothed and we reassembled primly in the front seats. I drove off.

The chastened atmosphere started to resume on the drive back to her pad, but not quite enough, probably because of the shortness of the drive.

I said goodbye grimly as we drew up but Angela said, 'Oh no, Jonno, I think you better come in for a coffee, with the amount you've drunk.' Christ: script by central casting.

Followed Ang. into a suitably immaculate block of flats, still possessed by the urge. Could tell she was too. We couldn't get in fast enough.

Both too wrecked for inhibitive embarrassing shuffles. Had a brief unthinking fag in kitchen while Angela went into the bedroom. Followed her in and there she was, undressed on top of the bed with legs akimbo.

Took all clothes off by the window trying to appear casual. Noticed that Angela hadn't closed curtains. Must have not done so purposefully. Wreckedly acknowledged that she was probably playing out a *10* fantasy.

Stood naked. Had a sneak look down: shit, bit bigger

than usual (believe me, have monitored). Must be all that rolling around in the Saab; build-up. Bet it's not as big as the Belgian's, though.

'Oh, *John*,' Angela said.

The 'John' momentarily shook me. Had always called me Jonno, Ang. had. The real intimacy . . . A tangle of reality wanted to descend but I pushed it away. Too late to go back.

Walked forward nonchalantly as if I always went around with it like this.

Went down on Angela. Christ, everything was so big down there: a great creamy thigh, clitoris like a life-size dangling Christmas light. Went back up, plunged my needy flesh into her needy flesh.

Shit, she was coming almost immediately. Never managed that before. Her face lighting up all pink. Well, she certainly had the illuminations down below, ha-ha.

Oh my God, and me . . . No . . .

After a silent pause I untangled myself, put underwear on and found fags. Offered Angela one. She took it. Never seen her smoke before.

Made a stupid joke about how, since it hadn't lasted very long, maybe it didn't count.

'Well, it wasn't nothing, John, was it?' Angela said.

Saw the realisation creeping over both our faces. Now we wouldn't even be able to get on with each other any more. In the office it would be terrible.

Angela was already reassuming about 80 per cent of the Angela I had known before that evening, putting on her night clothes with a thorough air.

I hastily put my clothes back on. Knew that Angela didn't want me to stay, and I didn't either. Said goodbye. Ran down the communal stairs.

Raining outside. It wasn't until I was half-way across the street to the Saab that I remembered I'd left my shoes and socks behind. Ignored it. Looked up. Angela was waving down weakly. Waved back weakly with the wet black street seeping over my feet.

Went home to my flat. Sat smoking almost till dawn, bowed: thinking, Carol, Carol, I have really betrayed you now.

Went in on Monday and Angela was sitting at her desk with a plastic bag containing my shoes and socks under her desk. Tony was away. Angela's desk area was strictly off limits to all except Tony so I don't think anyone had noticed the bag.

During one of my trips to the vending machine Angela gave me a nod to pick up the bag so I did. No words were exchanged. She had washed my socks.

I told Stanley, Angela told someone else and soon almost everyone knew. It was only a matter of time before Tony knew.

Adopted policy towards Angela of tentative normality overlaid with discernible sense of regret.

Didn't work. Felt terrible; didn't know what to do; did nothing. Angela seemed to be disintegrating fast. Her sense of order appeared to have imploded. No longer looked 'immaculate', came in without make-up on some days. Personally I thought she looked better without it, but you can imagine the shock in other quarters.

One day Tony called me in.

'You're a *bad* man, Jonno,' he said. He was almost shaking with rage.

'Sorry?' I said, though of course I knew what this was about.

'Am I to take it that Angela's wretched condition is due to your sleeping with her?' he enquired simmeringly with his eyebrows raised.

For a moment we both looked out through the glass door

at the back of Angela's head.

'Yes, I think so,' I said.

'Bad man, Jonno. You're a bad, *bad* man.'

Tony dismissed me with a flick of his soft lined newspaperman's hands. He was in pain.

I walked out, closing the glass door gently. Felt rather tearful like a child. Obviously, didn't actually cry. As I walked past Angela gave me a tangled semi-sympathetic look and our eyes met uncertainly.

My contract was up soon. I knew Tony wouldn't renew it and he didn't.

Soon lost touch with Stanley. Heard he got sacked for some minor expenses fraud, had given back Battersea pad to mortgage company and moved to country to do 'artistic photography'.

A few years passed. Worked for a succession of other newspapers. At the start I kept ringing Frank the DJ late at night, but he got pissed off so I stopped. Wrote almost every article completely plastered in Battersea flat, often in course of multi-day bender.

Found that if I drank steadily for a few days, I could burst through on to a landscape of perfect writing. Words didn't exactly tally when I read them back, but still.

Skin seemed to be able to take it. Every few days, ran blind drunk round Albert and Chelsea bridges to keep balance.

Then one week it didn't happen. Couldn't burst through on to the landscape. Drank and drank but I couldn't get there.

Purposefully missed deadline and put on answer-phone. Started writing letter resigning from current paper. Only a short note; took me a week to write.

Walked across Battersea Park to post it one mid-morning. It was a day before my thirtieth birthday.

Thought, Jesus shit, I'm as old as Lurch, and I knew I couldn't do this any more.

Passed running track in park. Some athletes and boxers running round. Found myself standing there taking genuine keen interest. Steam rose off the runners in morning air like off racehorses on Newmarket gallops.

Started talking to black guy called Alvin who was caretaker of hut by track. A bit mystified by my interest but friendly. Unusually for black guy, was great fan of Morrissey. Had tape on in background. This stemmed, apparently, from visits Morrissey had paid to track during period of interest in boxers. Alvin told me Morrissey came a lot for a while.

For some reason told Alvin that I was sleeping rough. Alvin said I could stay in the hut at night if I liked. There were showers in there and everything. Declined, sensing fantasy getting out of control.

Went out of park and over Chelsea Bridge, posted letter and hung around King's Road for whole afternoon, trying to suck in pure intent of 60s Boho ghosts through cracks in pavement. But none refracted through in new monied businesslike air. No cracks. Concreted over.

Realised that I seemed to be descending into very strange circumstances, but powerless somehow . . .

It began to get dark and I walked back over Albert Bridge instead of Batt. Bridge because of the beaut. lights. Half-way down the south side of Alb. Brdg. Rd I thought of Alvin and decided that I really should sleep rough, at least for one night.

Vaulted over the iron fence and made my way across the silent green park, to where the great wooden structure of the 1951 Festival of Britain had once stood and where the remains of the old funfair lay.

Almost all of it had been pulled down to make way for a children's playground but some of the old struts were still there. Found a sheltered place between a couple of struts.

Would normally have been drunk by this time of the night. Felt jitters. This was the first time the snakes came. I was unused to them and shocked. Decided to stay up instead. Had conscious, weird flashbacks: the struts were like the logs me and Stuart had used to build the camp and the harbour at the pond in the fields.

Dawn came and I collapsed with relief and had about three hours sleep. I woke up and began walking across the park towards the flat. On the way I heard a voice shouting my name.

'Jonno!' it said.

I turned round and saw Justin approaching. He had been a young pony-tailed photographer on the old paper and had modelled himself on Stanley.

'Shit, man,' Justin said. 'You look terrible.'

'Yeah, well,' I said. I changed the subject and a few trivial pleasantries were exchanged.

'Any news of Stanley?' I then asked.

'Oh, the old GWR?'

'No. Stanley.'

Justin did look slightly apologetic.

'How is he?' I persevered.

'Bad, I heard,' Justin said.

'Drugs?'

'And booze, that's what I'm told.'

'How bad?'

'As bad as it gets.'

'Shit.'

Justin and I said goodbye. Chastened by the encounter, I went back to the flat and rigorously cleaned myself up. Wondered what the hell I was doing. Thought about Stan.

In the next few weeks: gave the flat back to mortgage company, bought Dolly, started writing *Road Star*, moved to Suffolk without telling anyone, infused with new sense of jaundiced optimism.

For a while, proudly carried around memory of one night of sleeping rough like a badge of courage in the silent war. But after meeting the Colonel, obviously this paled.

15

Reconnaissance

Coming out of Elkie Brooks casino w. W. after 1-grand loss, remembered I'd left remaining 3 Gs of second instal. in Suff., so only had enough left for a couple of drinks.

Bus and walk to classy W. pub in S. Ken. Walked past Harrods. Still carpeted in flowers from period of mourning. Tourists taking photos of them.

Touched by actual sight of flowers but no longer moved. Bad luck to mourn after period of mourning over. Also poss. bad taste, ghoulishness and voyeurism – these almost certainly to be exploited commercially by enemy forces in silent war.

None the less, mentioned to W. as we walked past that it was the flowers that made you weep at the time.

'What, hay fever, John?' Walter said.

A good one, but didn't laugh.

Pub. Drinks. Au pairs. Suits (not like mine). No Chels. fans this time. Had only couple pints but walked out totally skint except for tube fare back to Lvpl St for train home.

Then found crumpled fiver in top pocket while on tube! Rich again! On journey back to Suff., invested fiver in extort. two cans of Strongbow, my usual train drink.

Sat in rancid smoker carriage by rushing dark window, reflecting that despite some unsavoury incidents the casino trip had actually been good prep. for A.C., and that also there now seemed some hope that distorted sense of reality might drop back into shape soon.

★

Arrived local stn 11.30 and drove home in hatchback. Poss. d.d. but if so only marginal. Shit, must pick up that bike from outside the station some time as well.

Went in with intention of making calls to US. Spent hour and a half rummaging through newspaper-strewn boxes looking for old journo notebook with Frank the DJ's number in New Orleans in it. Knew it was there somewhere. *Never* lose that. Yes. Found it. Still a long shot; can't have rung it for, what, five years?

Mixed giant Cuba to build up for phone call and probable crusher disappointment. Went through half the Cuba and chained a few fags. Picked up phone.

Ans.-phone. Unquestionably Frank's voice. Updated, sharper-delivery message, overlaid with new hipper 'mood' music: sort of deep-throat rapster soul. Amazing how even Magnum-type low-lifes like Frank can, in their own way, move with the times.

Put phone down and sat back luxuriating in knowledge of my access to Frank. Just stayed there with my eyes unseeing on the flickering crap-TV, occasionally reaching down to try the number again.

Finally got through to Frank himself around 3 a.m. my time.

'Yeah, I remember who you are,' Frank said convincingly. Gave him a quick run-down of the story again anyway. Frank listened with uh-uhs.

'You know, the funny thing about this kid you're talking about is she came back.'

Shit . . .

'When?'

'About four years ago. Then she left again after about a year and I don't know where she went after that. Strange chick . . .'

'No idea?' But Frank wasn't listening. He was telling the story at his own pace.

'. . . and then about a year ago I heard she was back in the dancing business and I was kinda surprised, y'know, because at her age. I mean, she must be twenty-nine, thirty . . .'

'Thirty,' I put in, but I don't think Frank heard.

'. . . and then I heard she was some kind of supervisor at one of the new big places they got over in Vegas. Y'know, booking the girls and all. Actually, I sent a chick down there from here. But this was a year ago. Things change . . .'

After Frank had finished I asked him if he had a name.

'Yeah. *Cowgirls.* They got two of them over there. *Cowgirls 1* and *Cowgirls 2.* You'd have to look in the two of them.'

So grateful to Frank that I asked him how Jim Gruber was. 'Dead,' Frank said. 'Y'know, it's funny, he finally got a fighter to challenge for the title. A kid named Frankie Mitchell out of Philly. He goes down there and he's staying at that place he always stayed, the, the . . .'

'Aladdin,' I contributed.

'. . . at the Aladdin and the night before the fight he just drops dead, right there in the lounge. I heard he was dancing with some chick. I guess the excitement finally got too much for Jim.'

16

Brand-new Second-hand

Day after phone convo with Frank the DJ, a def. levelling down of reality distortion occurred. Assumed my resumption of slow-drip process must be really kicking in.

As drove 'cross fields towards town and U-Bet, took in not only Pig City but also dark green slope of Dawson's Wood rising above (favrt. walk area for Col.) and beaut. deer-holding copses just before airfield.

Feel calm. Some depth and context coming back. Recent weeks on same drive only whizzing thoughts and narrow-channelled grey road disappearing under car.

Celebrated in U-Bet by putting on 57 × £5 e-w Heinz spread across three meetings. Croft Pool running again today. Put Croft in Heinz and also 25 e-w à la carte at 16s. Don't think coup will happen quite yet, but can sense it coming near. You can never tell.

When handed over notes – 570 Heinz and the 50 for Croft – you cld have heard a pin drop. Well, you probably cld have done but actually there was no one else in there. Eleven o'clock. The pensioners get up so early they were prob. having their lunches. Walked out of bookies on to utterly empty cobbled Market St.

Fairly sure this was the biggest Heinz ever placed in U-Bet, by massive margin.

Got back, rummaged around in a few boxes for an hour. Rang Pridwell on old Epsom number. To my surprise Prid himself answers phone. Now his office: accountant. Of course! Probably got the old man living in shed at bottom of garden w. his Bible.

Prid not at all surprised that I should ring him up after fifteen years. Sounds exact. same w. overlaid adult inflections. He asked me what I was *doing* now.

'Oh, writing, journalism, y'know. Usual shit.'

'Really?' Prid says w. hint of indignation. 'That doesn't sound like usual shit to me. It sounds very interesting.'

Incredible. Same rltnshp: immediately restacked.

Prid tells me Johnny living in San Francisco. Got 'consultancy' out there. Left army ages ago but may be still 'connected'. Prid hints sinisterly at some kind of mercenary activ.

Don't believe him. As well as super-efficient prag. side, Prid. has always had paradox. inclin. to extreme shoots of fantasy.

He mentions something about J. being involved at Drumcree. Fronting up baying pack of Loyalists or something.

Adds, 'But he won't talk about it.'

Got J. numbers off Prid.

Say we should meet for drink some time. Prid says great.

On a roll rang Johnny immed. When he drowsily answers, realise it must be c. 4 a.m. his time. J. doesn't mind. Same as Prid. Pick up immed. Shit, shld have done this years ago.

Say I'm going to Vegas for a few days. Will try to stop off in San Fran on way back. J. says will show me round. Is coming to Eng. soon after anyway.

'But I'm warning you, John,' J. adds. 'You won't recognise me.'

'Why not?

'Because I'm bloody fat and I've lost most of my hair and I look about forty-five.'

Say to J., 'Johnny, d'you think I'd give a fuck about that?' Must be true, though, if J. said it.

On a new roll rang old paper for Stanley's latest no. Angela left, so safe. Got no. and rang Stanley. Overreached myself there. Stanley not in. No ans. Probably not even Stanley's no.

Despite this, moved to study still on roll with elegant bott. of crisp white and watched Croft Pool not showing once throughout whole race. Good sign. Means coup must now be v. imminent.

Four losers and two e-w seconds at 1/5 odds from Heinz but seconds were both banker short-priced faves so work out return from 570 will be approx. 6.50. Can't go into U-Bet to collect 6.50 from world-record 570 Heinz, partic. in front of pens. Too humil. So won't. Will say must have been lookalike if they ask.

TV racing now off, and with 2/3 crisp white gone – plus earlier – and feeling slow-drip mellow, called Stan on dubious no. Stan answers. Doesn't sound like Stan at first but is. Diff. Stan. Not like Prid and Johnny H. Can't pick up.
    Ask Stan what he's up to, artist. photog. going well? and Stan says, 'Parallel universes.'
    Say, 'What are they?'
    Stan explains with a few aphorisms and I acknowledge, 'Well, Stanley, sounds like the same sort of thing as I'm doing.'
    Stan perks up. 'Really, man?' he says.
    'Yeah, man,' I say.
    'Shit, fucking great,' Stan says. 'Good to hear from you, John man. Unexpected, you know?'
    Talked brief Chels. but Stan not that int. except for checking results of course. Hasn't gone for yrs – last game midweek FA Cup replay v. Barnet, 199? Chelsea won three or four.

Very weird. Also my last game and Stan was there but didn't meet . . . Can't move around in seats in The Shed.

Mainly tho' I listened to dislocated sound of diff. Stanley voice.

Heard muffled clink of bottle on glass down line. Trying to conceal it. That act in itself humil. Echo of lonesome voice in empty room except for bottle and glass.

Can recognise. Have been there.

Well, technic. speaking, suppose I *am* there.

But Stan worse. Can tell. Got no one. Bad as it gets.

Nothing I can do. Doesn't want my help. Too humil.

No one else help. Can't see casualties like Stan in sil. invis. war. Anyway, the lines move so quick these days, like lightning. Never know where it's going to strike.

Got to dig yourself out of abandoned trench. No other way.

Asked Stan for a drink in Lond. next eve. before I left for Vegas. Gave time, name of pub etc.

'Yeah, that'd be cool.'

Knew already he wouldn't come. Blemishes? Wld hate to see blemishes on Stanley's beaut. exuding skin.

Poor Stan. Never really knew him. True original. Unlike me – brand-new second-hand,

> *Don't exalt, in your painted face, girl,*
> *Because underneath that face, you're just a disgrace.*

Most vicious song ever written, that. Good old Tosho, RIP. Fierce front-line warrior, tho' perhaps best left out of the generals' meetings.

Next day, drove out early for breakfast of Coke and Twixes at garage shop en route to London and Vegas. In shop decide against Coke as must stop these sugar bursts and instead opt for New Hombre Isotonic job.

Always avoided these before as I suspect enemy drinks 'em, but you've got to try everything once and also has value 33 and 1/3 per cent free.

Ring Rachel from garage shop, tell her I'm off. Back in three days. Don't tell her I'm going to Vegas. Thinks I'm going to A.C. Isn't keen on Vegas. Says it's been written to death (wish she wouldn't use that phrase). Most keen on Macau. Quite keen on A.C.

Able not to tell Rach under 12-grand good-faith operational rule: '. . . act in good faith towards her, *as far as is possible*' (p. 67).

Only going for three days because if don't find Carol, Vegas *not* a place to hang around in. If do find, have to come back anyway to nick final 4-grand instal. to start new life, assuming Carol hasn't got husband etc.

Able to nick money under 'necessary human survival' clause (p. 67).

This would mean I'd have to write the book, tho', under 'Scenarios' clause (3) (p. 67). Might soon have to invoke this clause anyway as estimate am approx.

5,500 down

after paying for 470 rtn ticket leaving 2,500 for Vegas gambling inc. long-range Golota bet before they put the final 4-grand instal. in bank.

Point out to Rach. that am having to make tiresome excursion to Oxfd St travel agent to pay for ticket in cash because I STILL HAVEN'T GOT THE BLOODY SWITCH.

She ignores.

Says, 'OK, see you when you get back then, bye.'

'*See*'? That's a new one.

Got in hatchback. Took sip of Isotonic. Disgusting. Screwed back designer lid and chucked bottle on to hatchback's ripped-up, virtually non-existent back seat. Drove off.

About ten miles down road-work-woven dual-carriage-way, hatchback starts overheating more than ever and all working lights on dashboard seem to come on inc. red 'Stop!' one. Knew I should have got Darren to have look.

But have been in this sitn before w. other cars, inc. Saab once, and on most occasions have brazened out the scare-mongering lights until end of journey. Dolly didn't have any lights. Drove on down dual-carriageway: only another 160 miles to go. About 400 yards after lights came on, spot trail of smoke coming out of bonnet. Convinces even me. Pull into lay-by where car full of pensioners with thermoses out were taking a break.

Open bonnet. Engine smoking and radiator fizzing as if it's about to explode. Approach pensioners asking if they have a thermos of water hanging about but am greeted like world-record mugger. Window opens approx. 1mm.

Am stranded ten miles e-w between my garage and next one at the great dual-carriageway supermarket. Put thumb out a few times but don't fancy it, them or me. See Isotonic bottle on back seat and pour entire contents into radiator nozzle. Discernible relief. Drive ten miles to great super-market and give rad. good hosing and top-up. Isotonic didn't seem to have done hatchback any harm. Didn't seem to have greatly enhanced its performance either.

Repeated the hosing process whenever saw smoke trail at approx. five further garages until at Chelmsford garage man told me what I needed was rad. sealant. Thanks for telling me earlier. Put sealant in and progressed London.

Bought ticket for 470 and waited fruitlessly for Stan in Soho pub, then went down to Walter's to hand back the keys feeling thoroughly pissed off w. both hatchback and W.

Despite this feel oblig. to tell W. I'm going to Vegas without him. He'll forgive me in time. Anyway, he can come and visit once I'm living out there, as long as we always meet away from the house, he doesn't bring

Graham, and never lets on he's my friend if Carol happens to be about.

W. and Graham were across the road in crap Rodrigo's eating squid rings and discussing latest escort-fondling experiences as I sat down.

'My one said she was too sore to go on,' Graham was saying. 'Quite proud of that, the amount of men she must of screwed.' Graham, you're right, you're such a big dick.

Tossed hatchback keys across squid to W.

'Sure you don't want it for another month, John, after you come back from Atlantic City?' W. says, friendly for him. 'Same terms?'

'No, I fucking don't,' I say.

W. went off bemusedly to bar to order another bottle of red.

'More radiator trouble, was it?' Graham says to me.

Jesus shit. Betrayal. W. *knew*.

'Walter normally puts two bottles of sealant in at a time,' Graham went on dully. 'Mad he is.'

Right then. Betrayal meets betrayal, sunshine. Won't tell him about Vegas. Probably never find out anyway.

W. came back carrying red.

'It's the Arc on Sunday, John,' he says. 'You'll be away for it. Want me to put the two grand on My Emma? Been laid out for it. Plus there's Newmarket the day before, thirty-runner handicap. All nags. Very open race.'

'Is it?' I say coldly.

'Yeah. Certainly not worth a lump-on, this race,' W. says w. deluded responsible air. 'You're a bit quiet tonight, John?'

Cursorily took care of business for while I was away. Issued Yellow Jersey Press cheques to W. for 750 My Emma Arc lump-on, plus at W.'s suggestion four 25 e-w fritterers on Newmkt hndcp hopefuls of his later choosing. Obviously after they'd all won he could send the cheques back.

Got up to go. Remembered where I was going. Felt a
dull emotional thud in my stomach, like a stone dropping.

'See you, John, and I might have a little fritter myself on
this Golota,' are Walter's parting words.

17

Heaven Thy Dwelling Place

Knew I shouldn't have brought Crombie as soon as I began two-stop criss-crossing of US dictated by unnec. cheapo 470 tckt.

Bloody practised air-travellers, the Americans. Use 'em like buses. Very good on the overhead lockers. Just as you've sat down looking around and then remembering to put your coat up they've nipped in and nicked all the space.

All seem to use these wheel-on portable-luggage carriers with fold-up frames. In terminals look like army trailing miniature field-guns. Sort of thing Pridwell shld have invented.

Problem was, Crombie kept sort of bulging up from between my feet, disturbing the drinks. Bad for Cromb. as well: shld never crease your special coat.

Non-smoking all the way. Thirteen hrs inc. terminals. No prob.: quite sanguine about not having fags for temp. periods, as long as you're not with anyone and nobody speaks to you.

Landed Vegas. Put Cromb. on and followed field-guns out. Eighty-degree blast so took Cromb. off on plane steps. Fuckin' *Vegas*, man! No, must curb.

Got cab to Aladdin. Talked cricket with Pakistani cab driver. Still took me extort. Strip route to see lights. Didn't complain. Never found Vegas lights beaut., tho'. Even when came in last mafioso days.

Now enemy moved in. Aladdin last authent. redolnt ex-Maf. joint in town [Not that Goodfellas allies. Self-intrstonly for Goodfells.] Booked into Aladdin. Late already, 11 p.m. Found out Aladdin about to close and be blown up in three weeks' time. Decent Reception woman almost tearful.

Touched but not sad as she tells me. Can't weep about buildings.

On way to room passed lounge area where Jim Gruber died. Room right opposite room where Elvis got married, alco bell-hop tells me. Believed him. Comrade. Tipped extravag.

Went in and sat down for while w. TV on, luxuriating in anonymity of jumbo-sized if old knackered American room. $35. Ah yes, excellent. Long time since I've been in one of these. Creeping sense of *déjà vu*, tho'. At least not New Orleans. Couldn't have taken that. Whole French Quarter probably a mall now anyway.

Wondered where *Cowgirls 1* and *2* were. Can't exactly go and ask at Reception. Probably cld in here actually. No, just get in cab. They'll know.

Not going tonight. Go tomorrow. Drank too much on flight. Be too wrecked and felt no poss. of exud. skin.

Had quick glance round room for unvarnished wood in case of jitters and poss. Vonze attack. Plenty unvarn. round edge of window frames. Won't be needing it anyway due to slow-drip.

Reminded me. Nipped down to Aladdin shop and bought DIY Bacard./Coke botts. Obese Midwest pens. and young redneck fams with babies in pushchairs parked by fruit machines. Small children in casinos? At midnight? Outrageous on all counts.

Ice machine right outside room. Several of them standing like noble sentries at intervals up long soiled corridor. Ice-bucket thoughtfully provided in room. Filled it up to rim. Mixed and drank a couple, chaining fags to get nicot. levels back up. Ah, America.

Slipped into beaut. melanc. writing mood. Rifled thru

room draws until found Aladd. writing paper and envelopes. Got out copy of 'This Sad Thing' poem I'd brought with me (not going to show Carol if find her; too mawkish, but OK for me). Read it. Shit, bloody good. Can't do 'em like that any more.

Won't try. Instead wrote short narrative poem involv. me and Carol set in Hong Kong. Wrote it to beat of old Pogues song. Never been to Hong Kong; always wanted to before handover; always seemed like my kind of place – our kind. Called it 'Kowloon Train'.

Read it back. Not that bad in circumstncs. Might be unintelligible if didn't know Pogues, tho'. Prob. shld send it to toothless Shane: he has a hit w. it and we both make millions. No, will give to Carol anyway. Author of 'My Forest' after all.

Plus exotic location may help reinforce allure of new life. And Aladdin notepaper means she has no chance of forgetting what hotel I'm staying at.

Folded 'Kowloon Train', put in Aladd. envelope and placed inside copy of Road Star I'd brought to show her I'd finally become a writer and to make her think I'm loaded. People always think writers are: incred.

Drank enough Cubas to put me out watching crap US TV unseeing. Beforehand, had quick watch of free 1-min. preview of subsriptn porn channel. Hard, brutal and ugly: US setting, two 21-yr-old porn actresses being gang-banged by series of big dicks whooping as they take turns; big dicks grab hold of porn actresses' hair for leverage as they do it, yanking hair and sneering; porn actresses seem rather to be enjoying it.

So that's what they're watching now, eh. Glad I'm out of it. Probably tailored to fantasies of new ultra-prag. women porn users. No inner life, ultra-prags. Thus when not pragging about occupationally have constantly to be entertained w. unintellect. stim.: new cars, expens. holidays, porn use (pens. diff.: can do what they want; deserve it; respec' to elders). Only have borrowed fantasy life, ultra-prags. Don't see real life. Distorted fantasy-driven unseeing grasp on reality.

Mind you, can't really talk on that score.

Finally went off around 5 a.m. Same as being home at cot., really, except for porn chann. and lack of crouching inert flies.

Woke up late, as desird: already used up chunk of day till eve. Cld do w. having someone around to use it up with. Don't want inner life until eve. Wouldn't mind having Deano to drive around with actually. Christ, did really say that? Time must indeed heal.

Bought local Vegas and other papers from crap redneck booze and knick-knack Aladd. shop. Golota–Lewis fight in A.C. tonight. Surpis. amount of pundits going for Golota. Thought they'd all be mugs and go for Lew. Fight starts 9 p.m. Vegas time. Showing on Caesar's Palace screen.

That's when I'll go: after Golota victory; shouldn't take long. Will arr. *Cowgirls* approx. 9.45. Thus will catch her if finishing early shift; but also be in postn to catch her if doing late. Know the 'dancing business', Frank the DJ and me.

Walked down Strip and saw sign for $1 Bloody Marys at low-end Barbary Coast casino. Along w. Aladd. and poss. Caesar's Pal., one of few bastions of neutral territory in increas. enem.-held part of Strip.

Good: breakfast. Ordered $1 Bloody, tipped barman extravag. and took Bloody to Sports Book area to examine odds for Gol. vict.

Jesus shit! Even-money fight! Well, Lewis only marg. fav. Suddenly realised: Golot. didn't have chance; it was Lew. vict. of course. What the hell had I been thinking about? Obvious outstanding value Lew. odds not overriding factor in decision: just knew. Must have forgotten: bloody underrated boxer, Lew.; raving cert.

From this moment on had absolut. no doubt about impending Lew. vict. Put 500 (dolls) on immed. in Barbary Coast. Probably a mistake for a purist gambler such as myself. Purist wld have walked up and down entire Strip looking for best- val. odds and then walked up it again to put bet on.

Decided this was what I wld now do. Saw 3,000 (dolls) ultra lump-on looming. Also way of passing time. Walked up and down centre part of Strip, then walked up again putting on three 500 bets. Golot. odds shortening all the while. Now genuine even money.

Lumped on remaining grand of 3,000 (dolls) when I saw that. Must be mug money going on Golot. Distorted odds. Polish émigré fans in A.C. lumping on sentimentally? Soon smart Vegas boxing money will come in on Lew. Got to take adv. now. After smart mon. comes in, Lew. prob. start solid fav.

After gettg rid of 3,000, stopped off at Barbary again for reviving Bloodies and covert examin. of annihilated wad.

Still had nec. hundreds to pay for $35 Aladd. nghts inc. minor wad for max 2 eves in clip-joint plus booze + fags dough. Christ, still rich if Lew. loses (imposs.). Incred. Bloody good idea coming to Vegas. Thank you, Carol.

6.30 p.m. alread. and time to start fight build-up in Caesar's. Spent 6.45–9 p.m. gettg. complet. wrecked sittg on stool at Caesar's lounge bar. Whole Caesar's Pal. packd w. fght-fns come to see big screen. In lounge bar, had own screens on banks of TVs suspend. above bar. Perfect. Didn't even need to move.

Sat next to redneck elder called Larry. Big talker and quizzer, L. Asked about everything. Never need much invitn. myself so tell him anything he asks, inc. 3,000 bet on Lew. and 12-grand bk idea. Larry impressed by 12-g idea. Great! Now it's Rachel, me and Larry as well.

At 8.50 made quick trip to Caesar's Sports Book – while

L. protects my stool – to check on late smart-money on Lew. and congrat. self on purist val. opportunism.

Can't believe it. Golot. now solid fav. Smart money must be on Golot. Oh well. Mugs. Makes you think, tho' . . .

Rtnd to Larry and watched Lew. knock out Golot. in 1 min. 30 sec. of 1st round. Jesus. I've won.

Larry tells everyone on our side of bar.

'This guy just won three thousand bucks on . . . what's the guy's name?'

'Lewis,' I say.

'On Lewis. Ain't that something?'

L. buys me drink and so does another man. I buy them immed. rtn drinks and stress haven't collected money yet in case any muggers present.

Left them and went up Strip collecting on Lew. bets, conscious of *Cowgirls* deadline arr. time. Strangely unexcited by money. Didn't care any more. Just stuffed in pocket and dashed up Strip to next pick-up at increas. speed.

Finished pick-ups 9.40. Just about to get cab when thought: can't. No. Have to eval.

Happened to be opp. Aladd. so crossed Strip and went to room. Took notes out of pocket, counted and placed on table underneath hanging reading lamp (reading lamp in Vegas?) wch cast warm yellow light on notes gently trembling from air-condtng in stack of hundreds: 5,800 dolls in total.

Sat thinking, watching trembling notes in yellow light. Not thinking about notes. Mind empty, desolate. No eval. poss. After 10 mins thought, I can't sit here all night. Got up, stuffed 5,800 back in pock., left room, got in cab beneath cracked light bulbs of giant Aladd. sign. He knew where. All do.

'1 or 2, man,' he said

'2.'

Drew up in dim-lit drive. Some sort of indust. area. Neon *Cowgirls 2* sign on top of big warehouse. Other cabs drawing up and leaving all the time. Cowboy bell-hops outside. Christ, some serious theme-park money in this operation.

Got out of my cab and watched people getting out of cab in front: four late-20s men, clean-cut but not exactly jocks, trendy clothes, more your thrusting media/film budding LA execs. Probably *are* execs. My, how time has strangely passed. One had a thin black roll-neck jumper on, neo-fascist scraped-back hair – ironic obviously – good-looking.

Went in past young would-be Goodfella behind till. Paid extort. $20. Noticed sort of mini-supermarket to right. Looked more closely: *sex* supermarket. Trolleys and every-thing. Dildos packed on shelves, tawdry extort. fantasy gear. Several checkouts. About the size of Supergrape.

Not many people in there, tho': prob. over-ambitious venture. Good. Only three or four US busnss miniature-field-gun-dragging types – expected – and . . . *two women!* *With trolleys!* Fucking hell. Where will it all end, man?

Remembered time sitting in Big O's when this black guy came in. Middle-aged. Obv. been a bit of a dude in his time. Sat down in front of me watching the dancers unseeing, chucking down the drinks, and then this one tear just rolled down his cheek. Something v. bad obv. happened. Some state arrvd at. Bad as it gets.

Then after the tear had rolled down he got up and left. Had just wanted to let something pass through him. Give him something; some kind of . . . solace.

Yes, solace, not bloody shopping.

Headed left into club. Bad vibes. No solace here. Big place, two floor-to-ceiling poles, dozens of table-dancers, all white, many East European-looking, excpt one black one just in case any politically correct cowboys there. While one dances, all rest circulate with commando-like efficncy.

Hardly 'dancing' at all. Much harder. No toggles. Apart from occas. pole-work, basic. static open flaunt. of genit. Not remot. arousing for old purist soak like me.

New Brutalist private-dancing booths line back wall for fake action, black PVC curtains suspend. from chrome bars. Fants. version of changing cubicles at Ippo swimming pool. House Goodfellas patrol outside curtains wearing walkie-talkie head-sets.

Christ, enemy even moved in to clip-joints.

Also small middle section. Seemed to be used exclus. for girls to bend down in front of men, who sat there watching.

Sat down behind scrape-back and LA yuppie friends. Tab.-dncrs flocking round. Smell money there.

Tab.-dncr came up to me. Looked remark. like Carol. Can't be. Too young. Slightly shorter and stockier.

'Hi, what's your name?' she said. No, wasn't. Broad NY accent.

'John.'

'My name's Brooklyn. Brooklyn by name, good-lookin' by nature.'

Thought, now there's a finely wrought line. No. No sneering. Rather sweet and eager-looking, Brooklyn. Must have just started.

Commando waitress came over like lightning asking, want to buy the girl a drink? I say sure. Better not take whole 5,800 wad out, tho'. Peeled off few notes from within pocket. Bloody awkward manoeuvre with such a wad, can attest.

7-up for Brook. I order a Cuba. Ah yes.

'I'm sorry, sir, we don't serve alcoholic beverages,' waitress says.

I beg your pardon?

'It's because we're a bottomless and topless club,' Brook. chips in. 'You can only get a drink in topless places.'

Meekly ordered Coke. Came back immed. in plastic

glass, costing extort. 10 bucks plus the 10 for Brook.'s. Who cares? Can afford. Easily. Absolute peanuts, 20.

Brook. goes on, 'There's a liquor store up the block. Some of the guys bring liquor in. It's OK so long as you keep the liquor in the wrapper.'

Didn't like generic assoc. with 'the guys' but bloody good of Brook. anyway. Even gave me directions.

Wld-be Goodfella stamped my hand on way out so I cld come back in. Cattle-brand motif. That's apt.

Walked block. Pocketd 3 miniatre botts Bacardi. Back past Goodfella and in pstn. in seat within 4–5 mins. Brook. now on stage doing frenetic elab. obv. self-choreogrphd dance set to Rolling Stones number. Exceptnl pole-work. Discern. less. genit. flaunt. Punters not imprssd. Murmurs. Bastards weren't even watching. Had turnd attntn back to circulating table-dancers. Constant traff. between tables and New Brut. cubicles.

Noticed scraped-back and co. cavorting w. four East Euro-lookg tab-dancrs. Scraped-back had one tab-dancr by hair, yanking it as he examnd breasts and genit. w. sneering lasciv. expressn. Must be the new thing. She obv. not happy about it, unlike porn actrss, but let him. That's not cavorting.

Head-set Goodfellas passing all the time but didn't intervne. Just glanced about caslly talkg into hd-sts. Hair-yankg mst be entire. norm. behav. in here then. Make fants. come true, eh. Bet no tab-dncrs do hair-ynkg at home (tho' have to ask Frank the DJ for defin. answr).

Brook. finished set. Obv. thinks it's gone great. Waves to me as leaves stage. Sweet.

Scanned around for other peop. with wrappered booze. Cldn't see any. Jesus shit, they're all in here *sober*. Gets worse.

Over next 10 mins made several v. furtive attmpts to transfer contnts of min. Bacard. bott. to plastic Coke glass.

After sev. abortd missions due to passing Gdfells, finally managed it. Big gulps, almost whole lot. Christ, relief. Imagine gettg the jitters in here? Jitters prob. come as relief actually. No. Never.

Brook. approached and asked me if I found liq. store. Nodded and offered her sip of remaining spiked Coke. She took and drained entire remains avidly. Steady on, Brooko.

She sat down. More extort. unspiked drinks frm commndo wtrss. Asked Brook. about Carol, supervisor?

Yes, there is a Carol, Brook. says, but she's not a supervisor. She did help booking the girls for a bit but she didn't like it and went back to dancing because there was more money.

Oh my God, it is her.

'Carol's really great,' Brook goes on. 'She kind of looks after me.'

Fumbled in pock. for Bacard. refill.

Said, 'Oh, does she?'

'Oh yeah, and she still dances and she's 27.'

Reflected, oh no she's not. Fuckin' Gdfells. Cldn't get refill in.

Brook. doesn't know whether Carol is coming in tonight. If she is, be late shift. Around 11. Oh well, in pstn now. Gotta stay. Not sure can go thru this again another night. Will do, of course, if nec.

Brook. finally got round to asking me for tab-dnce. Declined. She went off.

After midnight prag. punters joined by new influx of black guys and Mexicanos openly flauntg wrappered booze. Goodflls didn't seem to mind so started open. flaunt. myself. Rapidly poured in 2 remaing min. Bacard. botts and coupled w. earlier Lew. vict. intake was immed. complet. wrecked. Bad wreckd. Swimming-in-air bad wrckd. Cldn't move.

At this moment, Carol walked out from side entrnc.

wearing dayglo pink mini-dress wch still looked exceptnl. elegant on her beaut. tawny skin. More partic. there was a new air about her – more confident and mature (obv.) but also discern. matur*ity*. Knew exact. what she was doing in there. Unbridgeable space betwn her and punters. Cldn't touch her remotely even when they did.

Christ, so wish wasn't wrecked. How cld I . . . at a moment like this . . . ? Maybe she was wreckd too, like before. Wldn't notice. No. Cld tell she wasn't. Looked *clean*; w. a sort of wounded but unbowed dignity.

She, hustling some prag. punters for tab-dncs. Hadn't seen me. I watched her. She went off to cubicle w. one of punters for spcl dance bullshit. Relieved. Gave me 5 min. more recov. time.

She and punter back inside 2 mins. God, it rlly is commndo oprtn in here. Back at table punter went to pass her on to one of his friends. Carol was just leaving for cubicle when she saw me. Stood there lookg over punter's frnd's shoulder w. mouth open.

As they went past me she made slight detour and said, 'I'll be back in a minute, OK? Don't move, John.'

Tried to work out tone. Cldn't. Swooning thought clouds, falling.

She came back to punters' table and gave them some bllsht. All the while looking over at me, opening mouth and blinking.

Also cld tell she was stronger than me now.

Came over to me. Sat down close. Waitrss immed. hovered.

'You better buy me a drink,' she whispers. 'They're really strict in here.'

Ordered two Cokes and Carol said to waitrss to bring her a coffee. Coffee? Wtrss brought back coffee in cocktail glass.

Carol says, 'I thought so much how you'd look. And you

look just the same. But you're a little thinner. You've lost weight. John. How come?'

Cldn't answer. Speechless. Managed a shrug. She put a covert hand on my arm. Recognised the contours of her fingers.

'You know, we can't talk in here. The only way we could talk is if I gave you a dance.' She glanced back at cubcls. 'And I don't want to give you a dance.'

I got out, 'I don't want one . . . either.' Cldn't get tone. Not sure.

Carol says, 'I can't sit with you any more without a dance. They watch all the time.'

'Are you married?' I mumbled. Carol shook her head.

'Boyfriend? . . . Kids?' Still a real struggle to get words through the booze cloud.

Carol shook her head again. Didn't ask me anything. I shook my head anyway to indicate I didn't have any either. Girlfriend etc. She didn't seem to be listening. Just staring at me intently.

'You know what I'm going to do, John? I'm going to stand behind you like I'm not really sitting with you and like I'm just *there*.'

Carol stood behind me and stroked my suedehead with her fingers. I felt my head bowing. At the table in front of us I noticed Scraped-back watching. He had a hateful expression on. Like Potter's. As if to say: 'Oi! You can't do that in here!' Wanted to go and smash him in. But only fleetingly. So tired, wrck fatigue.

'I wasn't even going to come in tonight.'

'I'm bloody glad you did.' I said, trying to make the words somehow loop over my head.

'So am I,' Carol's voice said.

Two bldy cmmdo waittrsses were now hovering, as well as a vicious-looking young semi-uniformd crone (real supervisor?).

Carol quickly asked me where I was staying. Told her. She said wld ring and meet tomorrow. I got up and left.

In the cab on way back up Strip I realised the Arc wld be on in about an hour Euro time. Told driver to go to Caes. Pal. Prob. be on big screen. Walked in Caes. Pal. Sports Book. Looked up. Yes! The flawless Longchamps green.

Went there once w. Walt. years ago. Day trip. Bet on horse called Yawa. Pissed home at 20s on Paris-Mutuel ridden by Willie Newnes. Willie Newnes had fallen off horse in Derby that year. Flat race, so bit embarrsg. In Lngchmp paddock W. had shouted out: 'And don't fucking fall off this time!' And Willie Newnes had come over and told W. to fuck off.

Hd run along Lonchmp green in pouring rain w. Walt. shouting home Yawa and Willie Newnes.

Hardly anyone in Caes. Pal. Sports Book watchg Arc. Few redneck elders, couple of wrckd-lookg Leb. hombre guys drinking Chivases. Bloody alcos. For myself: mere bott. of Lite ice-cold beer simply in cause of rehydration.

Walked around waiting for Arc. Went outside smoking fag. Gettng light already. About 6 a.m. Arc at 6.30. Beaut. pink morning light on mountains round Vegas. Don't usually notice mountains when you're there.

6.20 and they're in the paddock. Saw my My Emma. Almost swooned.

Finish third ice-cold rehydrtg Lite. Casually lump another 1,000 (dolls) on My Emma at Sports Book window to go with 750 Paris-Mutuel already on w. Walt.

As they go down to start, have sudden Lew-vict.-style premonition that Oscar Schindler going to place. Shit, absol. cert. to place. Big price. Excptnl val.

Go back to window and put 500 (dolls) e-w on Oscar. While I'm there, toss extra 500 on My Em. to show she's still my special one.

Watch Arc. My Em. comes nowhere. Oscar, nowhere. Don't mind. Only money.

Wandered through into blackjack and roulette area. Attractvly unpopultd at this time morning. Suddenly new roulette system occurred: you put 10 consecutive 100 bets on 13 Black. One comes up: 3,600. Shld have done it when first got 12 grand, but with £1,000 bets. Just one 13 Black: 36K. And it wld have happened.

Still obv. 36-1 mug system, but had undoubted certain panache, and thus acceptable within true gambler aesthtc.

Peeled off 1,000 from dimin. doll. wad and approached roulette wheel manned by old prophet-looking black guy. Cashed in. Ten 100 chips. Began putting one on 13 Black each spin. Black prophet guy sussed what going on from second chip. He started willing 13 Black on. Cld tell he was gen. But didn't happen. 27 Red came up twice. Wasn't on.

Walked out of Caes. Pal. and realised I hadn't eaten for days. Had tried. Cldn't get it down. Havng met Carol, now knew this was emerg. sitn. Must get strongr. In emerg. stns only thing can get down is certain cheeseburger from heart of enem. terrtry.

Saw outlet opp. Caes. Pal. Went in shamefully and got burg. down. Worse, it ws quite tasty. Very little nutrit., tho'. Only felt slight surge. Had choc. milk-shake as well. All right. Enough.

Went back to Aladd., put remaing 1,800 of former 5,800 (dolls) wad on table under yellow reading lght and went to sleep.

Woke up around midday w. yell. lght still on and curtains still open. Shit, must have been rlly wrckd. Never usually sleep long in natural-light glare. Took couple of mins lying there to estab. that prev. night had not been a dream.

Felt butterflies start in stomach. Put hand on stomach to try and get closer to buttrfls. Yes, really happnd. Gripped hand on stom. to hold and cherish beaut. feelng.

After while took in dimin. wad on table and then *Road Star* lying next to it w. 'Kowloon Train' poem sticking out in Aladd. envelope. Forgot to give. Oh well. Give when see her today. Lay feelng bttrfls again for while.

About 1 p.m. got up, turned TV on and started watching audience-partic. talk-show unseeing. Coming nr hour of Carol wake-up and mst be ready both for call and/or crusher disappntmnt.

Then something drew me to aud.-participtn tlk-shw Serious shit going on. Theme writtn on bottm screen was: 'Tell Him/Her I'm Cheatin'.' Wife/husb. admits cheating w. 'other' to spouse on screen and then host brings out 'other' bearing flowers.

Fights erupt, broken up by Goodfll. TV-set security guards. Also bad genuine tears spilled by cuckolded wives/husbs. Host obv. delighted by fghts/gen. tears despite insincere calming gestures.

Am veteran of tasteless US aud.-participtn progs due to hrs of late-nght crap-TV viewng in cott. but nevertheless am shocked. Indeed, immed. recognise severe enem. gain.

Gen. dark recesses of soul exploited not as Art but as entertainment. Never seen this bad before. Crossed line.

Aud. go in seekng entertmnt. Can see they're slightly stunned at first by fghts/gen. bad tears. But by end are whooping and hollering cheers and boos. Converted without knowing it. Living dead.

Turned off TV. Bad karma.

By 2 p.m. convinced Carol wouldn't ring. No way of getting her excpt by going to club again. Have to avoid tht at all costs excpt if abs. nec.

At 2.30 she rang. Meet at Hard Rock Hotel 3.30. Don't know where is. Not on Strip. Will get cab. Wll be gd to ask cab driver to go to respectable venue. No. Not respectble ven., Hard Rock. Also enem. terr. But who's arguing?

Arrvd Hard Rock 3.20 having hd no booze all day. Hd beer at central bar from wch cld survey main entrnce. Because of no prev. booze, beer made me feel pleasantly heady: reminded of distant ancient orig. appeal of booze.

Only other peop. in bar area are Brit-pop support act playing Hard Rock tht nght: anoraks, shades on indoors and one with slimy anorak-hood up. Wld-be Youth but prob. mid-20s. One w. hood up goes to bar and demands beer from pro seasoned barman. Barman asks wld-be anorak Youth for ID. Great! Love it. Serves him right.

See poster for Morrissey gig playing Hard Rock in 1 week's time. Be back by then, having nicked remaing 4-grand instal. for new life. Wll take Carol, even tho' is at Hard Rock enem. terr. Haven't seen Morr. gig since early flower-throwing days.

Admittdly, great tragedist Morr. not rlly Carol's scene. Bldy Led Zep (even tho' at pres. Led Zep enjoying unfathmble 70s-retro hipness phase).

Never know, tho'. New maturity of C. may enable me to convert her to great tragdst Morr.

Had another beer.

Carol walked in wearing ankle-length Indian skirt, crisp navel-length shirt and shades. Looked v. cool, eleg. and strong and not at all like tab.-dncr. Took shades off in lobby looking around and put them in casually chic fawn soft-leather shoulder bag. Christ, she looks so perfect.

I practic. gallop from bar to lobby and embrace. Immed. pick-up. Immed. kiss. Feel contours of her tongue again. Too brief. Still can't believe am doing this in hotel lobb. but am helpless. Walk arms-entwnd to theme-park Hard Rock restrnt.

Even after finding Carol in *Cowgirls 2*, hd purposely avoided any eval. of new life. Ws still not sure and secretly regarded new life as only e-w chance and poss. even long-sht.

Now in Hd-Rck ws sure tht new life wld absol. piss home.

Ordered food. Arrvd. Left practic. untouched by each. She had hand on my arm across table. Only curs. retelling of interven. yrs. No point. Here now. Kissed again over table. Like swimming-in-air wreckd, but while still sober. Excllnt new discovery.

'John,' Carol said. 'Do you believe in reincarnation?'

Normally, dismiss as nutter-talk. But in present mood, believe anything. Shrugged.

'Because I really believe we must have met in a past life,' she continued. 'I think we're going to meet in a next life too.'

Just looked at her swooning.

She said, 'Let's go sit at the bar. I haven't been up this early for a *long* time. It's really great.'

Thought briefly: it's bloody 4 p.m., Carol. Didn't say this, obv. Peeled off few notes and walked w. her to bar. Sat down on stools and ordered 2 glasses white.

Still only anoraked Brit-poppers about in bar. They started making lewd sniggering glances at Carol. Ignored. Jerk-offs.

Leant on her and she leant on me. Broke off to go and get Carol pack of menthols from Hard Rock shop. Felt stronger with every step.

When I came back, Carol said she wanted to go. As we walked across sun-melted car park to cab rank I felt her new strength on my arm, but I was catching up.

In cab she gave address. Not her place. Just moving. Staying w. friends. Friend of a friend's address who's away.

Arrvd. Low-slung pink-coloured apartment compound. Security gates. Went into apartmnt. Almost like cabana. Aprtmnt empty apart from new expens. furnishings. Collapsed on bed, hung on for dear life.

Made love. *Love*. Exact fit. Home.

Afterwards, Carol fell asleep. I couldn't sleep. Paced softly round room.

Decided not to tell her I was going back to nick money for new life. Too much *déjà vu*. Just say going away for a few days; journo; Arizona or somewhere.

Watched her sleeping face and tiny heaving breasts and a strange thing happened. Reality distortion suddenly lifted, and everything was clear.

I thought of her life, all the wounding she'd suffered in places like those and I started to cry, genuine tears of reckoning: for her to have come through it, to have reached this workable stage with some dignity, strength. And then I thought of my own intervening life, and saw for the first time the actual poverty of the cottage, my study, the flies, the dirt and the booze, and I felt disgusted.

But it was over now. Fuck Marlsford: new life.

When Carol woke we walked out of the pink compound together up the block looking for a cab to take her back to her friends' house.

I saw a cab and hailed it, and before Carol went off we stood talking by the door.

'Don't come into the club again, John,' she said. 'It's not your kind of place, and they're so strict.'

'I don't want to come in again,' I assured her.

Gave her Arizona journo trip bullshit. She absorbed info without flinching. New maturity. The cab went off. Shit, forgot to ask for numbers.

Went to airport. Flew home via San Francisco.

Johnny met me at San Fran airport. He was right: *very* big; all blond curls gone. But same blue eyes. Same person. All other changes superfcl. I had three hours to kill.

He drove me to so-called 'bohemian' bar in centre.

Wood-panelled w. abstract pictures but long past boho days. Nice, tho'. Everyone smoking. Unusual for US outside Vegas.

'They're going to ban smoking in bars from January,' Johnny said.

'What are you going to do for fags?' I asked. 'Leave?'

'No,' Johnny said. 'I'm going out with someone. Non-smoker. She's a bit of a slapper but look at me. I'm too old for love.'

Shit, realised J. must be 33 too.

'No you're not,' I told him. 'You're only fucking 33.'

Mentioned Drumcree story but Johnny said that was just Pridwell fantasising. Told me about his army days in N. Ire. Said they'd done his head in. Then told me about this street fight he'd had in San Fran.

Guy came up to him, jock, threw a punch, and Johnny had just run away. Wasn't even hard guy. Cldn't believe his own reaction. Ran away, crying.

'I cracked, John,' Johnny said. 'Just fucking cracked.'

And every night since, Johnny said he remembered it. Feeling of shame. Physical cowardice. Haunted him.

I assured Johnny I wld have run too. Told him I had run many times. Told him about my two adult street fights; occasns when there was nowhere to run.

First time was w. m-class guy so knew it wldn't get too vicious even if lost. Tried to avoid. Never start fights but seem to attrct. He wanted fght. As soon as fght started knew I cld take him. Didn't hurt him. He conceded v. quick. He livng out m-c tough-guy fantasy.

Second guy v. diff. W-c vicious guy. Tattoos before tattoos fash. Just came up in empty street late at night when I was walking home half-wrckd. Started attacking. Backed me against wall: no escape. Thought: shit, gen. street fght. Felt my right leg shaking uncontroll. in fear. Knew if I lost he wld put boot in when I was on ground.

Hit him w. rt hand. Lucky punch. 99 times out of 100 wld not have connected w. same timing. Stood there watching him fall back on pavemnt, thinking Goddess Athena must be protecting me. Then he started getting up. I knew I had no more stom. for fght. Went up to him before he got up, grabbed his hair and lowered his head down on to pavement twice. Not too hard, but enough. Felt terrible tenderness doing it. Escaped.

When I got home I vomited. Not booze-sick, just sick at thought of what I had been involved in and what I had done.

After that, always ran. Knew how vicious it cld get. Ran. Told Johnny all this.

'You're right, John,' he said. 'It's the knowing that does it.'

Johnny not physical coward. Bravest person I've ever met. Once saw him take on two skins outside Harringtons in Epsom. Made them give up in end through sheer persistent evidence of his bravery. Never saw him lose. Just cracked. Something he'd seen or done in army or N. Ire. must have just emptied it out. Merely physical. Doesn't matter. Still there in spirit.

Me: def. physical coward. Now knew this from boxing and street fights.

I suppose trick is, like most m-c sneerers do, never to get involved in boxing or street fights and go through your whole life thinking you're really brave.

Also imparted this theory to J. He said it seemed true enough. Must be then.

After leaving boho bar Johnny took me on tour of San Fran. Saw desp. mugger area, the beaut. bridges stretching out in sunny haze and closed-off elevated freeway snapped in half like biscuit by 199? earthquake.

Johnny didn't use laden ashtray when driving about. Just tipped ash over whatever came to hand – seats, floor, dashboard. Followed his lead.

Brief stop for authent. takeaway Mexican. J. scoffed his down and ate half of mine too. Growing lad.

Drove me back to airport. Talked brief. by car door.

'I don't suppose you know what's happened to Lurch,' Johnny said.

'No. You?'

'No. Haven't seen him since that day on the Downs. Hope he's all right, though.'

'So do I,' I said.

Waved at car disappearing back towards San Fran. Johnny waved back with chunky fag-holding hand.

18

The Living Dead

Arrvd back London morning. Went straight to Oxfd St and bought another 470 Vegas tckt for four days' time. Only wanted one-way but 470 rtn cheaper. Stopped off in Ippo on way back. Last 4 grand instal. had arrvd in bank so nicked immed. in thick comb. wad of red fifties, twenties and tens. Now car-less and took extort. and unnec. cab home to cot. from Ippo instead of readily avail. local stn connctn.

Taking into acc. remaining est. 900 (pounds) from former 5,800 (dolls) wad, now est. am approx.

7,100 down.

Having nicked money, under 'Scenarios' clause (3) (p. 67), now have to write book, unless get surprise bg win enablng repaymnt of 12-G adv. Remaining. bettng strategy mst now be geared twards. long-shots in hope of surprise big win.

Will reserve 1,500 of remaing total 4,900 for lng-sht bets, leaving nicked 3,400 for new life. Ah, the new life.

For some time Rachel had been nagging me about 'getting in' more bets about 'footie' (still forgivable term in her case). Protest citing Barca v. Newcastle 250 ignored.

Next day was a Sat. and I decided to go down to Lond. again and see Chels. v. Newcastle – through inevit. Chels. vict. at least get meas. of revenge for cruel Barca 250 loss. Not that care of course within gamblr aesthtc.

Had lucky break on car front. Fri. eve. hd passing chat w. shear-holding beaut. Col.'s wife and mentioned sad loss of bth Dolly and W. htchbck. She said she and Col. were going to Spain for 3 wks next day and I cld borrow car, but wld I mind watering their plants while they were away?

Is Pope Cath.? Excptnl val. deal and bloody gd of beaut. Col.'s wife. W. shld take note.

Next morn. waved goodbye to Col. and wife in their sttn-bound minicab. Seized Col.'s immac. preserved htchbck and drove to garage shop to buy *Racing Post* thinking of surprse bg-win. horse bet that day as well.

Got bck, avoided disgusting fly-blown study and sat in relat. civilsd sttng-rm instead. No booze because of impend. Chels. drive and strict non-d.d. rule.

Opened *Post* and realised I was bored w. daily purist thorough exam. of form pages. Hd noticed excllnt strike-rate of Champ. Tipster Henry Rix and reflectd tht he ws not smug git after all, but actlly comrade in subsidiary war – to silent war – vs greedy bookies.

Decided I might as well just go w. Henry Rix's three selections that day, in singles, doubles and treble w. perhaps overall est. outlay of 300. Nothing extravag. Plus 100 treb. on Chels. vict. w. two other nag team victs.

Tght-bstd bookies won't let you bet singls on domest. foot. excpt when live on bldy Sky. Can't do tht on princip., obv.

Rang Walt. to say I ws. back and hear what he was tipping and made mistake of mentng H. Rix's excllnt strk-rte.

'Henry Rix, John?' W. said in *v*. indig. tone w. def. signs of anger. 'Well, if you're going to go with Henry Rix you can forget it. Fucking Henry Rix, John . . . ?'

Made hasty fake bcktrck in manner tht wld assure W. that I thght H. Rix a complet. nag just like he did.

For a moment reflected W. might be beset by touching fit of jealousy but then reasoned that almst cert. it was just he gen. believed tht any tipster apart fr. him was indeed complet. fucking nag.

'Shame about that Golota,' W. said. 'Didn't show anything. I had two hundred and seventy-four quid on.'

Odd figure either denoted extrem. diff. w. wch W. had assembled money for Golot. bet or nec. fraction of magical round sum tht wld have been collectd if Golot. won. Suspected former.

'Yeah, sorry about that, Walter,' I said.

'Doesn't matter, only two hundred and seventy-four,' W. said w./i. true gamblr aesthtc.

Felt oblig. to inform W. about sudden Lew.-vict. premontn.

'Oh, thanks John,' W. said coldly. 'You could have rung me.'

'I know, sorry. I was just walking up the Strip lumping all these bets on and I just forg . . .'

Jesus shit, let slip about Vegas. There was a pause.

Walter said hollowly, 'You mean you went to Vegas, not Atlantic City?'

'Yes. I did. I . . .'

'Well, in that case, John, I never want to fucking see you again.'

Didn't want to not see W. again, despite his horrendous faults, and mine. Nevertheless, felt my own anger rising.

A blazing bust-up ensued, w. W. citing great Vegas betrayal and me citing htchbck radiator issue, Coastal Bluff 750 immoralty and selfish unshared laying of Bosra Sham. Knew my betrayal was prob. the greater but he started it . . .

'If you want people to be sincere and generous towards you,' I told W., 'you should try being more sincere and generous towards them.'

Silence on W.'s mobile. Knew instinctvly I had wounded him. Surprised. Thought he was wound-proof.

W.'s voice came back on the line, emotion-cracked. Trying to hide it but it was def. there.

'John, I've known you a long time . . . it's a fucking shame it has to end like this . . .'

Never knew W. cld bleed outside. Thought he only bled inside, if at all. Felt bad, v. bad. Bleeding myself.

'I'm sorry, Walter.'

A pause.

'I'm sorry too, John.'

Heard a reassuring snigger. 'But I still don't want to fucking see you again.' Funny, W., hilar . . .

Discussed bets. Outlined strateg. for at least 500 long-shot lump-on. After respec. period of norm. bet discssn, put phone down.

Drove down to Chels. Game totally sold out. Bought extort. ticket for 80 from tout but w. my wad no prob.

Before going in Stam. Brdg. went to Fulham Broadway bettng shop and put on 100 Chels. treb. and 300 Henry Rix singls, doubs and trebs.

Walked in Stam. Brdg. Immed. bad vibe. Sneering English Gdfll. 'security' doing searches instead of police. Stan wld have hd no chance gttng flask in, let alone celery. No doubt got extens. c.c.-TV cams as well in case searches fail.

Once past searches, walked down new outer stadium walkway. Disoriented. Christ, cldn't even tell wch end old Shed End used to be. Ascended to seat. Am only one in row without extort. Chels. replic. shirt on. Same haircuts, too. Mandatory single ear-rings. Bad-cutter shaven cuts, not like FranCo's. Reminds me, must get another suedehead before set out again for Vegas and new life.

Behind in stand, extens. themed crap burger outlts and multi-snack area, enthus. popultd by Chels. fans all in replic. shrts, some in baseball caps over shaven skulls. Don't realise. Coverted w/o knowing. Living dead.

Terrible realisation: Stmfd Brdg. had become enem. terr.

Game started. Ian Rush was playing up front for Newc.
Good to see Rushie. Unfortntly for him, pace complet.
gone. No legs. Hope he scores. Obv. didn't air this thought
to living dead around me.

Living dead maintained hoarse cold vicious shouts
throughout game. Not just pref. win: MUST WIN. WE
MUST WIN. Uniform. Tried to suck something in.
Nothing there. Just coldness of living dead and their rthlss
exploitatn. by cocky overseeing enem. strategists.

Can't go for own reasons any more. Never go again. Just
follw results like Stanley. Watch on non-Sky TV when
occas. poss.

Chels. scored. Brave header by v. useful hard Uruguayan
interntnl. Leapt up but no one to dance with. Living dead
celebrated but soon not imprssd. Wanted two.

Thought about leaving early. No. Protocol. Always
scorned leaving-early brigade. Prags.

Final whistle blew. 1-0. Heard on tannoy tht nag teams
in 100 treb. hd lost. Only 100. Legged it out and bck down
to Ful. Broad. bttng shop. One of H. Rix singls hd pissed
home. Other two lost. About 120 rtn. on bet. Forgot noble
beast's name as soon as handed over slip for 120 rtn at
counter.

Gettng bored of all the names. Not imp. anyway.
Allotted names. Horse slavery. Accomplice if you back 'em,
except for My Emma of course (despite Arc loss).

Just stuffing 120 into jack. pock. w. other wad when man
bumped into me and approx. half entire wad spilled
fluttering down on to crowded bookie's floor in red fifties,
twenties and tens just as living dead were steaming in.

Guy about my age helped me pick it up rapido. Chels.
fan but not wearing replic. shrt, just carrying rolled-up
programme.

Thanks, comrade. Still a few of us left. For instant
considrd tipping him extravag. but then obv. realised not in

America and tht wld hve been both inappropriate and tasteless.

Walked back up New King's Rd. On crest of road saw two living dead in replic. shrts & b-bll caps w. a small boy, obv. one of them's son. Tho' the boy hd on replic. shrt and mandtry shaven skull, he was clearly still alive.

And as I walked past, I felt a terrible outpouring of protective sadness for this child, being born into *this*.

Almost stopped and patted the boy's head, but decided not to: one of living dead looked a bit snappy, and I didn't want another street-fght. So I walked on to the Col.'s immac. presvrd htchbck and drove back to Suff.

On the Mon. rang Rachel to inform her of 'footie' action and Lew.-vict. lump-on, expecting her to be elated. She seemed thoroughly unimpressed, but I sensed it was for a mysterious and unconnected reason.

'Have I done something?' I said finally.

'Yes,' Rach. said.

'What?'

'You're overdrawn on the twelve-thousand account,' she informed icily.

'What?'

Shit, yes, the Arc and Nwmkt cheques I gave to W. before going to Vegas. Forgot about those.

Felt juvenile and wholly incorrect fleetng sense of joy at havng got 12-G acc. overdrawn. Even I hdn't thght cld manage that.

'How much?' I said.

'£687,' R. said.

'I'll go and put it back now.'

'OK, bye then.'

Bad breach of gd-faith clause (p. 67). Peeled off notes, put in shrt pock., got in Col.'s car and drove down to bank in Ippo immed. to ward off inev. of forgetting later. Handed over notes. Took approx. 1½ hrs.

This meant now only had 3,213 w. wch to start new life, not counting dimin. orig. 1,500 reserved for surprse bg-win bets. Still, 3,213 a lot more than most peop. have when they start new lives in Vegas.

Came back and phone ws ringing: Rach. Told her I'd paid back money. She obv. astonished and v. impressed.

'Sorry. Sorry . . .'

Invited me to go to Nwmkt meeting w. her next day. Time we met. Go tonight, stay in nice hotel, visit gallops I'd talked about, then go to races. All expens. paid by Yell. Jer. excpt bet money. Obv., said yes immed.

Got bck in Col.'s car, drove to extort. hotel outside Nwmkt, parked amid prag. top-of-range new cars and booked in. Got there before Rach. Went brief. to extort. room – small, overheatd, who cares – and thence to bar where started reading papers amid framed prints of noble beasts while drinking not-bad near-deluxe modl. gin/ton. double.

Pick up my old paper first. No column this week by tolerance-fatigued Tom Layburn: ' . . . *is on holiday*', paper informs. Lucky Tom.

Went to obits. First obit.: Tony Bamber. Can't believe it. Sit staring at Tony's black-and-white silvery features and soft hands. Cancer, obit. says. Only 61. From way unsigned obit. written, think I recog. style of Harry Webb the sportswriter from legen. '76 Ali–Spinks N.O. bender. V. gd obit. Did Tony justice.

Did I really betray Tony with Angela? Dunno. Complicated one.

Rifle though other papers to see if any further Tony obits. None. Bastards. True newspaperman. He was.

Order second G & T, having wiped away tears. Tipped rest back. Hotel barman mistook red tear imprints in eyes for complet. wreckdnss and poured me second drink warily.

Later Rach. arrvd. Complet. inacc. telephone imaging: blonde, small to med., soft edges, no jackboots. Perfectly acceptable travelling companion in white-rasta saloon (if hd one).

Managed to remain respec' and not gt wrckd thr-out ave. extort. dinner. During dinn. R. produced photo-proof of 12-G bk jacket cover. Must be well into the writing, aren't you, John? 'Course, 'course, said nonch.

Stared thoughtflly at bk cov. Looked OK. My only suggestion – tentative – was havng a fag somewhere on cov., y'know, sort of smouldering there. Or maybe a butt? Don't think R. too impressed by my sugg.

Next morn., get up at unthink. hr to go and see gallops.

Wandered round centre of gallops in beaut. golden mist w. Rach. Past tried to come back but didn't let it. Don't need. Got future.

Went to races. Hd done detailed exam. of *Post* thru rest of morning in order cld exhib. impress. knowldge to R.

R. wanted to go Members. Tie-only. Hd to buy excptn.-val. £5 Nwmkt tie at Members' ticket office.

Fancied lng-sht noble beast in last race. Only had 500 wad w. me. Orig. plan to put almost entire wad on last race. In event, frittrd virt. all wad on earlier races. Only had enough left for 20 e-w. Came second. Still won over 100.

Between races, went to various racecourse bars w. R. Drank surpris. not-bad crisp white. Ask for glass and you get small airline-style bott. Val., must say.

R. got sweetly excited and distraught during passing races and I tried to join in as much as poss.

Didn't work. R. clever. Knew fake.

'You don't care if they win or lose, do you, John?' she said.

Protested obv.

Half-way thru, ws sitting in bar when Rach. said breezily, 'Have you heard about Tom Layburn?'

'No,' I said, v. much all ears.

'Hospital. Intensive care. Pneumonia and liver failure. Apparently when he woke up they said, "We're just going to administer some drugs, Mr Layburn."'

'Jesus shit,' I mumbled.

R. went on, 'And Tom heard the word "drugs" and thought it must be the police and said, "But I haven't taken any!"'

R. laughed.

'You think that's funny, do you?' I said. Just came out. Knew it was too New Brut. but sod it, he's a comrade, Tom Layburn.

Thought, Christ, they're dropping like flies: Stanley, Tony Bamber and now Layburn. Flanks threadbare, totally exposed to enem.

'Oh, I'm sorry,' Rach. said. 'I know it's not funny. It was crass of me to make a joke of it.'

Assured R. it was my fault and confidntly tipped her noble beast for next race. Came nowhere. Don't think she hd sniff of winner all day.

Left R. at door of minicab. Retnd cot. and packd bag for Veg. Played 'Nothing Lasts Forver' by Echo & Bunnymen on knackered tape-recorder all eve. drinkg Cubas.

Cld. have been written for me, that song, or Tony. Exact fit. Unrequited love. With rider in my case of course tht love was requited.

Took Cromb., 'Nothing Lasts Forever' tape, green suit & electrc typewriter w. me.

19

Among Fallen Shields

V. unfort. incident at Heathrow. Well, thought was v. unfort. when incident started. Was already in semi-floating state in x-ray handbaggage queue when spotted Angela approx. 10 yards away in adjacent queue w. balding midget type, obv. husband, who was loading Ang. vanity cases on to x-ray w. some diffclty.

Christ, Ang. must be 40 now. She had slight new image change w. prev. immaclcy. now overlaid w. def. hint of loucheness if in Jackie Collins sort of way. From her expens. Jack. Coll. outfit cld. tell the midget hd. plenty of dough. Or maybe Ang. herself now best-selling novelst.? Busnsswomn.? Doubtful.

My eyes met Ang.'s but we both pretnded. they hadn't. Thought: I know I wanted the past to come back, but not this bldy. much.

Even so, felt something else: in snatched glance, flow of immutable bond. Didn't want it, but it was there. Fusion of you and those you have slept with. An . . . eternal fondness. Shit, surprising. Ang. . . . Probably hates me. No, not prob.: cert.

Went through x-ray, passport areas and lingered in obscure parts of terminal buildng. until coast seemed clear.

After coast clear, wandered into deluxe but extort. duty-free zone to get fags and tcy to resume float. Was at check-out just starting to resume when sensed Ang. hovering; cld. smell her nice Jack. Coll. smell, five feet? No escape. She meant to be there. Brave of her.

'Hello John.'

'Oh . . . Christ, Angela!'

While shuffling about, noticed the midget at adjacent check-out w. fag boxes, perfume etc.

Said, 'Is that your . . .'

'Yes, husband,' Ang. said in auld Lincoln tones. 'His name's Jeremy.'

Jeremy eh. Well he can't help it.

'I suppose he's loaded, then,' I added, thoughtless.

'That's a bit forward, isn't it Jonno?'

Oh my God . . . my name on her lips . . . cruel refractive . . . Christmas light . . .

'But yes he is actually,' Ang. confirmed.

I mentioned Tony's name. 'Suppose you've heard.'

'About him leaving the paper?' Ang. said v. Jack. Coll. w. certain hauteur. 'Oh God Jonno, that was ages ago. And now he's left I can safely say . . .'

No, no, not leaving bldy. paper. Bldy. leaving the world. Tried to get this out but cldn't. Ang. overrode.

'. . . safely say I never liked him anyway.'

'Didn't you?'

'In fact I hated him.'

What?

'He gave me the creeps, Tony, with all his, y'know, pervy ways. I can say that now.'

Jesus shit. Would you ever . . .

In circmstncs., decided not to tell Ang. about Tony copping it. Saw low-slung Jeremy approaching grinning from check-out zone. We parted. I shook her hand. She kissed me on the cheek. During, felt flow of immutable bond again in both right palm and left gum.

Legged it last call to depart. gate and sat in arid plane w. mainly US fellow travellers, mostly pens., in rear crash-friendly sectn. where smoking used to be. Crafty. Enemy must still put obv. smokr. comrades there even though they've banned fags.

During take-off, tried to develop immut.-bond theory based on rueful idea tht .shld. have slept with more people. Not just in Britain, but in var. countries round globe. Worldwide network of imut. bonds. Mass fusion. Permanent float wherever you were.

Abandoned rueful theory after take-off when first trolley came round. Realized theory was both selfish and intellect. irrelevent since prob. wld. have slept w. more people anyway if hd. hd. the chance. Thought, how many has it been anyway? 35, 40? All right, 10? Looked around at US pens. Nothing to the Americans, 10. They get up to 30, 35, and they're just warming up, women as well as men. Amazing combo, the yanks. Puritan nymphos.

From trolley put back series of Cointeaus and crap red wines, my normal plane drinks. Slept.

Arrvd Vegas early aft. Bookd in Aladd. Drove around for a bit in cab scanning prospective residences. Walked up and down Strip. While walking down, ran into old mucker from boxing days called Frank Dean. Rich cockney. Lives Florida, Vegas and Lond. Invlvd. boxing but made money elsewhere. Sort of Ronnie from Cancún but w. ultra brains. Pretends he hasn't got them. Shields brains. Good move.

Always liked Frank. As w. Walt., know tht despite horror of his var. professions there is good in him.

Walked into Frank's Caes. Pal. suite. He always stays there.

'You should have seen this place last night,' Frank says. 'Condoms all over the floor. I had two in.'

'How do you pull them, Frank?' I say.

'Just offer 'em five hundred bucks, normally. You can do that sort of thing over here.'

Frank suggests game of pool at place he knows off Strip. Before doing so, informs me he has discovered cocaine at age of 41. Coke-fuelled often hilar. anecdotes spew out of his mouth. Offers me some from lavish stash. Decline. Cld do w. a drink, tho'.

Play pool w. Frank in nice sun-dappled gen. *Cheers*-style diner off Strip. Good to be in natural light instead of blacked-out casinos. Frank annihilates me 5-1, playing at frenetic Jimmy White Whirlwind pace. Hd proposed bets on games to Frank as well, at 1-1. He declined. Knew he cld take me. Cld easily have hustled me out of entire wad but just played straight-up. Nice guy.

Said goodbye to Frank and felt even logist. uneasiness about new Vegas life evaporating. Envisaged lazy Sunday aftns playing pool w. Frank in diner while Carol lounges on corner stool in her perfect way willing me on. Have to improve pool game.

Went back to Aladd. Was going to buy newspapers but thought, no. No need. Instead read fake gold-leaf Bible from drawer by bed. Ah yes, Revelation. The old Alpha and Omega, eh. Best-written vision of Apocalypse ever. Felt great afterwards.

Already realised that since Carol hadn't given me numbers, had to make nec. visit to horrific *Cowgirls 2*. Turned up around 10 that nght, breezed past wld-be Goodflla w. air of someone not part of scene. Own reasons, man.

Carrying in pock. copy of *Road Star* again inc. Aladd. envel. w. 'Kowloon Train' inside. Still hadn't given. As well as three minitre. Bacard. botts, also had in pock. 'Nothing Lasts Forever' Echo tape.

Had decided to give to Carol in hope tht she wld use to dance to instead of Led Zep and wld thus be more approp. linked to me every time she danced.

Turned left away from sex suprmkt area into tab.-dncg zone. Cldn't see Carol. No prob. Sat down, ordered Coke and poured Bacard. refill into Coke in practised casual manner.

Saw Brooklyn going past.

Said, 'Hello, Brooklyn.'

'How did you know my name?' Brooklyn said w. gen. appreciation.

You told me last week, babe.

In fact, shrugged rather awkwardly.

Brooklyn sat down. I ordered her a few Cokes, topped them up w. Bacard. – w. her connivance – and she drank them down w. customary zeal.

In course of this I gave Brook. abridged versn of Carol story and how far back we went; as far back as last week in enem.-held Hard Rock.

Brook. was awe-struck.

'You mean *you* saw Carol in the Hard Rock? You met her *out of here*? You know, normally that *never* happens.'

I shrugged w. air of hombre to whom these miracles do happen habitually.

Brook. took this as cue to tell me all about her fam. in actual Brooklyn and how she was hoping to move to Amsterdam because a *Cowgirls* outlet was opening there and *everyone* wanted to go.

About four-fifths thru this info Carol came up in pink dress and hovered behind table looking cross. Immed. sense tht crossness had nothing to do w. petty jeal. like before and was serious shit but tried to pretend was former, wishing Brook. wld go.

Eventlly Brook. went and I was left w. Carol glowering at me.

'I thought I told you never to come in here, John,' she said.

'I know,' I said. 'But you never rang to give me the numbers.'

'I know,' Carol said. Hard. Putting it on a bit but still hard. Shit, serious shit. Probly over. Why? Mentioned afternoon at Hard Rock as groped for something to say.

'You mean when you got me drunk?' Carol said.

'I didn't get you drunk.'

True statement. Hd noticed at time that she hadn't touched a drop of her white.

'OK, you didn't get me drunk.' Obv. this admissn hd no bearing on central thrust.

'I don't drink any more, John,' she went on. Informed me she had found her real Indian father. He bad sick w. booze. Now she had Indian name as well as Carol. Sounded like 'Raw Knee'.

'What do I call you, Miss Knee?' Stupid and inapprop., obv.

Still got small laugh out of Carol wch she tried to suppress. Told me it was one word. Even spelt it out. R-A-W-N-E-E.

Carol resumed hard air and said, 'You told Brooklyn we went to the Hard Rock, didn't you?'

Nodded.

'You know that could lose me my job, John.'

Good. No, not good really.

'If Brooklyn tells anyone I'm going to say you paid me a hundred dollars to see me at the Hard Rock and I shouldn't have done it. But at least I'll keep my job.'

No point arguing. Too humil. Obv., she had decided. In this sitn better off walking out. Got up to walk out.

She put hand on my arm. Must resist. No-win sitn.

Said, 'It's all right, Carol. I understand.'

Carol said, 'Give me twenty bucks.'

Said, 'What?'

'Just give me the goddam twenty bucks, John!'

Noticed young-crone real supervisor was observing at fairly close range. Gave Carol the twenty bucks.

Carol marched me back into fant. black-curtained chrome-hung cubicle. My heart felt heavy like a bad stone, whatever explantn wld now be given.

Horrible in cubicle. No space. Just the flapping fake leather and the rigid chrome.

'At least we can talk in here until the end of the song,' Carol said. 'I have to tell you something.'

Ah, so that's how they measure length of spcl dnces, is it? Songs. Bloody lottery. No val.

But had to make most of song. Had to know cruel details. Asked Carol if she had boyfriend, husband, honestly.

She nodded.

'He's the father of my child,' she said. 'That's what I had to tell you, John.'

A daughter. Three years old. I told her I was pleased for both of them, as well as being heart-broken, obv.

'Anyone I know?' I said of the father; meant rhetorically, sad joke.

'No, he's Australian,' Carol said. 'But he drinks too much beer just like you do.'

Thought: my darling, I have moved on considerably from beer.

Carol went on, 'And I suppose maybe he reminded me a little of you . . .'

Looked down. Don't want to hear this. Too bad.

I said, 'Carol, can I ask you something?'

She said yes with her beaut. lips that I no longer cld kiss.

'What the hell happened in Cancún the weekend before I came?'

'Oh, that. I guess I was just the weekend whore,' Carol said.

'Not with Ronnie.'

'Yes and Ronnie too.'

'Shit, fuckers.' Cldn't control anger. I punched a side of the leather cubicle and hit chrome. One knuckle started to bleed.

'Don't swear so much, John,' Carol said. 'They're really strict about that.'

Heard a new song starting up. Pointed this out to Carol w. a wordless signal of finger towards ceiling.

She noticed my hand was bleeding and reached out for it, but I withdrew. Put a tissue round it from green-suit pock.

Shrugged.

Said, 'Oh and I brought you something.'

Delved into jack. pock. and found several potential gifts: *Road Star*, 'Kowloon Train' poem and also tape of 'Nothing Lasts Forever' by Echo. Can't give her all of those in this sitn. Embarr. Took out Echo tape and handed it over.

'God! I love Echo and the Bunnymen,' Carol said.

Yeah, but not until they had recent belatd US hit. I was there sixteen yrs ago, sunshine.

Got up to go.

Added, 'Thought you might like to dance to it instead of that terrible Led Zep.'

Carol said, 'You know, Led Zep are really cool to like now. It's not like it was in Greece.'

Thought, Christ, so this is how it ends: w. a debate about Led Zep.

I got up w. real move to go. Carol put a hand round my waist but I brushed it away. Cld feel the still overriding strength in her hand. She still wanted me to go. I hoped it was painful for her, but that is what she wanted.

She quickly drew back curtain and scanned for young-crone supervisor, but no sign thankfully. I knew it was about to end w. no come-back but wanted to linger as long as poss. without humil.

Carol said, 'That's why we went to that place last week. You know, that apartment? I didn't want to go to your hotel in case I saw all your things. If I saw your things some of them might have reminded me and that's why I didn't go there.'

The second song ended and I said goodbye to Carol. We

hugged and I felt the contours of her fingers on my back for the last time.

Never really knew her. Even at start. Just expats thrown togeth. Tot. incompat. in fct. Just love. Why did I have to fall in lve w. tab.-dncr? Fuck it . . . oh Jesus . . .

And the last time in Vegas cabana – act of kindness? Women are capable of such kindness. Dunno . . .

I walked twrds exit passng Brook. bending down in designtd sectn. She looked up smiling, shade rueful from bendng-dwn pstn. Said, 'Hi, John,' and gave lttle wave w. one hand, almst overbalancng. Behind, two prag. punters – smug young m-c *couple* – examing Brook. genit. w. lasciv. exprtise.

Christ. Amazing. Whole prag. world become like Stuart and Julian except as legit. *adults.*

Went past would-be Goodfella at entrnce and he said, 'See you again, man.' Told him to fuck off.

Luckily there was a cab outside so I got in before wld-be Goodll. cld react and talked cricket with the Pakistani cab driver all the way back to the Aladd.

In the Aladd. felt cruel echo of swimming-in-air wreckd, but this time frozen in air, hanging, like doomed poised bung. jumper over canyon. Feared death for the first time. Cldn't. sleep. Thght., if I go to sleep I will die. Then I saw it there below, in the canyon, a great expanse of ancient tombs, in a sun-lit landscape, and suddenly I didn't fear it anymore. So before sleep came I got up hurriedly, walkd. out again and went to sev. casinos instead.

Changed my new-life money into dolls. Went to Caesar's Pal. in trance and did two 10 × 100-chip 13-Black runs w/o hitting. Black prophet guy wasn't there. Got two gay croupiers who wanted me to lose. Cld tell.

Wandered out and got cab to new off-Strip casino. Drank wine and playd bad incorrect b-j but won a bit even tho' noticed House were using tot. extort. *seven*-deck shoot. Crd-counting virt. imposs. even if was prof. gmblr attritnl type.

Had read somewhere tht instead of banning them, casinos now put top prof. gamblr crd-counting attrtnl b-j players on security pay-roll. Typical enem. move. Always knew prof. gamblrs were 9–5ers.

Walked over to roulette wheel. Only other person there was another young Goodflla type. Looked gen. Ital.-American at least. He was obv. losing badly and his skin showed how bad he felt.

Put 100 chip down on 13 Black. Goodfll. put chip on 13 Black too. Came up.

Left chip on 13 Black and put another on 27 Red. Again Goodfll. went in on my numbers w. 100s of own. 27 Red came up. Each just made 7,200 (dolls) on two spins of wheel.

Whooping by Goodfll. and puts palms out for me to slap. Oblige. He's like a big puppy.

In rare moment of rationality pick up chips and make to walk away fr. table. Goodfll. puts arm on my shoulder in panic.

'Man, you can't go now!' he says.

Mumble something.

'No, man, you bring me luck, man!' Goodfll. pleads.

Put chips back down on table. Thought, two more wins and I'll be able to pay 12-G adv. back. Spent next twenty mins putting 200 chips each spin on 13 Black, 27 Red and Zero. None came up once. I lost 7,200 plus further 1,300. Goodfll. lost more. Left him there, silent and destroyed.

They shldn't let people like that into casinos.

Carried on gambling and losing for next two hrs. Checked myself when realised down to approx. last 700 (pounds) of entire 12-G wad, or

11,300 down.

Must reserve 500 at all costs for final lump-on surprse bg win.

Now realise am in serious trouble. Rtn 470 flght doesn't go for six days. At least I got rtn flght. Shit! Hope it rains in Eng. and Col. wife's flowers are OK.

Can't afford Aladd. Go back to Aladd., check out, get cab and book into $80-week motel way off Strip. Ground-floor room w. reinforced anti-mugger steel door and window looking out on to desolate wino car park.

Stay there five days. Mainly sleep. Can't afford eat. Barely afford booze and fags. During day sometimes walk up to nice fam. suprmkt and wander round aisles sucking in atmos. w/o buying anything.

On sixth day check out and am walking w. bag near Hard Rock back to Strip about 1 p.m. when see Brooklyn looming up on pavement looking rather neo-Carol pretty.

'Hello, Brooklyn,' I say as she passes.

She stops and says, 'Oh my God, how did you know my name?

Scrutinises my face brief. and obv. has distant recollctn.

'Oh, *hi*. It's . . .

'John.'

'*Hi*, John.'

After six-day motel fast, reckon I still have 100 (pounds) to spare before vital bg-win lump-on money. Might as well spend it. Ask Brook. if she wants drink. Brook. doesn't refuse drinks.

'Sure, John,' she says.

Walk into Hard Rock. Almost exact same routine unfolds. Try to avoid subjct of C. but Brook. obv. great C. worshipper and delghtd to be follwng in her Hard Rock footsteps.

Theme-pk restrnt, untouched food. As well as tarot cards, Brook. even talks about reincarnation. Must have got that off C. Dunno, tho'. Everyone seems to be talking about reinc. these days. Must be fear of great 2028 asteroid.

Found *Road Star* in pock. Showed Brook. Shameless. She dlghtd as she examnd. Told her she cld keep it. Didn't give her 'Kowloon Train', tho'. Send tht to toothless Shane.

'I'm so lucky,' Brook. reflected. 'Everywhere I go I meet these influential people.

'Influential', eh? New one. Brook. tells me again about going to new Amsterdam *Cowgirls*.

'How old are you, John?' she adds.

'Twenty-nine,' I lie.

'You know that's funny, because in your book . . . *Rod Star?*'

Christ, cldn't make it up.

'*Road*,' I corrected.

'In your book it says here you were born in 1964 and that makes you . . .'

'Yeah, yeah, I know, thirty-three. Sorry, Brooklyn.'

'It's OK.'

Bloody hell. Clever as well.

Thence to bar. Same barman. Exact. same scene excpt for absence of Brit-poppers and I was drinking Cubas instead of wine. Brook. drnkg Cubas too and both chaining fags. W. each Cuba, Brook. gttng. more and more attrctv. Sense recip., but admitt. gttng wrckd in terrible *déjà-vu* thin light.

Brook. hovered near my face in wht wrckdly seemed to me clear invit. to kiss. Kissed her. She responded. Jesus, in a restaurant again. Her mouth tasted of spearmint chewing-gum.

'You know, I'm really attracted to you, John,' Brook. said after kiss.

'I'm really attracted to you too, Brooklyn,' I reciprctd.

Finished drinks and walked out in glare across Hard Rock car pk towards cab rank w. my arm round her waist. Solid feel, Brook. Build 'em strong in actual Brook.

Shameless snogging at cab rank. Stirred up fake love feeling. I will fake love anyone who fake loves me.

Brief. imagined future life w. Brook. back in Suff. Walks in Dawson's Wood, perhaps running into the Col. and beaut. wife. 'Oh hello, Brooklyn my dear,' Col.'s beaut. wife says as we stand beneath green canopied trees.

No, cldn't really see it.

Just as well I cldn't because then Brook. says sweetly, 'John, you know that hundred dollars you paid Carol to go to the Hard Rock? Do I get a hundred dollars too?'

'Haven't got it on me, Brooklyn,' I say.

'Yes you do,' Brook. says, w. eagle-eyed glance at remains of annihltd wad in my shrt pock. Peeled her off a 100 (dolls) note.

She gave me phone nos. Two. One a mobile. Took ages for her to write down on scrap of paper in childish neat hndwrtng. Wondered if they were real? Wldn't ring 'em anyway. Brooklyn got in cab, waving and blowing me kisses. Watched her go.

Ah, life: the things it throws up.

At Vegas airport termnl sat drinking Cubas in bar thinking about Carol's conversion from gen. lost romant. to workable semi-prag. Not unusual conversion. Still bloody diff. to effect. Wish cld do myself sometimes. Well done, Carol. Really pleased for you.

Toasted Carol's conversion in all termnls and flghts from Vegas bck to Lond.

Arrvd back Suff. late aftn next day. Felt v. bad phys. Knew hd crossed line. Hd to stop off at local stn bogs for severe vom. and dia. Staggered out past still padlocked abandnd bike. Rlly mst collect.

Mst eat. Too far fr. emerg. burgr joint. Went to meglo butcher and bght beef for Greek *stifado* stew. Bought onions and other ingred. Also matrl for immac. *meze* tray. Might do trick. Got to try get down.

Went back cott. and bloody walking-carpet straggly dog came trotting up on doorstep. Told it to piss off. Didn't. Came in w. me instead. Too weak to argue. Stood lookng at me in kitchen w. tongue hanging out. S'ppose you want some food. What is it you give dogs? Dog food, isn't it? No chance in here, son. Think it's a girl actually. Long-range examin. of undercarriage. Yes. Def. girl dog, I think.

Went to cupboard and gave her packet of ridged sour-cream-and-chive lux. crisps instead. Lapped 'em up on floor. And licked floor afterwds. Incred. May have underestimtd dogs. Cld be val.

Sat bowed on stool by stove making *stifado*. Looked great. Sauce just right constit. Assembled immac. *meze* tray. Took both to sttng-rm. Cldn't get one mouthful down. Dog follwd me in. Started chucking chunks of *stifado* on ash-covered stone fireplace hearth for dog. Lapped all up. And ashes.

Thought of name for dog: Molly. Unorig., but cldn't expect to expend val. energy thinking up orig. dog names in my condtn. Just thought of Dolly and went thru alphabet.

Molly started scratching at front door so let her out. Around 2 a.m. after watching crap-TV, I gamely tried to get down final glass of Cava and erupted w. v. v. bad vom. Crawled up to starry chamber, lay on bed and tried to brazen out. Imposs. Vom. on bed. Jesus shit! Blood. Blood in vom. on white sheets.

Staggd to bthrm. Whole bott.-sized gush of blood came out, like bott. of noble shrapnlld Leb. Musar being poured. Slightly baked colour, tho'. Musar bott. left out in Med. sun.

Now gttng ser. worried. Thght, what a waste. Not even in love w. the bottle like they say you're suppsd to be. Always been more in love w. cert. people than the bott. Just habitual, really. Occuptnl haz., temptn of empty room combined w. natural inclin. twrds and liking for booze.

Cld ring Marls. and gt him out but cldn't face it. Drive to Ippo hosp. instead. Got yellow towel for poss. vom. en route and tk Noel Edmonds bott. h.-mde cherry brandy for company. Obv. won't drink, even me. Managd to chain few fags down drvng.

Blood-vom. on Casualty floor. Admttd immed.

Exmnd by ultra-prag. young late 20s male doc. wearing disgust. cornish-pasty shoes. Still told him exact. detls of booze intake. Honesty best pol. w. docs., howev. prag.

Doc. examnd my face w. profess. interest and said, 'Yes, and I see you've got all these blemishes. Do you always have those?'

Blemishes! Moi! I *don't* think so, doc.

Haven't looked in mirror for some time. Shit, must be true.

He picked up phone. Rang internal.

'Oh, hello, Giles,' he said. 'Sending a long-term alcoholic up to your ward. Shld be wending its way up there shortly.'

Sorry? 'It'. Excuse me, doc, but I am here within hearing. I am flesh and blood. Mentally if not physically. Equal curing rights, man.

Arsehole. 'Specially w. shoes like those.

No one ever called me tht before. Not even Marls.

Woke up next morning having stomach examnd by beaut. young femle doc. w. pure face and innocnt clean-smelling hair. Tried to read her name from tag but it was pinned on her white coat rght on top of a gntly heavng. breast so thght impolite to look.

Anyway, immed. recognsd her as the Goddess Athena in one of her guises.

She did exact. same routine on stom. as Marls. but it was more like a soul massage, really.

Thght about surprs. bg-win lmp-on bets to avoid embarr. arousal.

She told me I was going into endoscopy next day a.m.

Gullet job. Have to stay in till after tht at least. Prob. more.

Took news casually and smiled. Do anything the Goddss Ath. says, even endosc.

Lay all day in sunlit ward listening to imag. convos.

Heard Jimmy White, Gary Glitter and Max Bygraves discussing booze, gambling and torch songs.

Gary said: 'One night I just lay down in the kitchen and stayed there for five days, covered in my own filth. Couldn't get up. That's when it happened. After that. I knew it couldn't get worse.'

Jimmy said: 'Bit early in the day for that, isn't it? I've been there a few times with the old booze, you know. AA and all that. And GA, Gamblers Anonymous. I done the lot. I've been very irresponsible with money. I basically spunked it. At lightning speed.'

And then Max Bygraves said: 'When I was ten I used to sing to the men in our flat by the Rotherhithe tunnel. We used to swim in the Thames. Terrible rats. They couldn't afford to go out, the men. They had a crate of beer. The beer was a lot darker and stronger then. It was black; stout. I found out the songs that would get to them. They liked the tear-jerkers best. You couldn't go wrong with a torch song like:

> *Don't know why*
> *There's no clouds up in the sky*
> *Stormy Weather.*

Jimmy White and Gary Glitter nodded.

The night was coming in the ward. I knew the jitters would too. Thght maybe I cld brazen out till the crying dawn. Fell asleep sometime in the early hours.

When I woke up, it was still night and the Fonze was leaning by the beaut. illumin. fridge door wch. stood ajar at the end of the ward filled with botts of G. Pils. Excllnt.

Hadn't noticed that before. I got up and walked towards it. Saw Brooklyn was standing by the Fonze w. her arm round him. Bit taken aback but because it was the Fonze, I didn't mind.

'Hi, Fonze,' I said, reaching for the fridge door.

'Hey-y-y, John,' the Fonze said w. his trademark low-slung dble thumbs-up. Brooklyn said 'Hi' too. It was only then that I smelled the terrible waft of his breath, and knew. Snakes began tumbling writhing out of the fridge all over me. They were big ones too.

Desperately I searched for unvarnished wood in the ward to get rid of the scheming Vonze. Reached grasping for the window frames, but they were metal. Finally found some unvarn. by crawling underneath the ward Sister's desk at the other end of the ward.

It was there an old English-crone nurse found me and woke me up. I crawled out from under the desk. She led me back by my arm.

'Now what are we doing up at this hour?' she said as we walked.

'Let's put you back in your nice, warm bed, shall we?'

Lucky she woke me up. Bldy. good of her. Hd good feelng towards this Eng. crone.

Morning came and somehow I must have managed to leave the hosp. Cldn't remember the exact details. I noticed my plastic hosp. tag was still on my wrist. Fingers trembling slightly on steering wheel of the Col.'s immac. preservd htchbck. Shit, rlly mst get something down. Emerg. burger jt?

I was just arriving at the pond in the fields. On the way, I hd picked up a kiddies' fishing set fr. shop in town. Embarr., but only thing avail. Also no real bait, so hd got crap wrappered white loaf from Co-op. Aware it was stupid compulsn but just knew I hd to see pond again.

I parked the htchbck at the top of the hill.

Everything was just the same, except for a sign saying 'Cycle Route' where the old by-road sign had been.

The bread kept flaking off the hook when I cast, but it didn't matter. For more than an hour I watched the secret mirrored surface, the fish rolling by the lilies. Through the trees round the pond, the green and straw fields stretched out under the evening blue.

Then a car drew up. Two figures got out, a father and his small son. They eyed me suspiciously. I was wearing the green suit and must have indeed looked v. suspic. standing there holding the kiddies' rod w. my plastic-hosp.-tagged wrist. Mght be mistakn for obv. loony.

Didn't feel like company in weaknd state. Anyway, felt I'd seen enough of pond. Hd sucked it all in.

I scrabbled away from the pond's edge, spilling bread crusts from my suit pocket.

'Just going!' I called out to the father and son.

'Any luck?' the father called back, suspicion still in his voice.

'No,' I said. 'But it was probably just the bait.'

He paused before saying, 'Luncheon meat's as good as any.'

Now they were approaching. I recognised Stuart before he recognised me, but only by a second. I took in the dull righteousness of Stuart's sturdy frame as it advanced. He had lost some of his hair and his stubble was prematurely greying, but I could tell Stuart was just the same.

'Stuart!'

'John. Well, this is a surprise. It's a good job I know you. We get a lot of kids up here, messing about, dropping litter. That's what I thought you were at first.'

'What, you live here?' I asked.

'Oh yeah. Well, in the village. Moved up here about five years ago. Took out a lease on the pond. Now I lease it to the angling society.'

I joked that I should have got a permit. But Stuart didn't see it as a joke.

'Obviously, if it was me, John . . . ' he said. 'But Jumbo runs the angling club. You know Jumbo?' I shook my head, obv. 'He's the one you want to see. First bungalow in the village, opposite the church.'

'Right,' I said. 'Well, I'll nip down there now.'

'He'll be grateful for your tenner, Jumbo will.'

Stuart's son began walking round the pond. Stuart started after him, but then paused, eyeing the crusts of bread on the bank, and my Vegas betting slips on My Emma and Oscar Schindler, which had fallen down there too.

'Rats are the only thing,' Stuart said. 'Clearing up the litter. That's the only rule we have.'

I waited for Stuart to pass. I picked up the crusts. I heard his voice calling from the other side of the pond.

'You can't miss Jumbo's place! There's a burger van parked outside. He sells burgers on the A14, and jumbo sausages. That's why he's called Jumbo!' Stuart added amusedly.

I walked across the fields and through the folding hedge-rows back to the Colonel's car, clawing at the midges with my hands.

Strange. Thought I might have been upset discovering Stuart owned the pond. Even cried. But actually I felt rather good. I knew I didn't need to see the pond again.

And at the bottom of the hill there was a further bonus when I encountered Jimmy White, Gary Glitter and Max Bygraves on horseback being serenaded by the old gypsy organ-grinder like you used to see on Omorou St . . .

What?

Jesus shit. It was a fucking dream. And such a perfect

238

denouement too. I felt myself moving. Forced open my eyes. Saw the sickly-green trolley beneath me and the pale hosp. colours going by. Stopped outside rm w. sign readng 'Endoscopy'.

Lookd around for the Gddss Athna. Nowhere. Just the porter and the old Eng.-crone nurse.

Ws wheeled in. New male Endosc. doc. Ultra-prag. Lookd like right psychopath.

He happily stuck thin Black Mamba-like tube down gullet. Jesus H.! Uncontroll. vom. but nothing coming out and he stuck at it w. Blck Mamba while Eng. crone cupped my head stroking.

'It'll be over soon,' she was saying. 'Just relax, love.'

Almost blckd out. Psycho doc. concrnd for moment. Withdrew Mamba, but then rammed it back in when saw I ws compos.

Ten mins of this, man.

Not advsbl. In fact, wld def. have legged it in real life if hd known in adv.

Finally ended. Came up for air covrd in snot and vom. trails.

'I thought you did very well, dear,' Eng. crone said.

I: lost for wds.

Wheeled bck to ward. Brief vist from Gdds Athna and Asiatic new doc. Trained as barman at Orleanna Hotel. How *were* Iris's pubes, Dr Ng?

Oh, turn it off.

Lay throughout night listening to the sounds of the ward. All oldsters apart fr. me. Some rt on cusp of the end. Lstnd to their rasping breaths. So many fallen shields. They were beautiful in their way.

'But mine is too new and polished, and I too young to join them,' said the newly recruited youth, as he spoke to the general on the grisly field. 'My mother herself made sure to polish this shield for me this morning, before I set off.'

With a covert sign, the general ordered his swarthy adjutant, FranCo, to lead the youth off to the exposed flank. There the young recruits and old soldiers were dying like flies, to buy time and preserve the hardened troops for the final rearguard.

And, even years later sitting by the fireside with his faithful hound, FranCo would weep at this memory every night . . .

The next morning, ws releasd fr. hosp. on Willie Ng's orders despite some opp. fr. the Gddss Athna my protectr.

Nwmkt meetng in four days' time. Mst go. Srprse 500 bg-win lmp-on. Johnny be here by then. Go w. J.

Staggd out of hosp. twds Col.'s immac. presvrd htchbck. Fell over on way. Shit, nvr bn ths weak. Mst hve emerg. burg. Hope psycho doc. not around. Mght use a pretext to book me in again for more Mamba.

Dr. to burg. jt. Got some down.

Needed sound-track. No working tapes now tht gvn Carol tape w. 'Nothing Lasts Forever' on.

Stppd in Ippo and wnt to enem.-hld record-shop outlet. Even in disgust. condtn got serious eye fr. 15-st. French or Belg. au pair.

Cldn't think wht to buy. Mstly CDs anyway. Who the hell has CD plyrs?

Suggs solo album? N/A. Terry Hall? Nada. Bldy outrage. Geniuses.

Great trgdst Morr.? No, bad enough inside my own head. Ultimate *generalissimo* prophet king the great Bob M.? No, don't want old songs.

Cassette box caught my eye: Finlay Quaye. Oh yeah. Young guy. Seemed promising. Saw him on some crap-TV awards show backed by three noble rastas wearing white hats. Fin. Quaye voice remark. sim. to tht of grt prophet king Bob M.

15-st. au pair came up to me at chckout holding Janet Jackson CD. Said she didn't want J. Jack. CD 'cause alread. hd, but wantd somethng sim.

Directed her to Pogues compiltn. Shld give her a shock.

Go back, rest up, eat only Grk yoghurts w. honey and drnk only min. wtr for three days before Nwmkt lmp-on: that's what I'd do.

Stpd off and bght Grk yogs, hon. and extort. botts Ital. min. watr.

Turned Col.'s immac. car radio on. Racing. Sprinting beasts. Fucking, what? Croft running. *'And Croft Pool now showing as they pass the two pole.'* First time I'm not on. Bound to be the coup.

Croft 4th. Thank God for that.

Bldy straggly walking-carpt dog on doorstp again when arrvd. What was . . . ? Oh yeah. Molly. Let Molly in w. me. Gave her some crisps.

Mst not start lovng dogs more than humans: Hitler syndrome.

Strtd going twds stairs and strry chamb. Cldn't face climb. Went stud. instead. Put two chairs togeth. Too cramped. Got blanket from dwnstrs cupbd. Put on floor. Put Grk yogs and extort. min. wtr in new fridge.

Lay on stud. floor for three days w. Moll. at feet eatng/drnkg yogs/extort. min. and listng to Finlay Quaye on crap tape-recorder by head. Just kept trnng tape over when awake – 50, 60 times?

Occas. hd to crawl to frnt door and let Moll. out when heard scrtchng at door. Don't they do dog-flaps these days?

Finlay sang on in his beaut. voice about chicks, food and rasta 'Igh.

. . . *Money in my pocket but I just can't get your love* . . .

Been there, star. Been there . . .

Pure confidence song. Reminds me of a beautiful boxer I once knew. Not Derek Jay; a proper one. Should get back in touch, maybe send him the tape . . .

Must have that drink with Pridwell sometime as well . . .

. . . My generation, got to stand up in love. . . .

Christ, for a relative nipper, Fin. had all the . . .

Must have that drink with Pridwell sometime as well

. . . *My generation, got to stand up in love* . . .

For a relative nipper, Fin. had all the refs. Cld be the new *generalissimo*.

Question was, if srprs. 500 bg win not occur and have to write 12 G bk, where to write it?

No, of course 500 bg win occur. Inev.

. . . *You will survive, soldier. And your soul is good* . . .

Thanks, man. You too.

Greece?

Forget these American chicks. And English chicks. Stick to Greek chicks in fut.

No. Forget all chicks. Stick to crones.

Saw one once in this white-stoned village in the south. Peloponnese. First went one early spring when I was 20. Incred. place. When first went, only accessible by sea and 50km dirt track. The steep village paths were populated by a strange big-headed cat family. Locals squeezed lemon juice in their eyes when cats appprchd tavernas. Thought tht ws a bit extreme. Made the big-headed cats' eyes go milky and half-blind.

Not much food around for anyone in winter. In winter, the stray dogs tht scavenged round the village ate stones: just passed the stones through their bodies, got something out of them, enough to survive the winter. I myself witnessed a dog eating a stone.

Then I went again ten years later and everythng hd changed. A motorway hd been built to within 30km of village and now a hydrofoil stopped there every day from Athens. In summer, village hd become chic retro place for Athenians' second homes.

Athenians brght pets cats w. them for summer and within three yrs of their arrival the entire family of milky-eyed big-headed cats had died out.

The stray popultn had been decimated. The dogs no longer ate stones. In summer, those tht hadn't starved to death in winter just followed the tourists around pitifully.

All this, in ten years.

Still mght go there to write 12-G bk. Knock off 750 wds a day while crone ferries up exquis. *meze* trays and jugs of barrelled pink *hyma* wine.

Not really booze, the *hyma*. More like medicine.

Little wooden skewers of *souvlaki* on tap.

No, go there and write another book. 200 wds a day. No, 100. No, 10. Entire bk of poetry intellgble only to me. Take me years. But I would have done it. Yes . . .

Felt myself drifting off to sleep again, w. warm feeling of forthcoming 500 surprs. bg-win vict.

Tried to turn over on hard stud. floor. Cldn't. Eng. stone, see. Ungrooved.

Listnd to Fin.

. . . *She will die. I will follow* . . .

Or was that 'guide'? Hope so, for both their sakes.

20

Crazee Mental

Well, this was it. The last 500. We were half-way to Newmarket, me and Johnny. I could see the British Sugar factory coming up on the right, the smoke spewing out and then dissolving into the miles of fields on either side.

I touched the thick wad of notes in my pocket, fifties and twenties. I'd grown used to the wads. It would be strange not having them there. But maybe they would be, if Crazee Mental won.

Walter had tipped me Crazee Mental that morning on the phone. 'If it doesn't hang left it'll win,' he'd said. Walter was less angry than usual – I could tell he was genuinely excited. The odds in the paper were 20-1. 'Forget the odds,' Walter said. 'This isn't a fritterer. This is a lump-on.'

Walter was even going to come up to Newmarket to see Crazee Mental win, until he'd found out Johnny was coming. 'If the most boring person in the entire universe is going to be there you can forget it,' were the exact words.

Johnny flicked cigarette ash out of the car window with a thick forearm. 'Amazing to think that every bag of sugar comes from that one place,' he observed.

Johnny was driving slowly. Ever since he'd moved to San Francisco he kept to US speed limits, even on motorways. Lorries sandwiched us in the inside lane. The clock was broken in the ash-covered car. We must have missed the first race already. Soon we'd be missing the 1.20 too. It didn't matter. I'd only have put on fritterers. Now I could lump the whole 500 on.

The world seemed curiously refracted. Only simple images and thoughts came through. It was good sitting there, listening to the hum of the engine, and the familiar amble of Johnny's conversation as it went from Gulf War torture tactics to the non-smoking in Haight-Ashbury bars and this girl who'd once left him for a jockey he was sure was Frankie Dettori.

'So how's Walter?' Johnny went on.

'Fine.'

'I always liked Walter at school, even when he went a bit crazed,' Johnny said. 'I know he hated me, though.'

'No,' I reassured Johnny. 'Anyway, school's a long time ago now.'

We came into Newmarket in the drizzle, past the bronze statue of Hyperion in the high street, the drizzle skidding off Hyperion's hooves in fast drops, then on up the incline towards the course. An old steward waved us on. We were the only car on the road. Where were the other cars? Maybe we were too late.

Johnny spent ages executing intricate parking movements in a field behind the grandstand. I felt the car going into another reversing manoeuvre so I opened the door and jumped out. I grabbed my *Racing Post* and umbrella from the moving doorwell and started running towards the grandstand. I heard Johnny stop the car abruptly and come padding through the wet grass behind me for a few steps. 'What's wrong!' Johnny was shouting. 'Calm down!'

But he couldn't keep up. Fifteen years ago Johnny would have killed me over that distance – any distance. Then I heard his panting die away, and the distant clunk as he went back and locked the car with his zapper.

I ran through the turnstile and past the paddock, and through the tunnel underneath the grandstand up into the public enclosure where the bookies' boards stood. It was a Tuesday meeting and the crowd was thin.

The wind rattled the boards and flicked the used pink betting tickets along the concrete. I saw Crazee Mental's name on the board but there was no price yet. There must be at least twenty minutes to go. I realised I hadn't had a drink for days and that I'd have been drunk by now if it was still Vegas time.

I walked back and found Johnny ordering a seafood-cocktail sandwich from a van by the paddock. I saw the sleek hinds of the horses pacing round, but I didn't look closely because that's when you lose your nerve. I walked into a bar instead with Johnny alongside, bits of seafood and pink mayonnaise spilling out of his mouth.

'So what about this girl in Vegas then?' he said when we were standing by the bar with our rehydrative pints. 'Rona, wasn't it?'

'Rawnee.'

'How old was she?'

'Nineteen,' I lied. I don't know why.

'They always are,' Johnny said sagely into his pint. 'They always are.'

We drank down our pints and walked back through the tunnel to the boards. Crazee Mental was 25-1 in places. But the first bookie wouldn't take a 500 single bet. I didn't try another. I gave Johnny half the money and we spread it around the boards. In all there was 400 on the nose, plus a 50 each-way saver even though Walter would have disapproved.

As I put the saver on an old jockey with shiny eyes was standing by the board. He winked and said, 'If he doesn't hang left your horse'll win.'

'Thanks,' I said.

Hardly any of the bookies used tic-tac signs any more. They all had runners with mobile phones patrolling the boards. They must have known about the money going down on Crazee Mental from Johnny and me, but the odds didn't come down at all. They must have known and just thought we were idiots.

The horses cantered past towards the distant stalls with the jockeys chattering. We took up our normal pre-race positions on the rails with our backs to the course. I thought about a panic bet on the favourite but then remembered I had no wad.

I thought about the 12 grand, and for a second the used pink tickets swirling on the ground weren't tickets at all but pieces of skin, my skin, and each piece shed was a bet I'd had or something that had happened, so that as I glanced from ticket to ticket I saw a hotel room in Vegas, and Coastal Bluff's bridle swinging uselessly in the air, poor Coastal, and the dim walk to the entrance of *Cowgirls 2*, and going back and the cab reeking of perfume, and the winnings from the Lewis fight on the hotel room table, next to a Bacardi bottle, in a stack of hundred-dollar bills.

Then I turned to face the track and the empty green beyond, and it was as if all the used tickets had been gathered up behind me and sucked back, their skin rejoining my skin, so that I was living it again from the start – no time limit.

For a moment I wondered if perhaps I had died and was in the process of reincarnating.

Shit, never wrote a will. Only one thing: bury my heart with wounded Knee's (when she follows).

'Fag?' I heard Johnny's voice say. Oh, obv. not reincntg. I took one from the packet and lit it from his stub. I could feel Johnny's gaze on me intently, in a way that people who don't know you couldn't do. The stalls snapped open and they went through the first furlong all running promisingly straight.

'What is it about this horse?' Johnny said. 'Normally you don't care whether they win or lose.'

'Well, if Crazee Mental doesn't win I'll have to write this book,' I told Johnny. 'But it's not just that.'

Author's Note

Crazee Mental came second.

All amounts and subjects of bets are true. On occasions the sequence of bets has been changed.

All the characters and all the rest are fiction.

J.R.
Athens, March 1998

Acknowledgements

For their companionship and food parcels during the writing of this book in Monemvasia, Greece, I would like to thank my sister Kate, Akis Kapsis, Mamma Kapsis and especially my parents John and Jay Rendall.

Above all I would like to thank Rachel Cugnoni (no relation) for the special trauma of being my editor.